# DUST OF LIFE

DUST OF LIFE

Children of the Saigon Streets

LIZ THOMAS

HAMISH HAMILTON
LONDON

First published in Great Britain 1977
by Hamish Hamilton Ltd
90 Great Russell Street London WC1B 3PT

Copyright © 1977 by Liz Thomas

SBN 241 89489 1

Printed in Great Britain by
Elliott Bros and Yeoman Ltd, Liverpool L24 9JL

To my Mother
and to the Children of Saigon

ILLUSTRATIONS

Between pages 72 and 73

1a Tuyet, Father Hoang, Mai and Chao in the courtyard of Te Ban prison with other girls from Le Lai.
1b Girls in their cell in Te Ban, with Tuyet and Mai in the front row.
2a Liz's home for girls. No, Van and Hoa standing in a row and Cu Ly, Lien and tiny Thanh are kneeling in front of them.
2b Younger brothers and sisters of the girls in Liz's home and children from Le Lai
3a Boys outside their cell in Te Ban
3b No and Lien distributing fruit to the older women prisoners in Te Ban
4a Beggars outside the cathedral in Saigon
4b A small street boy with a huge bag of rubbish

Between pages 136 and 137

5a Liz helping to treat a young opium addict suffering from malaria in Te Ban
5b The burial of Mai, the young girl Liz found on the steps of Saigon hospital
6a Liz working in a refugee camp outside Tay Ninh City shortly before the take-over
6b Liz giving bread to the refugees from Tay Ninh

7   Refugees living on the streets in Saigon just before the take-over
8a Street children in Da Nang
8b Resettlement camp on the border of Quang Tri province. The women are armed with rifles

Map (drawn by Patrick Leeson)   Page 10

PROLOGUE

When I was about fourteen years old, I decided I wanted to go to Vietnam. I had been reading about the war in the newspapers and had watched reports of the fighting on television. I kept on thinking about the poor Vietnamese people and children now losing their homes and families because of the war.

I thought how terrible it must be for people to see their homes burned down and their whole village destroyed by fire, and to become refugees wandering around the countryside until they found new settlements. I thought about the children who had been killed, and the children who would return to their villages in the evening and find their homes destroyed and their parents dead.

I used to think a lot about the war. How long would it continue, and what would become of the Vietnamese people? Whenever I heard anything about Vietnam, I did not just hear and then forget, but would go on thinking about what I could do to help. I used to send what money I had to Vietnam, but just to send money to various organisations wasn't enough for me. I had to go there. Perhaps I could not do much to alleviate the misery of Vietnam at war, but at least I could try to contribute in some way.

I was still at school near my home in Sussex and Vietnam seemed so far away. I had no idea how I was going to get there, and yet somehow, deep inside me, I always knew that one day I would live in Vietnam. My first love had always been for animals and I had wanted to work with horses. Then when I thought about all the suffering in the world, I thought it would be selfish of me to indulge in my own pleasures. How could I devote my time, my love and care to helping animals, when there were so many people to be helped first?

I left school when I was sixteen, having obtained three Ordinary Level G.C.E. passes, and looked for a job where I would be helping people. I wanted to be a nursing cadet but at the time I was too young. I decided to work in a hospital in order to gain experience, and the only job available to me, because of my age, was that of a ward domestic. So for nearly a year I worked hard cleaning the wards and learned a lot about life in a hospital. I used to enjoy working at the weekends because when the wards were short-staffed I would hurry through my own work and then help the nurses look after the patients. I wasn't allowed to do very much, but when I worked on the geriatric ward I used to help with the feeding of the patients, walking them out to the bathroom, and sitting them up in bed when they slipped down. I also had my first experience of death on that ward. An old lady died and I asked one of the nurses if I could go into her room. I just wanted to see what she looked like. I felt a little nervous, but there was no need to be. The old lady looked just as she did before and I almost expected her to sit up and start breathing again; but she lay so still and looked so pale.

When I was seventeen I left the hospital so that I could do some preliminary nursing before I started my training. I wanted to gain as much experience as possible. During the next year I worked with physically handicapped and mentally retarded children, old people and then private patients in a nursing home. I used to enjoy work in the nursing home because I nursed both medical and surgical patients, learned how to care for patients receiving intravenous infusions and blood transfusions, and how to care for patients post-operatively. I also discovered the needs of a dying patient, and how to nurse the unconscious.

Just before my eighteenth birthday, in May 1970, I applied to the Middlesex Hospital in London to do my two years practical nursing training to qualify as a State Enrolled Nurse. I decided on the shorter nursing course because I wanted to be a good practical nurse and have direct contact with the patients, whereas the three year State Registered Nursing Training would have involved more ward management and administration. I also thought that the two year course would enable me to go out to Vietnam a year earlier. During my first year I worked on both medical and surgical wards and in the operating theatre, where sometimes I was allowed to 'scrub-up' and assist in minor operations and where I also had the opportunity to watch many major operations. I also worked on orthopaedics and did plenty of night duty which I really enjoyed. During my second year I worked on paediatrics, geriatrics and the patients 'recovery unit' and finally in neurology. I loved every minute of my training. I took my Assessment of Pupil Nurses in General Nursing in the spring of 1972, and on 26 May I had my results from the General Nursing Council. I had passed.

I had started to apply to go out to Vietnam when I was nineteen years old and had completed the first year of my training. I remember sitting down with the telephone directory and looking through the Yellow Pages, writing down the names of all the voluntary agencies and charities I could find who were assisting in overseas work. I wrote to over thirty different organisations but they all said that I was too young and too inexperienced to go. However, I was determined not to be put off by these objections and tried other outlets. I even applied to the British Army and finally to the American Embassy. I spent one whole afternoon in the American Embassy, where they put me on to the Air Force, told me I would have to emigrate to the States for two years, become an American citizen, and finally go out to Vietnam through the U.S. Air Force.

I never gave up hope. I would go to Vietnam even if I made my own way over-land, even if I had to walk. I would get there somehow. I even thought of appealing on the radio or television or of putting an advertisement in the newspapers. Then one day, after almost a year of applying to be sent out, one small British Charity called the Ockenden Venture wrote to ask me if I would like to go for an interview. This was my great day, the day I had been waiting for. I felt as if I were nearly there.

Again, they felt I was too young and were afraid that the conditions in Saigon might upset me, but they finally accepted me because of my determination. I was so happy, for it looked as if my dream was coming true. I was going to Vietnam, to Saigon, where I was going to work in a large orphanage which the Ockenden Venture helped to support.

I rushed back to the nurses' home where I was living and

telephoned my parents to tell them the good news. My mother could hardly believe it, but she was happy that at last I could do what I really wanted and did not stand in my way. She was so kind and understanding. She said she never wanted me to turn back one day and say, 'Well I couldn't do that, because my parents stopped me.' Everyone wished me lots of luck.

By the time I left the hospital the flight times had all been arranged and I had my visa from the Vietnamese Embassy in London. The hospital gave me my vaccinations against smallpox, T.A.B. and cholera, polio and tetanus. I left the Middlesex Hospital in July 1972, spent one month at home with my family, and flew out to Saigon on 16 September, 1972, on an evening flight from Gatwick Airport.

My suitcase contained six cotton dresses, a pair of jeans and a pair of sandals, soap and one hundred sachets of shampoo, which we worked out would last me for a year if I washed my hair twice a week. I filled the rest of the suitcase with baby powder and zinc and castor oil cream for the children at the orphanage. I also took all my medical books and my mother baked me a lovely fruit cake. I gave all my clothes away. I didn't think I would need them any more and thought it better that they should be used rather than just hang in the wardrobe.

I remember leaving my home on that September evening, ready to fly out to Saigon. I felt quite calm as we drove to the airport, but rather excited. I had never flown before and wondered what it would be like. I couldn't really believe I was leaving my family as I walked through the departure lounge. My mother looked as if she wanted to cry but she didn't. I had a big lump in my throat and so I had two stiff gin and tonics before I got on the plane. I didn't sleep at all during my flight from London to Singapore; I just gazed out of the window and thought how beautiful everything was. As morning came the sky was full of colour, red and orange and yellow. I could see the stars shining in the black sky, now turning to a dark blue, and towards the East I could see the sun rising. I noticed quite a lot of lightning as we came towards the East.

I thought about Vietnam and wondered what it would be like to work in an orphanage there. I also thought about God and I felt that He was really close to me. I have never been a very religious person, but I have always had a strong faith. I think it was this faith and my belief that God was with me that enabled me to carry out my work in Vietnam.

We arrived in Singapore at seven o'clock in the evening. I checked through customs and found a taxi to take me to my hotel. It was a long drive, but very fast, and on the left hand side of the road. I really enjoyed the warmth and felt very comfortable. The driver spoke English and I told him I would be leaving for Vietnam the next day. He told me I would have to leave from another airport on the other side of the city and arranged to meet me early the following morning to drive me there.

When we arrived at the hotel I thought the driver had made a mistake. It was so expensive and luxurious, with a huge entrance hall and reception rooms. I checked in and sent my mother a telegram to say that I had arrived safely. My room was large and fully air-conditioned. There were various switches and buttons all over the wall. I pressed all the buttons and lights appeared over the two beds and the full-length mirror that stretched from one side of the room to the other. I put on the radio and television but couldn't understand much of what was said.

I went downstairs to the hotel restaurant. It was huge and everyone in it looked so rich. I couldn't go in, not by myself. I wouldn't have known what to do. Outside the hotel there were limousines and chauffeurs, uniformed porters and more rich-looking people. I wondered what they thought of me. Perhaps they thought I was terribly rich as well.

I started to walk along the street. It was hard to believe I was in Singapore. I turned away from the hotel and came to an area where the streets were much narrower. There were many more people around. I could see that they were much poorer, most of them earning their living by running open-air restaurants and cafés. I walked through the narrow rows of tables lining the street and as I did so small boys ran out and persuaded me to sit down. I wasn't hungry, so I ordered a gin and tonic. Young boys started performing professional card tricks. Their clothes were torn and dirty and they looked as if they hadn't washed for weeks. I noticed there were a lot of girls walking about, chatting and laughing amongst themselves on the street corners or sitting down at one of the tables.

It wasn't until later that I realised they were really men, dressed up as women and wearing women's clothes and heavy make-up under their wigs.

I knew it was getting late but I had no idea of the time. A few streets away, I could hear music playing and I went into a discotheque. I met some other English people inside and we had a few drinks together and danced. I felt very happy. It was about five o'clock in the morning before I left and took another taxi back to my hotel. I felt very tired and had a quick shower to revive me. At seven o'clock my taxi came and I left for the airport. I did have a bit of a headache.

I had already spent the thirty dollars I had brought with me from England. I didn't think I would need any more money, but when I checked in my luggage I was asked for ten dollars to pay for the airport tax. I sat down on my suitcase and wondered what I should do. There were not many passengers for the flight to Vietnam, but I did approach one man who was a U.S. Air Force pilot. I told him that if he could lend me ten dollars I would pay him back on arrival in Saigon as someone was meeting me there. He was very kind and gave me the money.

I boarded the plane and when we took off I wished I hadn't had so much to drink. My head ached and I felt very sick. When the air-hostess brought us a tray of food I couldn't eat anything and just asked for a travel-sickness pill. It was only a short flight to Saigon and I dozed off to sleep. When I awoke the plane was already coming down to land. I looked out of the window and saw the city of Saigon.

It was about eleven o'clock in the morning as we flew down the runway. Everything was bathed in brilliant sunshine. As I looked out of the window I could see rows of U.S. aircraft and nearer the airport some American soldiers stripped down to their waist and stretched out on the wings of their planes, drinking cans of beer and smoking as they watched our plane come in.

The pilot asked us to remain in our seats until the airport security police had come aboard. Two policemen arrived. They were slim, with tan-coloured skin and dark hair. Around their waists they wore a bullet belt and a gun which hung loosely in its holster. They searched the plane and between the seats before allowing us to disembark. I stepped off the plane and put my feet on the ground. I was here. I was standing on a part of Vietnam.

It was very hot and a warm breeze was blowing as I walked across to the customs. I collected my luggage and met Mrs Beach, the lady with whom I was going to work. I felt a little better as we got into the car and drove away from the airport into Saigon. The first thing I noticed was the goats grazing just outside the main building of the airport. They were left to wander freely.

The streets were crowded with people riding on Hondas and bicycles, moving in and out amongst the cars. I noticed that the people riding on the passenger seats were sitting sideways and I wondered why. I learned later that it was supposed to be harder to throw a hand grenade sitting that way. There were not only two people to a Honda. A whole family would ride along on one. Usually the father would drive and the mother would sit on the back holding her baby, with the rest of the children sitting in between. I saw as many as six on the same Honda, with the extra child standing in front of the father and holding on to the cross bars. Further down the street we came to a set of traffic lights and to my surprise many Hondas didn't wait at the lights, but would go up on the pavement and come down onto the street again on the other side. The Hondas seemed to rule the streets and pavements. Luckily the traffic moved slowly and there were not many accidents.

I watched the Vietnamese people and thought how slender and hollow-cheeked they looked. I loved their tanned skins and their black hair. Most of them wore peasant clothes, and many had holes in their shirts. The women wore black satin pants and Vietnamese-style working shirts that allowed them plenty of freedom. Some of the younger women were wearing 'ao-dais', the traditional dress, tailor-fitted at the top, worn down to just below the knee, and open at the sides from the waist to the hem. Ao-dais were made in many different colours and usually worn over black or white satin pants. The men were wearing light trousers and open-necked shirts because it was hot at this time of day.

As we drove away from the airport, we passed the U.S. army hospital, comprising six white-washed buildings quite separate from each other. The buildings were spaced in this way so that in the event of a rocket attack only one building would be destroyed and not the entire hospital. We drove into Cong Ly street, the main street from the airport to the centre of Saigon. On either side there were large French colonial-style houses with magnificent white porches where mostly the Americans, or the more wealthy Vietnamese lived. Each house had a garden, surrounded by high walls covered with barbed wire. We continued down the street, past a beautiful Pagoda on the right hand side, and over a bridge crossing a small, very dirty-looking river. Rice grew on the mud banks of the river and small wooden houses were built along the edge of the rice fields.

We turned off Cong Ly street and came into a much poorer area. Here there were no more French colonial-style houses, but much smaller Vietnamese houses with flat roofs and white-washed walls. Most of the people here seemed to be using the front of their houses as shops. The houses looked so poor and over-crowded, and between them were many shacks made out of cardboard boxes and corrugated iron where whole families were living. I could see chickens and very scrawny-looking dogs running around and noticed what a lot of rubbish was thrown into the streets. The pavements were lined with drink-stalls selling beer, bottled fruit drinks and coconut milk. Women were selling bowls of Vietnamese soup from large saucepans burning on charcoal fires. On the street corners were small boys who had set up their own Honda repair shops.

This was Saigon, and it was just as I had imagined it to be. I looked forward to the days ahead of me, working amongst the children at the orphanage and finding my way around the city. I wanted to become part of everything I saw. I wanted to be amongst the people, close to the poverty. This was my life, and it was just beginning.

CHAPTER 1

About fifteen minutes after leaving the airport, we arrived at the house where I was to live with Mrs Beach. It was only a small house with white-washed walls, and a high wall covered in barbed wire surrounded it. We rang the bell and one of the Vietnamese helpers ran over to open the gate and let us in. There were about ten children playing in the courtyard, watched by another Vietnamese helper. Mrs Beach told me that these were the handicapped children who came to the house from the orphanage each day. Here they were able to receive a little extra love and attention, nutrition, a daily bath and the exercises they needed to strengthen their limbs.

Even though these children had suffered so much they were extremely brave, and when we entered the gate they expressed their happiness by laughing and waving. I went over and picked up a little boy. He was about four years old. His legs were paralysed and hung limply under him, the muscles almost completely wasted away. His arms were so thin and very weak, probably from lack of use. He laughed and looked round, his eyes not really focusing on anything. His stomach was distended, his nose and eyes were running and his ears were infected.

We went into a large living-room. Two ceiling fans were on and the room was quite cool. There was a sofa and a few easy chairs and I sat down thankfully. I was tired from lack of sleep, my legs ached and my ankles had swollen in the heat. Mrs Beach offered me some cool beer to refresh me. I drank it because I didn't want her to know I had been out all night. I explained that I felt very tired because of the travelling and because I hadn't managed to sleep on the plane.

We drank our beers and then had a lunch of rice and small

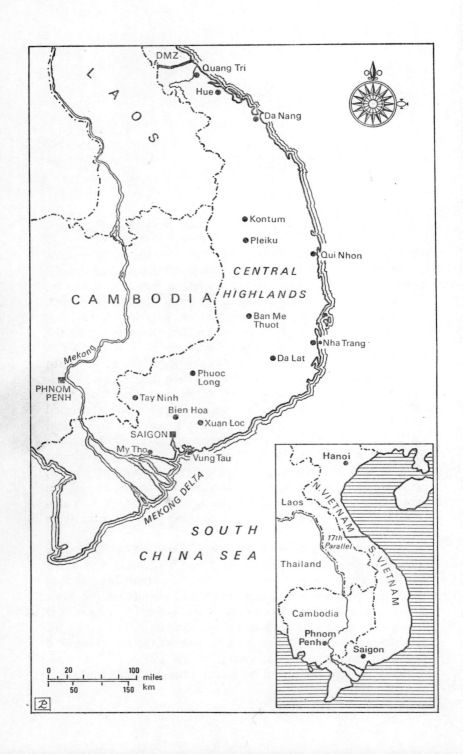

buffalo steaks which were very tough. We finished with bananas and coffee and talked about the orphanage and the children, and the best way to help them. Mrs Beach asked me if I would like to start work in the babies' room. I was to work with the Vietnamese women already there and was to teach them a little more about the care of young children. I agreed and by this time I was beginning to drop off to sleep over the table.

The house itself consisted of the living-room, Mrs Beach's room which was also used as an office, and another bedroom used as a treatment room for the children. At the back of the house was another building, comprising a kitchen, a classroom for the children and a rest room for the Vietnamese women. On the floor above were three bedrooms, two already occupied by Hom and Co Tu, two Vietnamese girls who had taken short courses in teaching and were now working at the orphanage. I took the third room.

It was a square-shaped room, medium sized and painted in a shade of light blue. The furniture consisted of a wooden bed, a wardrobe, a table and one chair. There were shutters outside the windows and inside they were covered by a mosquito net, very old and full of holes. The windows had no glass. I closed the shutters and put on the ceiling fan. It was a very noisy old fan and it blew the dust round the room. There were even cobwebs on the window frames and walls. I also noticed about six or seven lizards on the wall and chased them out before I went to sleep. They seemed to stay on the wall or the ceiling but they didn't really bother me. I just hoped they would not fall off the ceiling and on to the bed when I was sleeping. I threw a sheet across the bed and was soon fast asleep.

A couple of hours later I was awoken by the sound of the children playing. I washed my face under the cold tap, put on a pair of jeans and went down to find Mrs. Beach. She was helping the women bath the children. She told me the children would be going back to the orphanage soon and that we could go back with them so that she could show me round. We finished bathing the children, using soap and cold water from the hose pipe. We dressed them in clean clothes and sat them down on small tables and chairs ready for their tea. They each had a bowl of rice, with soup made from meat bones and vegetables. The older children fed themselves, sorting out what they didn't like and putting it on the other children's plates. The younger children had to be fed, and when they had had enough, they would just spit it all out again and hold their lips tightly together. We also gave them some sweetened condensed milk to drink diluted with water—there was no fresh milk in Saigon. Then we sat them on their pots and waited for the car to come to take us to the orphanage. Three Vietnamese women helpers who only spoke a few words of English tried to tell the children my name. The children couldn't pronounce 'Liz' and called me 'Ly'. My new name was 'Co Ly' which in English means Miss Ly.

Our transport arrived, a small van with three rows of seats. Somehow we all managed to squeeze in. Mrs Beach used to pay the Vietnamese driver a small monthly salary as the van was privately owned by him and didn't belong to the orphanage. As we drove along I noticed what a keen interest the children took in all that went on around them. They were laughing and chatting and looking out of the window. I felt just as excited as they seemed to be.

There seemed to be no traffic control at all, except for the occasional lights. The streets were crowded with mini-buses that ran on a lambretta engine, with the driver sitting in the front with two rows of seats behind him for about five people to sit either side. Usually there was a small boy who, balancing on the step with one hand on the roof, would collect fares.

There were small, dilapidated blue and yellow taxis, pedal cycles, motor cycles and bicycles. The police jeeps were bottle green and white with red flash-lights, and then there were the U.S. army jeeps used by both the American and Vietnamese soldiers. There were a few privately owned cars, some of which were the big American cars used by military or government officials, doctors, lawyers or the more wealthy Vietnamese. Huge army trucks rattled along the streets, transporting soldiers or carrying supplies and ammunition. Lorries were used to bring the fruit and vegetables from the countryside to the Saigon markets.

The streets were swarming with people. Women carrying two baskets on either side of a wooden support which was balanced over one shoulder, were selling their produce. Families had set up small stands and were sitting on chairs behind selling cigarettes and tobacco, American chewing gum, Vietnamese-made sweets and ampoules of sterile water for intravenous or intra-muscular injection. Children were just coming out of school, dressed in blue skirts or trousers with white shirts and wearing open sandals. They walked along in groups, laughing and talking, or rode away two and three together on a bicycle. They looked very thin and many wore frayed shirts and broken shoes.

Then there were the Army Republic Vietnam (A.R.V.N.) soldiers wearing either jungle green or green and brown camouflaged uniforms. They looked very young and anxious. All young men over the age of seventeen had to enlist but many tried to avoid doing so. In 1972 there were about a million soldiers in the South Vietnamese army. I also noticed barbed wire everywhere, outside almost every building. On the corners of the streets were the barbed wire barricades, pushed to the side during the day, and pulled across the street during the hours of curfew.

I always loved the streets of Saigon. There was so much to see, so many people to look at, so much to learn. Walking wasn't very easy in Saigon, firstly, because both the streets and pavements were full of holes, and secondly, because there wasn't much room to walk between the street stalls. The food-stalls served as small cafés, with tables and chairs set out in the street. They sold various Chinese and Vietnamese soups, rice dishes with an assortment of cooked buffalo steaks, pork, chicken, fish, shrimps or eggs. With every dish the Vietnamese people always had 'nuoc mam' which was a very strong fish sauce, usually with red peppers chopped up and added to make it very hot. 'Nuoc mam' smelt very bad but tasted very good, although few foreigners ever ate it. All these dishes were very cheap, about 100 to 150 piasters each. When I first arrived 500 piasters equalled one dollar. If you wanted to buy food to take home they would put it into plastic bags for you. You could buy as much or as little as you liked.

Drink-stalls lined the streets and small coffee shops were usually set up outside important buildings. The coffee shops were built out of wooden or cardboard boxes and corrugated iron. The tables and chairs were wooden and the girls who served the coffee would collect the water from a tap in the street and boil the water on small kerosene stoves. In Saigon, when we drank coffee we always drank a glass of Chinese tea afterwards. There were pots of tea on every table and a glass of iced tea would cost only 20 piasters.

You could also buy plastic bags full of iced tea or water or you could just buy a block of ice. Most people were too poor to be able to afford a refrigerator. Usually those who did own one would put a notice on the wall outside their house, and all day long little children would be sent over to buy ice from them. Even the owners of the coffee shops didn't always have a refrigerator and would keep an ice box. Down towards the river front was a huge ice factory. People would either go and buy ice from the factory, or wait for the ice-men who pedalled their bicycles all day long through the streets, selling blocks of ice.

Most of the poorer people in Saigon who smoked didn't buy a whole packet of cigarettes. They would buy five or ten at a time and you could, if you wished, just buy one cigarette. American cigarettes were very popular and there was quite a well-established black market for them. The English 'Capstan' cigarettes were also in demand. Vietnamese cigarettes were very strong and un-tipped, so only the old men smoked them. They were hand rolled cigarettes and sold very cheaply in packs of fifty.

On some of the main streets in Saigon and especially round the markets, the stalls would line the pavements in a continuous row. They would sell all kinds of goods and there were different areas in Saigon for buying and selling different things. The largest market was situated in the centre of the city. It consisted of a large square building, with smaller stalls which looked like open-fronted shops, in a double row all round the outside.

All the food was sold inside the main building, with different places inside the market specializing in a particular food. There was the meat section, the fish section, and other sections for fruit, vegetables, Chinese foods, tinned foods and dried foods, noodles and rice and also flowers. You couldn't buy fresh milk, but you could buy tinned milk and also American margarine and processed cheese.

In the fish section, most of the fish were sold live. You could choose what you wanted and then give it to the woman selling the fish who would chop off its head with a very sharp knife and prepare it for you. Chickens and ducks were always sold live and you killed them yourself at home. You had to barter for anything bought in the market or elsewhere in Saigon for otherwise you were overcharged. Foreigners had to be particularly careful. The fish section was constantly under water because of the live fish. The women would sit barefoot amongst trays of fish and eels because it was too wet for shoes. Even when we walked through the fish section, we had to roll up our trousers and wash the backs of our legs and feet where the water had splashed when we got home.

The men and women working in the market would start setting up their stalls and preparing the tables for display at about five o'clock in the morning before the market opened at six. Some people would sleep all night in the market, either in swinging hammocks suspended between the stalls, or covered with a blanket on top of their stalls.

Every day they would sell completely fresh food. The lorries and trucks would start arriving at about five and they would unload wooden cratefuls of fresh fish covered in ice. The fruit, vegetables and meat lorries would also arrive and suddenly, the whole market-place would be teeming with people unloading and setting up their stalls, brewing coffee and cooking rice.

The smaller shops round the outside of the market would open at about eight o'clock. They sold everything from clothes, materials, wedding-gowns and wigs to handbags, shoes, make-up, jewellery and toys. The surrounding streets were also full of activity with people buying and selling or just shopping. Outside almost every shop there were stalls. If there was any space between the stalls on the pavement someone would come along and spread out a plastic sheet and set up a display of fruit. Sometimes people would sell mangoes and pineapples piled high in wicker baskets along the sides of the streets.

Children were sent out by their mothers to sell their home-made cakes. They walked along the streets with the tray either balanced on their heads or under one arm, calling for people to come and buy. Small boys would wander the streets with a string of balloons to sell. Beggars would either wander round inside the market begging for money, or if they had lost their legs or suffered from leprosy, they would lie down in the street outside, their arms outstretched.

Then there were the street boys who would gather round the food-stalls and wait for people to leave their tables, eager to grab the left-over food. Some of the street boys would come and beg. They were usually sent by one of their parents, and they had to collect money to help support their families. Others preferred to work for their living and would shine shoes, equipped with shoeshine boxes which they made themselves, containing shoe brushes, cloths and shoe polish. Some of the boys would watch people's parked cars for them and be paid about 30 piasters a time. This was a quick way to make money on busy days.

Outside the market place the cyclo and lambretta drivers would gather, waiting to pick up a fare. There were people with privately owned two-seater Hondas and motor-bikes who would also give you a lift, for a fare. This wasn't really allowed, but it was another easy way to make money.

In any crowded area of Saigon there were always small groups of boys, commonly known by the Vietnamese people as 'cowboys'. These boys would spend the day milling their way between the crowds, trying to steal. Some boys liked working independently but most preferred to work in groups, so that they could help each other out in times of trouble. Sometimes the boys would work for an older man or pimp. At the end of each 'working' day the boys would bring their money to the pimp who would look after them in return. They would see that the boys had enough to eat, provide them with a place to sleep at night, and look after them if they were sick. They would allow the boys a little pocket money and very often try to help them if they became involved with the police.

The boys worked professionally. They would mingle in the crowds with a small razor between their fingers, allowing them to slit open your bag and make off with your purse. They were so quick that you never felt anything at the time. In more desperate cases the boys would snatch neck chains or with a quick flick of their fingers steal earrings from people's ears, and then just as quickly disappear into the crowds. I used to watch small boys working round the market place, running swiftly after Hondas and bicycles, and stealing raincoats or shopping bags from the back of the Hondas.

The older boys who worked as 'cowboys' would very often steal a Honda and change the number plate and serial number. Then they would ride the streets together with a boy sitting on the back, snatching people's handbags from under their arms as they went along. Sometimes the boys would ride up beside someone already riding in a cyclo and try to grab a bag, or even a watch from the passenger's wrist. They would carry a sharp knife with them and slit the straps of a shoulder bag or camera hanging over a pedestrian's shoulder, and as the bag or camera fell, they would catch it and speed away again. Theft was commonplace in Saigon.

Sometimes, if people who had been robbed raised the alarm quickly enough, the police would chase after them, but usually the 'cowboys' would escape. Sometimes the police would shoot after the boys but as the boys always disappeared into a crowd of people, it was often the passers-by or even children playing along the roadside who were hit by the bullet.

The police patrolled the city either on foot or in jeeps. Usually they stopped people for traffic offences as this was the quickest way to make money. For whatever the traffic offence, you could always pay yourself out of it. The police could ask for any amount of money, and if you refused to pay you could be arrested and even beaten up. Once I remember the police stopped people for not crossing the street on a zebra crossing, although there were few zebra crossings around. They fined them 200 piasters on the spot—about 20p.

Corruption was rife in the police force. Even people who had committed quite serious crimes could buy themselves out of prison if they had enough money. A policeman's average monthly wage was so low that he could not even afford to buy enough rice for himself and his family, let alone send his children to school or pay water and electricity bills. The police would even receive money from the street children and homeless people in return for letting them sleep in the street or around the market places at night without fear of arrest.

Most Vietnamese could not afford to send their children to school, and even if they had sufficient money to pay the school fees, they could not afford to buy the children's school clothes and keep them supplied with exercise books and pencils. Nothing was given away in Saigon. Welfare, state or social services didn't exist. It was easy to understand why there were so many poor people and children in Saigon, making a living as best they could from the streets and from ther people.

The orphanage was in the centre of the city, directly opposite a market. On the other corner of the street was a cinema. Just outside the orphanage was a large rubbish dump, used by the people working in the market and by the people who lived in the houses nearby. In Saigon there were no house to house refuse cleaners. Everyone would throw their rubbish on to a dump in the streets, and eventually the refuse collectors would come and take it away.

We drove into the courtyard of the orphanage, through the double iron gates which bore the sign HOI DUC ANH, which in English means 'Association for the Protection of Children'. Inside the courtyard there were little children playing, dressed in grubby, ill-fitting clothes and without shoes on their feet. As we got out of the van the children ran over to us, their hands outstretched, and threw their arms around us in a hug, longing to be lifted up and held. I picked up one child in one arm and another child in the other arm. The children were fascinated by the colour of my hair and also by the gold cross and chain that I wore around my neck. They were beautiful, with their jet black hair falling over their faces, and their big, dark pleading eyes. I thought how brave these children were, living in such poor circumstances, and still laughing and smiling despite all the suffering and hardship of their young lives.

A few of the younger children were running round without any pants on. Their bottoms were covered in sores and red marks and you could see their distended stomachs under their shirts. I noticed that practically every child had some kind of scar on its arms and legs, probably left behind from old sores. Many of the children still had open sores which were painted over with Mercurichrome, a red coloured lotion which acted as a healing aid. I wondered how the children managed to survive amongst all the dirt and the filth of the orphanage.

The courtyard was fairly large and used as a playground by the children. There were two walled-in flower beds with barbed wire over the walls and small flowering shrubs growing inside. People used to park their cars in the courtyard and pay a small monthly fee to the orphanage. The courtyard was filthy, although it was swept twice a day.

The orphanage looked derelict and consisted of three buildings overlooking the courtyard. There was a bakery on the fourth side. On the left hand side was the office. It was filled with empty tables and chairs and a few U.S. army lockers at the back. There was one filing cabinet in the far corner of the room with a few files in it. No one worked in the office and most of the time the room was left empty, except for the occasional meetings of the principal and the 'Cao-Dai' ladies, members of a strict religious sect, who ran the orphanage.

Co Thanh, a young Vietnamese nurse who was in charge of the babies' room, lived in a small room next to the office. Co Thanh was married and lived together with her husband and four children in that tiny room. The only furniture she had was a wooden bed, on which she and her husband and children all slept together, and a wardrobe. The room had no ventilation and no windows. Co Thanh cooked on a small kerosene stove just outside their room and washed from a nearby tap.

One of the children from the orphanage ran to tell Co Thanh I had arrived and she came down to greet me. She welcomed me in the few words of English she spoke, laughing as she did so to try and hide her shyness. She was very thin, but extremely pretty, and she had a quiet, reassuring voice. She wore a white cotton uniform over white satin pants and held up her long black hair in a French slide. Despite her poor living conditions she always looked neat. Her children were also clean and tidy, and although very poor, they wore clothes that at least fitted them.

The second building, which adjoined the first, consisted of a large hall downstairs and three large rooms above. The first room upstairs was the toddlers' room for children aged from one to about three years old. The second room was for older girls and the third stood quite empty, except for a small altar in the far corner decorated with flowers.

The hall downstairs was used mostly as a dining-room for the children, set out with four rows of long wooden benches and wooden tables where the children would come to eat twice a day. They usually ate at about eleven o'clock in the morning and four o'clock in the afternoon. In the mornings each child would be given hot bread fresh from the bakery—about half a French loaf each. At one end of the dining-hall was a small stage used for pantomimes put on by the children during festive seasons. The hall was light and airy, with ceiling fans and open shutters at the windows.

Next to the dining-hall was and open kitchen which overlooked a very dark corner of the courtyard. It was very dark and had no water or electricity. Inside there were two Vietnamese women working, cooking the evening rice in huge black pots supported on brick frameworks over burning charcoal fires. They were both on the plump side but had happy-looking faces. They turned to greet us, smiling happily and chatting amongst themselves. The women were dressed in patched black satin pants and old cotton shirts held together with safety pins as substitutes for buttons. In the middle of the kitchen was a large wooden table. Underneath the table were chicken hutches, full of chickens. An old dog which looked as if it had mange was scavenging around for something to eat.

When the women needed water they would carry it in plastic bowls and buckets from a tap opposite the kitchen, attached to the wall at the side of the third building. The tap was left constantly running and so this part of the courtyard was always wet and damp. Here the women would squat down or sit on very low home-made wooden stools, chopping and preparing fish and vegetables on wooden boards—they used very sharp kitchen knives. As the cooks prepared the food, other women from the orphanage would come and do their washing there or even bathe their children. Then, when everyone had finished, everything would be washed away together with buckets of water.

The only toilets in the orphanage were in this same dark, wet part of the courtyard. There were four toilets and each was a hole in the ground with a step on either side for squatting down over the hole. However, the toilets were so dirty that they were rarely used and the stone steps leading down to them were covered in human faeces. The children were probably afraid to go into the toilets because of the rats and so they just used the steps.

This damp part of the courtyard, so close to the kitchen, was an ideal living and breeding place for rats. I used to hear people say that there were twice as many rats in Saigon as there were children, and certainly the orphanage had its fair share. The rats were big, some about nine inches to nearly a foot long. When I first saw them I thought they were kittens because they were so big. The rats were something we came to accept, and had to live with.

The third and largest building contained three classrooms. The first classroom was empty and used as a junk room. The second classroom was run by Hom, one of the Vietnamese girls who lived at the house with us. There were about thirty children in Hom's class, aged from about seven to ten years old. They were seated neatly at individual desks and chairs learning arithmetic from the blackboard.

The third classroom was run by Co Tu, the other girl who lived at the house. Co Tu taught the younger children aged from four to about six years old and invited us into her classroom. She was rather plump and spoke English quite well, laughing all the time. The classroom was very decorative with paintings by the children put up on the walls and Chinese lanterns which Co Tu had made hanging from the ceiling.

The children welcomed us by folding their arms and bowing their heads which was the way children were taught to greet older people. Then Co Tu made the children sing. I noticed how happy they looked and how much they seemed to be enjoying their class activities. I really admired their courage.

Next to Co Tu's classroom was the sewing room. Here there was one middle-aged Vietnamese woman, very thin and shabbily dressed, working away at a sewing-machine. She stopped work to greet us and seemed a little embarrassed at her poor appearance. The clothes she was trying to mend looked beyond repair. This was another tiny room without ventilation and with no windows where the woman lived together with her children.

Room 4 was the largest of the rooms on the ground floor. It held about forty children aged from four to about six years old and also the handicapped children. Although Room 4 was a large room, there was little ventilation and the air smelled of urine. There were stale urine patches all over the tiled floor, especially at the end of the room used by the handicapped children.

Unfortunately, it was sometimes believed by the Vietnamese people that severely handicapped or disabled children were often people who had already lived one life in this world—a life of evil and misdoings—and that they were re-born severely handicapped for their second birth, as a punishment for their first life. Before Mrs Beach came to the orphanage, the handicapped and mentally retarded children were often just left to lie on their wooden beds all day, often in their own excreta and urine. If they fell off their beds they would be left on the floor. Nearly all these children were covered in sores on their arms, legs and backs. They all had otitis, which is an inflammation of the ear; they all had pus in the corners of their eyes and sores round their mouths, where the flies would settle. Some of the mentally retarded children were also deaf and dumb and would lie staring at the ceiling, hardly aware of their surroundings.

These children were fed twice daily, once in the morning and once in the afternoon. They would be removed from their beds and taken into the stone corridor outside. There the children who could feed themselves would cope as best they could and those who were totally incapable were fed by one of the woman helpers. Sometimes, when the children were left alone to feed, the rats would hover round them, waiting for a chance to snatch away the food. Often a child was so terrified that he would just gape at the rat finishing his meal. The children were quite aware of the rats, yet in their handicapped condition there was nothing they could do, and they would look on helplessly.

When the handicapped children had finished eating, they were left where they were, until they had had their bowels opened. Then the women would wash the children down with cold water, using their hands, and return them to their beds. Buckets of water would be thrown over the corridor and the remains of the food, the excrement and urine were all washed away together.

The babies' room, where I was going to work with Co Thanh, was on the second floor of this third building. It was light and airy, with windows on either side and two ceiling fans. There were three rows of cots, with ten cots in each row. The youngest babies were put in the first row. The women wrapped the new babies in cotton sheets or towels, binding their arms and legs so that they were unable to move. I thought the babies were beautiful as I walked up and down, but when I picked them up I realised how dirty and smelly they were.

Again, like the handicapped children in Room 4, the babies were left on their backs twenty-four hours a day. The only time they were washed was when they had their diapers changed and that was a quick wash under the cold tap. The older babies, aged from about six months to a year old, didn't wear diapers and when they were dirty the women would often smack them. All the babies had black and blue bottoms from bruising, either as a result of being smacked or virtually thrown into their cots.

The babies were fed four times a day, with about eight ounces of warm diluted tinned milk. They were never taken out of their cots to be fed. Instead, the women would settle each baby on its back, put the bottle in its mouth, and put a pillow under the bottle to keep it in an upright position. After a couple of minutes the women would come round and collect up the bottles again, regardless of whether the baby had finished his feed or not. Some of the babies were slow feeders. Others dropped their bottles and so would lose their feed. When the women had collected the bottles together they would drink the left-over milk themselves, or give it to their own children from the same bottles. Most of the babies were very underweight and thin.

As I walked between the rows of cots and picked up the babies I was aware of the women watching me. Co Thanh was explaining to the women in Vietnamese that I would soon be coming to work with them. Although these women were very poor and didn't care much about their work or themselves, I always found them easy to work with. Most of them had lost their husbands in the war and were unable to support themselves and their children elsewhere. They worked at the orphanage in return for a roof over their heads and their daily share of food. They had practically no possessions of their own and scarcely any clothes. Each month they were given a little pocket money, about 600 piasters—at that time the equivalent to 70p in English money. Perhaps once a month the women would buy themselves a little extra fish or a piece of meat and a present for their children.

Mrs Beach introduced me to Ba Sau, the woman who was in charge of the older children. Ba Sau was the most feared woman in the orphanage, both for her appearance and her strictness. She was a very thin, middle-aged woman, whose most prominent feature was a false eye which didn't fit properly and protruded slightly from her eye socket. She never wore the eye straight and it looked as though it would pop out at any minute. She was very strict with the children and would often beat them with a stick.

There was also a treatment room on the second floor. It was a fair-sized room with ceiling fans and closed shutters at the windows. It was covered in dust and smelt very musty. There were several glass cupboards in the room, filled with various surgical instruments which were never used at the orphanage and a few boxes of old medicines which had been donated by the Americans. Most of the medicines were tranquillizers and anti-depressants—hardly of use to the children.

Before we left we went to meet Ba Kieu, the principal of the orphanage and a member of the 'Cao-Dai' sect. 'Ba' was the Vietnamese name given to an older or married woman. Ba Kieu lived in the upstairs part of a house next door to the orphanage, across from the market place. She offered us some Chinese tea which was very refreshing and had a woody taste and aroma to it. Ba Kieu spoke excellent English and told me how pleased she was that I had come to work at the orphanage and care for the children. I liked her immediately. She was rather a fat lady with a very kindly-looking face and a soft voice.

After our meeting with Ba Kieu, Mrs Beach and I went home. Darkness falls quickly in the East and it was dark by 7 p.m. Mrs Beach spoke in French to the taxi driver, explaining to him where we wanted to go and bargaining for the price. Whenever you took a taxi in Saigon, you had to agree the price with the driver first or else you would end up paying double. I wondered how I would be able to make my own way around Saigon, not speaking French and unable to pronounce or remember the Vietnamese words. There still seemed to be just as much traffic on the streets. There were very few lights and the streets were mostly lit by the little oil lamps which the women hung from their food stalls.

Before I went to bed Mrs Beach told me that there was a curfew every night between 11 p.m. and 6 a.m. in the morning. She explained that sometimes during the night we would hear occasional gun shots, but that it was usually just the police shooting into the air having spotted someone out walking. I went to my room and stretched out on the bed. I was very tired but I couldn't go to sleep. I kept thinking about the orphans and all I had seen. I thought of the children in England, loved and cared for by their parents, living in their own homes, wearing their own clothes and having plenty of food to eat. Here in Saigon were children who were virtually ignored, with no one to love or care for them. I could not wait to start work.

CHAPTER 2

I felt rather lost during my first few days in Saigon and not very useful. I couldn't possibly find my way round by myself since I did not understand one word of Vietnamese. Vietnamese is a tone language and depending on the tone level at which you pronounce it, one word can have up to five different meanings.

I spent all day at the house with the handicapped children, helping to feed, change and play with them. I helped the polio children into their calipers, and with the aid of crutches, they would start walking up and down the driveway. The children were full of enthusiasm and easy to manage, appreciating all the care and attention they were receiving.

We wanted to try to make the severely handicapped children who were still unable to walk and the mentally retarded children play together—something they hadn't yet learned to do. By interesting the children in playing we made them exercise their limbs at the same time. Gradually they became more aware of their surroundings and began to take some interest in what was going on round them. We began by persuading the children to play with sand or water, in order to make them use their hands. Later we brought out small toys, threw a ball to them or built up piles of bricks. One thing the children always loved were balloons. Sometimes the children would respond quickly, sometimes they seemed to shut themselves away from us and throw anything we gave them to play with away. The polio children always responded quickly and were quick to learn, but the mentally retarded children took much longer.

Every morning Mrs Beach would give one of the women helpers money for the market and she would buy enough food for the day for everyone. At about 11 a.m. we would give the children their lunch. Mrs Beach had taught the children to sit up at small wooden tables which she had made, instead of sitting or lying on the ground to eat. For some of the children it was the first time they had ever had their own little wooden chairs to sit on. The children ate mostly rice, with a little meat or fish or vegetables. Even when we offered them more meat or fish they would often leave it, because they were not accustomed to eating it. Some just ate plain rice with a little soup to moisten it.

When the children had finished eating we would settle them down to sleep for their afternoon siesta. Most of the children slept in the classroom after we had put plastic mats on the floor and turned on the ceiling fans to cool the room. One of the Vietnamese women would then cook for us and we would eat the same kind of food, usually meat or fish with vegetables and rice, followed by bananas. We would sleep for an hour or so as well since it was far too hot to do any work.

During the rainy season, between April and September, it would usually pour with rain early every afternoon. The rain would last for about an hour and then the skies would clear and the sun would come out. The first time I heard the rain I thought a pipe must have burst in the house. It was as if someone was hurling buckets of water out of the skies. It really poured and the streets were quickly flooded because most of the drains either overflowed or were already blocked up. It was an ideal time for children to run out and take a free shower and the poorer people would collect the water in buckets to use later for washing and cooking.

In the afternoon we would wake the children up at about 2.30 p.m. and give them all a shower. We would fill our bowls with water and wash the children thoroughly with soap, rinsing them off under the hose. The children loved splashing around in the courtyard and splashing us. We would then help the polio children into their calipers again, encouraging them to put them on by themselves. Then Mrs Beach and I would start the other children playing again, making them do exercises on their paralysed limbs.

The other Vietnamese women would help us to delouse the children's hair. We washed their hair with special shampoo and combed it through with a fine tooth-comb, removing dead lice and nits. We used to clean the children's ears with cotton wool twisted around fine toothpicks which we dipped in hydrogen peroxide. We bathed their eyes with warmed normal saline and applied eye drops to the children with conjunctivitis. We also had to cope with the occasional roundworms which the children either passed in their stools or vomited. Some of the worms were nine inches long, and about half an inch in diameter. They really frightened the children who would scream out, wondering what on earth was happening to them. Other children had ringworm, a contagious skin disease caused by a fungus. This usually started on their heads and we would have to shave off their hair.

Every day we treated coughs and colds, chest infections and common diarrhoeas. Each child received supplementary vitamin pills. When they were really sick, perhaps with a high fever, we would keep them back at the house and I would look after them. We could usually diagnose and treat the children ourselves but if they were seriously ill we would take them to the children's hospital. Doctors in general practice were few and far between and rather expensive.

When I first started working at the orphanage I used to wait in the morning for the van to arrive, bringing the handicapped children to the house for the day, and travel back to the orphanage in it. Every morning Mrs Beach got up early and cooked a large saucepan of meat and vegetable soup for the toddlers and I would take the soup with me. Just before midday she would send a Vietnamese boy who owned a Honda to collect me so that I could come home for lunch. At about two o'clock in the afternoon he would drive me back to the orphanage again. In this way I slowly began to recognize and remember the streets.

The first morning I started work in the babies' room I arrived equipped with soap and towels, baby powder and zinc and castor oil cream. I wanted to improve the health of the babies, and the first thing I did was to clean them. There was no sink in the babies' room itself, but there were two sinks in a little room adjoining it. I found two plastic bowls and one baby bath. I washed out the bowls and filled them with warm water. I laid a towel out across the draining board and the women brought me a pile of clean baby clothes and diapers.

I had thirty babies to bath and I wondered how I would

manage to do them all. I began by bathing the smallest babies and worked my way round the room as fast as I could, carrying babies from their cots to the sink, bathing them, and then carrying them back again to collect the next baby. I bathed each baby in a clean bowl of warm water and I also washed their hair. Dirt had collected and hardened under the babies' arms and between their groins. When I washed off the dirt I could see that underneath their skin had become sore and infected. I washed and dried the babies, powdered them and applied the zinc and castor oil cream under their arms and between their legs. All the cot sheets needed changing because they were either still wet or smelled of stale urine. After about the sixteenth baby I began to slow down. Tired as I was, I forced myself to keep going and eventually they were all bathed, in clean clothes and lying in clean cots.

As soon as I had finished I reached for my packet of cigarettes and stood outside on the veranda overlooking the courtyard. As I inhaled the smoke deep into my lungs I thought back to the time when I was nursing, working on the pædiatric ward, with perhaps just two or three babies to care for. How things had changed. Co Thanh and the women had just sat on the floor all morning playing with their own children and watching me work. However, I could not hope to build up a good relationship with them if on my first day I started to tell them what to do. Also, I had to remember that these women came here long before me, and would probably remain long after I had left. I felt sorry for them. I just hoped that by setting a good example they would perhaps try to copy me. Before I left for lunch, Co Thanh came over and whispered, 'Co Ly, number one.' Mrs Beach told me that the Vietnamese called all foreigners either number one or number ten, depending on whether they liked you or not. Number one was very good and number ten was very bad. At least I had made a start.

Despite the heat, at 2 p.m. I was back in the babies' room. Co Thanh was not there and the rest of the women were asleep on the floor, resting their heads on their arms with their children beside them. The shutters were closed and the ceiling fans turned on to cool the room. I tiptoed round, careful not to wake anyone, for most of the babies were asleep too. When the women awoke they were surprised to see me again. At 2.30 p.m. the babies' milk was brought in. I started to pick up the youngest babies, holding them in my arms and feeding them from the bottle. I realised the women were watching me all the time. I had only fed three babies when they came round and collected the bottles again.

Later in the afternoon one of the women went out and bought some sticks of sugar cane. When she came back she offered me one and the women all watched to see how I would cope. I looked at them, waiting for them to eat first, so that I could follow. The woman who bought the sugar cane bit the end of her stick and ripped off the outer skin with her teeth. Now it was my turn. I tried to follow her example, but my teeth were not as strong as hers and I could only bite off small pieces at a time. We all started to laugh. When I did finally manage to bite into it the taste was delicious. We sat down on the floor eating our sugar cane together, chewing on it until all the juice was extracted, and then spitting it out. From that time on I felt they had accepted me.

For the rest of the afternoon I watched the babies play and helped them take their first steps. The women seemed to be discussing me in great detail. They were very inquisitive. They compared the colour of my yellow hair to their black hair, my blue eyes to their dark brown eyes, and my high nose to their flat noses. They would come and touch my nose, smile approvingly, then put their hand to their own nose, laugh shyly and in English say, 'Number Ten'. They constantly touched and pinched my nose. They would come and feel my hair, twisting it up on top of my head, in the same style as they did their own. They would even put their hands round my waist to feel how fat or thin I was and felt my arms. They were interested in my clothes and in the material of my jeans and T-shirt. They studied my feet carefully and noticed the arch on my foot which all Europeans have, their own feet being very flat. They tried on my shoes in turn and made me try on theirs, all the time busily discussing and comparing. They loved to watch me smoke a cigarette and blow the smoke down my nose. They would take a cigarette and try to copy me, laughing and coughing as they did so.

I could not imagine English girls touching their friends and acquaintances as freely and openly as these women did amongst themselves. But then women in England had everything compared to the women in the orphanage—their own homes, their own clothes, make-up, husbands. These women had nothing, except their own children and each other. They were not sexually involved with each other, but because of the way they lived, a bare human existence, they were beyond self-embarrassment. They washed together, went to the toilet together, fed their babies together and slept together. Most of them had no alternative.

The women would always openly breastfeed their babies, wherever they were, sitting in the market place or riding in one of the lambretta buses, and no one ever took any notice. They would usually continue breastfeeding their babies for as long as they had their own milk, sometimes for as long as two years. If they had enough milk they would often breastfeed another baby as well. The poor people could not afford to buy milk and if the baby wasn't breast fed, it would probably be drinking rice water. Even when their breasts were quite dry mothers would still allow their children to lie down at night and go to sleep sucking their breasts, but I think this was a form of security for both mother and child. When people have nothing they need one another. This was apparent in the relationship between the women, and in the mother and child relationship. The warmth, love and comfort of the human touch between mother and child seemed to make up for some of the things they didn't have.

I never knew the women's names. They never called each other by their own name. The only time they would use a name was when talking to each other and referring to someone else. The women always called each other 'chi' which in English means sister. The men always called each other 'anh' meaning brother. Even their own children were rarely called by their own names but by the word 'em' which could mean either a younger brother or sister, or child. A husband, when talking to his wife, would call her 'em' and the wife would call her husband 'anh'.

Brothers and sisters in a Vietnamese family would call each other 'Chi Hai, Chi Ba or Chi Tu', 'hai', 'ba' and 'tu' being the Vietnamese words for two, three and four, thus meaning 'Sister number two, sister number three and sister number four'. It would be the same for the men, 'Anh Hai, Anh Ba, Anh Tu'. Sometimes a mother of up to nine and ten children would name them in numerical order. That was how I got my own Vietnamese name, 'Co Nam', which meant 'girl number five', as I had been born fifth in my family.

There was not a great variety of Vietnamese names from which to choose and if mothers did actually choose a name for their children they would name them after something that had a beautiful meaning, like the sun, or flowers, or a precious stone. Vietnamese family names were nearly all the same. I think there are only about one hundred different family names in the whole Vietnamese language. The most common family name, and used by about half the Vietnamese population, was Nguyen, the family name of the President Nguyen Van Thieu. The family name always came first. Usually, if it was a male, 'van' was the middle name, and then the person's own name came last. If it was a female, 'thi' would be the middle name, and so I was Nguyen Thi Nam. A lot of young people chose their own names when they grew up, and would only use their real names for official purposes. The Vietnamese for 'Mr.' is 'Ong' and older men who were not personal or family friends were often called 'Ong Hai, Ong Ba, Ong Tu,' and likewise the older women were known as 'Ba Hai' Ba Tu, Ba Nam.' Because of these customs I seldom knew people's real names.

I worked really hard during my first few weeks at the orphanage. I usually arrived in the babies' room at about eight o'clock and would start my round of baths. I enjoyed bathing the babies, but bathing thirty at a time single-handed was exhausting. At least their general condition began to improve and the sores under their arms and between their groins were gradually disappearing. Sometimes I stood at the sink feeling ready to drop. It was so hot that by the time I had finished the baths I was soaked through because of perspiration and being splashed by the babies.

The women still did not help me but rather looked upon this time as a relaxation period, since I relieved their work load. I did not like to ask them to help because they did spend practically twenty-four hours a day in that room, and were probably sick of the sight of babies. They were quiet, terribly thin, and had a melancholy look about them. I wanted to help them and was glad to be able to relieve them for a couple of hours each day. They would use this time to do their own chores for they had to do their own washing as well as their children's. An old washing-machine stood in the corner of the room, and one of the older girls was responsible for washing all the babies' clothes and diapers.

The older girls in the orphanage would come in and ask if they could wash their hair in the second sink. While I bathed the babies in the first sink, they would be washing their hair in the second. Someone else would be filling bowls of water for washing in the middle of the floor. The floor was always covered in water and I used to take off my shoes and roll up my jeans to stop myself getting too wet. Women from the babies' room would come in and urinate with their children, squatting down on the floor next to me. I didn't notice at first, but when I felt something warm running under my bare feet, followed by a bucket of water over my legs, I realized what it was and immediately replaced my shoes.

When the women urinated over the floor, washed away the urine and proceeded to set up a small gasoline stove to boil up the rice and cook the fish, the smell and the heat were too much for me, and I would lean over the sink and vomit. But I was determined to keep going, and would wash my face under the cold tap, and continue my work. Working conditions in Saigon were far from easy and words cannot describe what it was really like. You had to be there, to feel and experience it. I cannot therefore describe adequately the smell of the place, but I was at first overwhelmed by it.

Some of these poor babies were covered in boils. They seemed to appear mainly on their faces and over their heads. We had to shave off the babies' hair to reach the boil more easily and to prevent further infection from the hair. Then Co Thanh, who was an expert at excising boils and very gentle, would take a sharp razor and open the boil in the middle, squeezing out all the pus. Then she would fill a syringe with an injection of penicillin and irrigate the wound, and finally cover it with a clean dressing. I frequently picked up boils myself and she used to treat mine in the same way. The women also went through my hair to delouse me, but at this stage I was still free of head lice.

The babies never had any toys to play with. One afternoon Mrs Beach and I went to the market and bought a bag full of small plastic toys. They were very cheap, bright and colourful, and I thought the babies would like them. They did, and so did the other children in the orphanage. By the end of the week every single toy had disappeared and the babies had nothing left to play with. The next time we bought toys for them I took them all home with me. They still disappeared but not quite so quickly.

As I started to find my way round Saigon I began to stay later at the orphanage and returned home in a taxi. When I first started to use the taxis, I would write down the name of the street on which I lived and how much I was prepared to pay. The problem was that many of the taxi drivers could not read, and I, being unable to pronounce the names correctly, used to end up all over the city. Most of the taxi drivers, seeing that I was a foreigner, would immediately put up the price, but I always refused to pay more than 150 piasters for my ride home.

To the Vietnamese people every foreigner was an American and the Americans always had 'beaucoup money'. The Vietnamese people had never heard of England or the English. There were only about one hundred British people altogether in Saigon, and most of the other foreigners were Americans in the U.S. Army. If you were not American, you were bound to be French.

Most of the taxi drivers could understand French, but only a few words of English. I would often hear the driver muttering, 'You—American. Beaucoup money. Me—Vietnam. Tee tee money,' or 'You—Cheap Charlie. You number ten.' If the taxi driver couldn't read the name of the street on which I lived he still pretended he could so that he wouldn't lose the fare. He would drive to the nearest hotel and try to drop me off there, but I never paid up until I had reached the correct destination. I remember one taxi driver asking for something like 1000 piasters instead of 150 at the end of the journey. I handed him 150 piasters and he threw them back at me. Then he started shouting angrily at me in Vietnamese and proceeded to drive off in a fury down the street with me still sitting in his cab. I opened all the taxi doors, and each time he reached back and closed them I opened them again. He was afraid of damaging his taxi and finally let me out. With an angry look on his face he accepted 150 piasters. I walked home feeling rather sorry for him but nevertheless could not be swindled like that.

I used to arrive home at the end of each day feeling worn out. Mrs Beach and I would sit down over a cup of tea and sometimes eat some small Vietnamese cakes or biscuits. I have always had a very sweet tooth and I missed my mother's homemade fruit cakes more than anything else in Saigon. After tea Mrs Beach would catch up on her administrative work and I would fill up the washing-machine in the courtyard and wash the handicapped children's clothes, smoking as I worked. Then I used to sit under the cold tap in the shower and cool off. It was so hot in Saigon that even when I took a shower and had cold water running all over me, I could still feel myself sweating.

The women who worked at the house during the day went home quite early in the evening, so Mrs Beach would cook supper. Sometimes I would cook, but I didn't enjoy doing so because the kitchen was too dirty. Every time we opened the oven door there would be a huge rat sitting inside which would quickly disappear down a hole in the back of the oven. I used to tiptoe into the kitchen and quietly turn the gas full on in the hope that I could gas the rats. Later I would turn off the gas and open the oven door to see how many I had killed. They always seemed to manage to escape down the hole. Mrs Beach used to set rat-traps in the kitchen at night, baiting them with a piece of meat or cheese. The rats were so crafty that they knew just how to take the meat or cheese without being caught in the trap and we never caught any.

Rats were not the only problem; insects were a menace too. You couldn't leave a bowl of sugar or anything sweet around because the ants would always find it. Even when we put sugar in an air-tight jar they seemed to get in. I think the ants must have sat watching and waiting, because whenever I put a spoonful of sugar in my coffee, ants would always be floating around on top. At night, when we were sitting eating our meal, other little insects would come in and fly round the fluorescent lights. There were literally hundreds of them and they were always falling down dead onto the middle of the table or into our suppers. We would just pick them out of our food and continue eating.

I always went to bed early partly because I was always tired, and partly because there wasn't much to do between the hours of curfew. My body ached and I lay awake for hours. Try as I might, I couldn't forget the orphanage. Every time I closed my eyes I saw the babies lying in their cots. I would be back there again, bathing babies, changing babies, feeding babies. I used to wake up suddenly after dozing off, thinking I had fallen asleep while working in the babies' room. Then I would wake up again later in the night, careful not to move, thinking the babies were asleep on my bed with me. I couldn't stop thinking about them. My mind seemed to be running away with me. I had never had that kind of experience before.

On some nights I was too hot and uncomfortable to sleep. Eventually I would get up and sit outside in the courtyard smoking, listening to the sounds of the night. I could hear the crickets in the grass, hear the cats crying as they explored the rubbish heaps looking for something to eat. The crack of rifle fire would echo through the darkness causing the dogs to howl. Sometimes I would listen to the distant gunfire all night long.

I would go to the kitchen for a glass of iced water. Rats would scamper out of my way, darting into the corner. I could see cockroaches running over the top of the cooker, the top of the table and along the draining board. They would run over my bare feet and I would take the broom and swat them, killing as many as I could and leaving them for the ants to devour. What a place to be.

As time went on I gradually started to remember a few words of Vietnamese. The first word I learnt was 'cam on' which in English means 'thank-you'. I don't think there is a Vietnamese word for 'please'. I also learnt how to greet people and to enquire after their health. Then I started to learn how to count, first up to ten, then to twenty, then to one hundred and so on until I reached a thousand. Counting was very useful as I could now barter over how much I paid for things. By the end of my stay in Vietnam I could understand the simple language of the poor very adequately and was able to converse with them quite freely.

When I first arrived in Saigon everything was still very cheap, although prices began to rise gradually. I could buy a packet of cigarettes for about 10p in English money. I smoked Vietnamese cigarettes made from American tobacco. They were menthol cigarettes but much cheaper than ordinary ones. Most Vietnamese women didn't smoke and Vietnamese girls never did. I never smoked in the street or in public, but I chain smoked when I came home at night.

I had volunteered to go to Saigon and was not paid. Mrs Beach gave me a float of about 5000 piasters for daily expenditure on taxi fares, medicines for the children etc. Every month she gave me 12,000 piasters for pocket money—about ten pounds. As soon as I got my pocket money I would buy cigarettes and go to the market to buy some fish or fruit for the women in the orphanage. Sometimes my mother would send me some money and I usually shared it out between Co Thanh and the other women who worked in the babies' room.

The average Vietnamese was paid very little, the monthly wage being between 12,000—14,000 piasters, which would not even buy a whole sack of rice. Because the people were so poor they were always trying to make money on the side. They had to—to survive. Some people would do almost anything for money. In some cases, if the price was right, men would kill for money. You could not escape from the poverty in Saigon. There were no fat or overweight Vietnamese people. Their diet consisted mainly of boiled rice, with a little meat, fish or vegetables. The Vietnamese would fight over what English people give to their dogs.

When the Vietnamese bought a chicken they would take it home and kill it themselves. This was done by twisting the chicken's neck and slitting its throat with a sharp knife. They would let the blood drain out into a clean bowl and afterwards plunge it into hot water to loosen its feathers for plucking. Chickens were usually boiled and made into a curry. The whole chicken would be chopped up and put into a saucepan of boiling water. The legs and feet went in as well as the head and neck. The congealed blood of the chicken would be boiled as well. They ate everything, including the blood. Mrs Beach always roasted her chickens but when I lived with the Vietnamese I used to eat chickens the same way as they did, blood and all.

The Vietnamese had no love for animals and were rather cruel to them. They didn't mind dogs but they hated cats, believing that a cat brought bad luck to the household if it came into the home. Dogs were never treated as pets and were only given boiled rice to eat. They were never house trained but they soon learnt to be clean for fear of being beaten. Sometimes they were beaten to death. They were skinny, full of mange and covered with fleas. The streets were so crowded that dogs were often knocked down by a car or a Honda and most of them limped. If a dog died in the street it would just be thrown onto the rubbish heap, providing an easy meal for another hungry scavenger.

One morning on my way to the orphanage, I saw the children gathered round a small tree in the courtyard. There was a tiny kitten in the tree, soaked to the skin and howling its head off. The children had been trying unsuccessfully to drown it in a bowl of water and had then taken it into the courtyard to see who could throw it highest into the tree. One of the older children would retrieve the kitten each time and it would then be thrown up again. I rescued the kitten and rubbed it dry in the babies' room. It disappeared during the morning and I discovered that one of the women had thrown it out. They could not understand why I bothered to take care of such a helpless little creature. The taxi drivers refused to have a kitten in their cabs, and I had to walk home that day. I only managed to keep the kitten a few days for one of the women finally threw it over the wall when I was not there. I often found kittens in the street but despite my efforts they usually died.

There were so many rats in the orphanage that every night the older boys would set the rat-traps to try to catch a few. One morning, they did catch a huge rat and brought the trap into the courtyard. The children poured gasoline over the rat and the rat's fur caught alight and slowly burned. The children let the rat out of the trap and threw stones at it as it died. It was a horrible sight, blood and guts all over the courtyard, and the poor pathetic creature trying to escape. I turned my head and was sick.

The Vietnamese seemed to like horses more than they did cats and dogs. There was a riding school in the centre of Saigon. The teaching was done in French and the pupils were mainly French or American. It was quite expensive and few Vietnamese could afford to go. In the suburbs of the city there was a large race course and there was a race-meeting every Saturday afternoon. Later, I sometimes went to watch with the girls from my home. Vietnamese horses were much smaller than our own British horses.

By the end of October the babies' condition had improved considerably and the women at last began to co-operate, taking it in turns to dry the babies as I bathed them. They started to take the babies out of their cots and allow them to crawl on the floor and play. At feeding times they would let the babies have their bottles for longer and most of them had time to finish their feed. Common ear and eye infections began to clear up because the babies were so much cleaner and boils began to disappear.

Every week I scrubbed all the cots and put them out in the sun to dry and the women washed the floor twice a day. Gradually the old smell of stale urine began to disappear and the babies' room became the cleanest room in the whole orphanage. The women were still not very gentle with the babies and most of them had black and blue bruises on their backs. They would put the babies on the table in the middle of the room to change them and then go away to do something else. Sometimes the babies would roll over and fall off the table onto the floor. One baby died after a fall, early in the morning before I arrived. The women never said anything to me but having spent so much time with the babies I knew them all and realised he was missing. They eventually admitted that he had been put outside on the rubbish heap in the street.

Sometimes I did not bother to go back to the house for lunch but stayed in the orphanage. I started to eat the same food as the women and in the early afternoon I used to lie down on the floor, rest my head on my arms and sleep for a while. I even started to wear Vietnamese clothes, black satin pants and an old cotton shirt, and pin my hair up in the Vietnamese style. Ba Kieu, the principal of the orphanage, seeing that I liked the Vietnamese clothes so much, made me another pair of black pants and a beautiful white ao-dai. She even went to the market and bought me a pair of shoes, handmade with dragons made out of sequins on them. I was slowly losing contact with my own people and hardly knew any other foreigners in Saigon. I was so happy amongst the Vietnamese that I only wanted to be with them.

I remember when Mrs Beach took me to the British Embassy. It was only a small building and stood opposite the American Embassy, on the main street that led to the 'Doc-lap' or Independence Palace. The British Embassy was the coldest place in Saigon and when you came out the heat really hit you. Mrs. Beach and I used to go in to have a quick look through the British newspapers. This reminder of England never made me homesick and although I missed my family and would have loved them to visit me in Saigon I had no thoughts of leaving.

Mrs Beach and I would be invited to the British Embassy homes for cocktails or dinner. One evening we were invited out to dinner and I changed out of my Vietnamese clothes and put on a dress, although my legs were covered in mosquito bites. We took a taxi to our host's house, which was very large, beautifully furnished and with air conditioning throughout. I took an immediate dislike to it and although everyone was charming to me I wanted to go home. We sat down to a dinner of fine English food which was followed by coffee and liqueurs.

Somehow it just didn't seem right to me, the English living in such splendour in a city full of poverty, and the poor Vietnamese who lived in such squalor having to wait on the British hand and foot. I felt embarrassed as the Vietnamese servant served me and would rather it had been the other way round. Perhaps I was wrong, but after seeing how the women at the orphanage lived this luxurious way of life made me uneasy . . . it was all out of proportion. It made me sick at heart and I never went back to the Embassy again.

I didn't have much contact with the Americans either. President Nixon had already started to withdraw the American troops and although there were still about 50,000 regular soldiers in South Vietnam they were gradually all leaving. Some of the U.S. army officers stayed behind as civilians to act a military advisers to the South Vietnamese army. Many had a Vietnamese wife and had started a family. The soldiers returning to the States would take their wives and girlfriends with them, rushing off to the lawyers' offices to make out marriage licences, passports and exit visas. The Americans were very unpopular and disliked by the Vietnamese. The lowest wage for an American soldier in South Vietnam was 1,000 dollars per month. They bought whatever they wanted without having to ask and at night they threw away their money in the bars, on drink and on women.

Many girls and young women became prostitutes because it was a quick way to make money. Some of the women who worked in the bars or stood on street corners really hated the Americans and they hated what they were doing even more. Most of the girls would only sleep with an American and not with a Vietnamese because the American paid more. And often the girl would slip away during the night with the American's watch and wallet.

A married Vietnamese man would often send his wife out at night to work in one of the bars. Boyfriends would hire their girlfriends out for the night, providing the price was right. A young boy would take his sister out on the back of his Honda and would ride around until he saw an American. Then in pidgin English he would say: 'You want number one girl, you want my sister'. And very often the girls couldn't speak a word of English.

The Americans didn't eat Vietnamese food. Their own food was flown over to them from the States. When they had surplus food stuffs, especially loaves of cut bread and cartons of milk, they would distribute it to the orphanages in Saigon. As soon as their truck drew up in the courtyard the children would run over to greet the men and then sit quietly eating the bread and drinking the milk.

The Government of South Vietnam was against adoptions of Vietnamese babies as these children would grow up to be the future citizens of Vietnam. The boys would be needed for military service when they were of age. Vietnamese babies were sent for adoption only when agencies found them piled into orphages suffering from malnutrition and under-development.

There was one American I got to know in the U.S. Air Force. His name was Bill and he was married with two children. His wife was in the States and as Bill was shortly to leave Vietnam he wanted to adopt a baby girl. Bill came to the orphanage nearly every day to look for a little girl but although we had many babies who were true orphans and available for adoption, Co Thanh was very reluctant to let them go. He always brought something for Co Thanh and the women, such as soap from the American P.X. or sweets for their children, and medicines for us. He also obtained a large double stainless steel sink which he had installed in the babies' room.

Two well-dressed Vietnamese women also frequently came in to look at the babies and would talk at length to Co Thanh. Then one afternoon, just as I was returning to the orphanage, the two women passed me in the courtyard on their way out, carrying one of our babies. The baby was dressed in new clothes and wrapped in a clean shawl. I went up to the babies' room and there was Co Thanh looking very happy and holding quite a lot of money in her hand which she was about to share out with the women. I realised immediately what had happened. Co Thanh was negotiating adoptions quietly on the side and making money from it.

Bill had come to the orphanage with adoption papers he had obtained from a Vietnamese lawyer to make the adoption legal. He would pay the lawyer money and not Co Thanh. Horrified as I was to think that people were actually capable of selling a baby, I saw the advantage of the system. The baby would benefit because he would go to a real home and the poor women helpers would have a little money for themselves. It was a sad state of affairs but I had to accept it. I told Bill about Co Thanh's practice and although at first he was reluctant to comply he finally came to an agreement with her and was able to take home his baby girl.

I learned later that mothers who could not afford to support their own babies or even very young children would quite often sell them to someone else. When they went out to work they would try and save enough money to buy their child back again but more often than not they left them in the new homes. I knew of women who sold their babies for as little as 10,000 piasters, less than ten English pounds.

A negro American came to the orphanage and just seemed to want to look round. He saw we didn't have much and brought us an old refrigerator and some U.S. army lockers. Then late one evening when I was not there, he came back again and filled the children's dining-hall with chairs and tables, refrigerators, U.S. army lockers, old beds and electric fans. I thought how kind he was to have brought them for us and we decided what could be used in the orphanage and what might be useful to Mrs Beach back at the house.

Then suddenly one morning a Vietnamese Major and some of his soldiers came in and inquired after the missing items. I didn't know at the time that the American had come to some arrangement with the Vietnamese Major and that all the things had been stolen. I discovered that the furniture and the refrigerators had merely been stored in the orphanage and that the Vietnamese Major had come to pick them up and sell them at a profit in the market. The Major looked everywhere for the 'interfering American woman' as he called me, but I stayed well out of sight because I had no intention of giving anything back. After all, our children needed the things far more than he did.

As the babies continued to improve and the women were beginning to take more care of them, we began to think of ways to help the other children. Mrs Beach had started play therapy sessions for the toddlers, paying a small monthly salary to two Vietnamese girls to go into the orphanage every morning and afternoon to play with the children. We were able to obtain toys from the Gordon Barclay Fund, another small British charity working in South Vietnam. The Gordon Barclay Fund had two well-equipped vans and their workers would visit various other orphanages in and around Saigon, introducing the children to simple, educational toys and teaching them to play.

In Saigon a public health service, child care officers or baby clinics did not exist. Most of the two hundred children in the orphanage had never been vaccinated. If disease or illness struck it spread quickly. Vaccines could be obtained from the Pharmacy if someone was prepared to administer them to the children. I suggested we should start a vaccination programme for the children and both Co Thanh and Ba Kieu agreed it would be a good idea. We obtained a supply of polio vaccine and bought sugar cubes to take away the taste. The children lined up outside the babies' room and as they came in we gave them each a sugar cube to swallow. In about two hours we were finished.

We also collected a supply of smallpox vaccine from the Pharmacy. Again we worked in the babies' room because it was the cleanest room in the orphanage. We burned a small oil lamp so that we could sterilize the needles as we administered the vaccine. We vaccinated all the babies first and then the children of the women who worked in the room. Next we called the other children together, and as they came in we scratched a small surface of the skin on the upper, outer side of their arm and administered a small drop of the vaccine to each child. We were soon finished and when the children appeared with a small scab over their vaccination site we knew they had all taken.

The children who had been brought to the orphanage shortly after birth had never known their real parents or what it was like to live in a proper home. They often slept three to one bed because there were not enough beds in the orphanage for all the children. The children liked to sleep together because the knowledge that their friends were close by provided them with a little comfort and security. They often clung onto each other as they slept, with their arms and legs entwined. With other children around them, they were not afraid of the women who sometimes beat them, or of the rats.

Children who were brought in from the streets, however, missed their freedom, missed not being able to please themselves, and could not live in the confinement of the orphanage. They managed to survive on the streets because they had always done so. They knew the places where they were most likely to get some food when they were hungry. They found themselves a place to sleep at night, either in the empty market place, or under a newspaper stall. They slept in shop doorways or on street corners and knew how to avoid the police.

Most street children preferred to work rather than steal for a living. They would shine shoes, watch cars, sell newspapers or walk the streets selling bread; others would sort through the rubbish dumps in the street, collecting glass bottles, tin cans or old used paper—anything which could be sold and used again. There were many more street boys than street girls. Usually the girls stayed at home to help their mothers or would go to the markets with their mother and sell something. There were some girls on the streets, but only a few. They would sell flowers and peanuts to the Americans, and when they were older would work in the bars.

Some children were brought to the orphanage by the police having been found wandering around the street; some were brought in by one of their parents and then abandoned. Children of about five or six years of age who were brought in and suddenly separated from their families could not accept the change in their surroundings, but nor could they have survived on the streets. They often tried to run away and would walk the streets for days on end, without food, without shelter, searching in vain for their parents. Sometimes the children would be knocked down by a Honda in the overcrowded streets. Eventually they would be picked up again by the police and brought back to the orphanage.

If a child frequently tried to run away and was repeatedly brought back by the police, the women would shackle the child to a bed. Often the child was terrified, alone during the day with perhaps one or two physically handicapped or mentally retarded children as his only companions. And always the rats.

Such was the case of a six-year-old girl whose mother was Vietnamese and her father American. After the father had returned to the States, their mother could no longer afford to support her children and she had therefore brought the little girl and her older brother to the orphanage. They were very beautiful, looking more American than Vietnamese and both had very blonde hair and very pale skin. The Vietnamese considered a white skin beautiful compared to their own yellow skin.

The little girl was very afraid and kept trying to run away. The police would bring her back and in the end the women shackled her to one of the beds with a chain fastened to her ankle and locked to the bed. She cried all day. She was so afraid that she refused to eat and became very thin. Her hair became infested with head lice and the women chopped it off. Due to lack of washing and always wearing the same dirty clothes she contracted scabies. The sores which formed as a result of her constant scratching became infected and the infection spread to her eyes which she had rubbed as she cried.

We immediately contacted HOLT, a large American adoption agency which operated in orphanages throughout South Vietnam. Its aim was to send as many half-caste and black American children and babies back to the States as possible. HOLT sent one of their Vietnamese social workers to the orphanage. Contact was made with the children's mother and their home situation was assessed. The mother agreed that she could no longer support her children, and the little girl and her brother were taken away from the orphanage into one of HOLT's homes. Later they were both adopted by the same American family so that they could stay together.

Most Vietnamese families had eight or nine children, sometimes more. There was no birth control and many babies died before they were a year old. In some cases babies were fed on nothing but boiled rice water and at such a young age they could not survive; other babies died from sickness and neglect. I remember one baby who was brought to the orphanage by the police after they had found him wrapped up in newspapers on the steps of a cinema. During the night the rats had torn the newspaper away and had bitten into the baby's head and body. When the baby came to us he was suffering from malnutrition and rat bites. I took him home and bathed him three times a day in warm saline water, applying clean dressings to his wounds each time. I fed him with sips of warm milk, first every hour and then once every two hours. He slowly improved and was able to contain three hourly feedings. He would not have survived conditions at the orphanage and so we referred him to an adoption agency when he was well enough.

There was only one rehabilitation centre in the whole of South Vietnam and it attempted to cope with the physically handicapped and war-wounded people and children. The centre was close by, in the street next to the one where we lived, and we used to take handicapped children there to be examined by the doctors. The waiting list at the centre for surgery was already over one year long. The centre was very large and well equipped with modern apparatus. They had a highly skilled team of trained doctors and nurses, orthopaedic surgeons and physiotherapists, both American and Vietnamese. In front of the building was a large garden with grass growing, tall trees and flowering shrubs. There was plenty of space in the courtyard where people could exercise and practise walking.

There was also a plastic surgery unit in Saigon called the Barsky Unit. It was started and sponsored by an American group of doctors and nurses, some of whom remained behind to work together with the Vietnamese doctors and nurses to train them in plastic surgery. The Barsky Unit had all its equipment flown in from the States and it was used for specialized plastic surgery and skin grafting. The Unit was attached to a Vietnamese hospital which specialized in neurology and was situated in Cholon, the Chinese area of Saigon.

The Barsky Unit dealt mostly with children who had been severely burned, especially those who had been burned by napalm. When the Americans dropped napalm on believed Viet Cong contested areas, there were often children working in the fields along the roadside. When the napalm fell on them it continued burning through their flesh and burned all the skin away to the bone. These children needed months of skin grafting and specialized nursing care.

Mrs Beach planned to accompany a group of our polio children to England for further treatment and surgery. She told me that the Ockenden Venture intended to send out three more nurses to complete our team. This would enable us to expand our activities and to start to help the more needy children in various other orphanages in Saigon. The first two nurses were due to arrive while Mrs Beach was still away and the third was to fly to Saigon with Mrs Beach on her return journey, and would eventually replace her as team leader. It was now November and I had been in Saigon for two months.

CHAPTER 3

Mrs Beach spent several hours each day in the city, going from one Ministry to another. She had to make out birth certificates, collect identification papers, passports and visas for the children before they left for England. It was impossible to get anything done quickly in Saigon and any dealings with the Vietnamese Government always took ages to complete. I used to travel with Mrs Beach so that I would be able to find my way around during her absence. I needed to know the whereabouts of the various Ministries with which we were most likely to deal, and I had to be introduced to the Ministers who could help us. I also needed to know where the bank and the post office were. We would take a taxi into the city centre and then walk, because most of the buildings we had to visit were in the same vicinity.

All government buildings had soldiers and police outside who were on patrol, and before we entered the building we would have to show our I.D. cards. The Ministry of Social Welfare, which we visited first, was badly in need of repair. It was fairly large and consisted of small private offices and long narrow corridors. The windows along the corridors had no glass but the green rusty shutters were always kept open for ventilation. Early in the morning the Ministry was alive with bats which hovered round the high ceilings and flew in and out through the open windows. There were even wild birds nesting inside. The floor was tiled and in places the tiles were so badly broken that they left huge holes in the floor. The walls were painted over with white-wash, and the paint had peeled off where the rain had leaked through the roof, leaving brown, rusty stains down the wall. On other parts of the wall the plaster had fallen off, leaving patches of bare brickwork. The electric wires for the ceiling fans and lights had fallen out of the wall and were tied back in place by a piece of string or stuck with sellotape. The rooms were covered in dust which blew in from the street outside, and were littered with torn-up paper and rubbish piled up in the corners and left. No one bothered to clean it up.

The Ministers to whom Mrs Beach introduced me were all very nice, and they tried to be kind and helpful. They all spoke English very well and many of them spoke French. Most of the Ministers had either visited the States or Paris, and were quite interested to know we were from England. We were always offered Chinese tea to drink in the course of the interview. Every time we called we were always asked to return the following week. Either our papers had been misplaced or they just hadn't done anything. When we did finally obtain our papers we had to run from office to office trying to get various signatures. Even then we would be asked to come back the following day. It was time-consuming and expensive to make any progress and we had to be patient.

The Vietnamese girls who worked in the Ministry as secretaries just used to sit about all day, usually doing their knitting. There were plenty of typewriters around, donated by the Americans, but many of the girls couldn't even type. There was no filing system in the Ministry and files could never be found when needed. They were stacked in wooden cupboards on shelves that were about to collapse and when the cupboards were full they would be left on the floor. They were either nibbled at by the mice or made sodden by rain leaking through the roof.

There was a great deal of corruption in the various Ministries. Papers could be obtained quickly or forged if you were prepared to give a hand-out. People made money by forging false birth certificates, I.D. cards, marriage certificates or any other official paper. Then when someone in the corruption line had to show their files, mysterious fires would break out and the papers would be destroyed so that no one was found out.

The Ministry of Social Welfare stood on the top left hand side of Tu Do street. Tu Do means freedom in Vietnamese. On the opposite side of the street stood another similiar building, the Ministry of the Interior. It looked very old and was also in need of repair. Inside, there seemed to be even more confusion than in the Ministry of Social Welfare. It was usually very crowded and we always had to wait for up to four or five hours just to see someone for five minutes. There were no lavatories and there was nowhere to get a drink.

At twelve o'clock midday the post office sounded a siren which could be heard all over Saigon, alerting everyone that work was over for the morning. People took a two hour lunch break and a siesta. If you hadn't succeeded in seeing anyone in the morning you would be handed your I.D. card and asked to return at two o'clock in the afternoon. Although the Ministry opened at two o'clock no one started work until about three o'clock, and then at four thirty everyone packed up and went home. If you had still not been seen, they asked you to return either the next day or the following week.

The Ministry of the Interior was more corrupt than the Ministry of Social Welfare because it dealt with all official papers. The passport and visa section was the most corrupt because it was difficult for the Vietnamese to leave Vietnam. Unless they were prepared to pay for their papers they could be delayed for months on end and often lost their chance of leaving. I saw people inside the Ministry shake hands with an official and hand money to him at the same time. Another way was to put money inside an envelope, inside a file, and give it to the official under cover. The official would then disappear for a minute to check how much he had been paid, and if it was enough, he would come and give service to his client.

The Ministry of the Interior overlooked a small square on the opposite side of which was the cathedral, a very beautiful, elaborately decorated old building which had been built by the French. Beggars used to gather on either side of the cathedral steps. Some mothers would dress their children in torn clothes and make them sit and beg next to them. The mother would usually have a baby on her lap sucking from her breast and when people walked past she would lift up the baby in the hope that they would give her something for it. The babies were often 'hired' out specifically for begging.

On the right hand side of the square was the post office. This was a very large building divided into different sections inside. There was a large courtyard in front filled with tables displaying writing paper, envelopes, air mail paper, birthday cards and post cards for sale. Over the main entrance was a large clock and underneath, sitting on the steps again, were the beggars. Many were hardly able to support themselves in an upright position; but when the police appeared, they would forget their disabilities, quickly get up and run away. They would wait somewhere out of sight until the police had gone away and then return to their positions.

Whenever we received packages sent to Vietnam we were notified by the post office and had to go and collect them. We could not take away the parcels unless we showed our I.D. cards and returned the form of paper sent to us, duly signed. The packages were opened in front of us and we then had to show the contents to the customs officer. He would check through the items sent, unfolding clothes, opening any packets and taking the tops off bottles to sniff their contents. If he was satisfied you were allowed to leave after paying the tax. Any packages that arrived and were not claimed were never returned, but shared out between the people working in the post office.

My younger brother used to send me cigarettes and the customs officer made me pay a fine, saying I could not receive cigarettes because they were already manufactured in Vietnam. If I paid the fine, he would put the money straight into his pocket. If I offered him some cigarettes, he would forget the fine and allow me to receive as many cigarettes as I liked, providing I always remembered him.

Tu Do street led from the cathedral down to the river front and was the main centre of attraction for Americans, journalists and visiting tourists. The hotels most frequented by foreigners were on Tu Do Street, including the famous Continental Palace Hotel. The Continental hotel was the centre of activity at night, with an open bar in the patio of the hotel, overlooking the street. This was a favourite haunt of the American soldiers, a place where they could drink beer and wait for the girls. Waiters dressed in white jackets would serve them either Beer '33' or Bière 'Larue', the only two beers made in Vietnam.

Night-life started early in Saigon because of the curfew at eleven o'clock. As the late afternoon sun disappeared behind the red and yellow clouds of dusk, silhouetting the trees against the skyline and throwing huge shadows across the city, Tu Do street cast away its melancholy daytime mood and suddenly came alive. The bars and the night-clubs, the American and French restaurants, the pizza houses and hamburger bars all opened their doors. Soft music filled the night air, against the background din of Hondas and traffic. Pretty girls hidden under heavy make-up, wearing mini-skirts or tight white trousers and low-necked sweaters, drifted into the street, ready to face the night ahead of them.

Small boys in torn clothes and mumbling 'pidgin' English, tried to sell 'Stars and Stripes' or the 'Saigon Post' to the Americans. Barefooted girls sold flower chains and peanuts. Wounded Vietnamese soldiers and young drug addicts sold paperback books, paintings, carved wooden models and hand-painted lacquer ware. Old women sat in the street selling cigarettes. The night air was hot and humid. The mosquitoes played around your bare ankles. Taxi drivers and cyclo drivers queued up outside the night-clubs, waiting for a last double fare from an American. The police drove up and down in their jeeps, making arrests and taking prostitutes soliciting in the street off to jail.

At about ten thirty, just half an hour before the curfew, the bars and night-clubs emptied. Vietnamese girl singers belonging to young 'pop-groups', the bar girls and the Americans once more filled the street. Taxi drivers and cyclo drivers disappeared in different directions, hurrying to get people home in time. Newspaper stalls and cigarette stands were folded up and cleared away. The street children vanished to find a safe sleeping place for the night.

Tu Do street was also the centre for foreigners during the day. Between the bars and night-clubs were numerous small gift shops, selling souvenirs, ceramics and lacquer ware. There was a tremendous craze for china elephants and all the Americans were buying them before they returned to the States. A number of Indians lived in Saigon and many of them had opened gift shops on Tu Do street. There were also hairdressing salons for men and women, a beauty clinic and sauna bath.

The money changers used to collect on Tu Do street, hanging round in shop doorways waiting for the Americans to pass. They always worked in pairs, one acting as a lookout for the police. They were expert at their trade, changing American dollars for toilet paper wrapped up in a Vietnamese money note and vanishing before the American had time to check his money. The main foreign exchange banks were in the smaller side streets, together with more bars, night-clubs and restaurants. The larger commercial banks in Saigon were towards the river front. Foreigners had to be particularly careful on leaving the bank in case they were followed by a group of 'cowboys' and later attacked and robbed.

The Mekong river was very beautiful and symbolised the simplicity of the lives of the poorer people. All day long the ferry-boat crossed the river, transporting people living in the village opposite to the Saigon markets. Industrial factories lined the far banks and in front of the factories were wooden houses built up over the river. The occupants had no sanitation, running water or electricity in their homes and drew water from a nearby well for cooking and drinking. They bathed in the river and children often fell in and drowned. The rats thrived in all the filth and mosquitoes and flies hung like carpets on the wind. On the Saigon side of the river, to the left of Tu Do street, stood the South Vietnamese navy headquarters. Warships and passing freighters filled the port. On the right hand side of the river was a floating restaurant which was popular with foreigners.

A railway track led away from the side of the river into the city. The train ran through the centre of the streets with all the people, Hondas and traffic swarming round it. Usually it was a goods train pulled by an old steam engine. The train moved very slowly, the driver constantly blowing his whistle and often having to stop and wait while people cleared the line. The track ran in front of the banks into Ham Nghi street, another busy market place. Women and children would rush to move their chickens out of the way and fold up small tables laden with fruit which they had set out along the line.

The railway station was opposite Saigon market. The trains only went as far as Bien Hoa, about fifteen miles away. Because of the war most of the railway track north of Bien Hoa had been blown up and was unsafe to use. The trains entering and leaving Saigon were crowded with people coming in from the country-side to buy and sell in the markets. They would bring their pigs and chickens on the train with them, along with their children. Any available space was taken by the soldiers travelling. If there was not enough room inside, people would climb up and sit on the top of the carriages.

Most people travelling from Saigon to the countryside went by road. Ramshackle buses crammed with people left the city all day long. The first buses left early in the morning just after curfew had lifted. People travelling over long distances did not like to go through the countryside at night for fear of being ambushed by the Viet Cong and the buses usually stopped when it was dark. It took about three days to reach Da Nang and Hue in the north, and the bus used to stop over-night at small towns along the road. Towns and villages in the Delta could be reached in one day.

The main bus station was on Petrusky street, towards Cholon. Petrusky street was a long street and buses lined both sides of it. In front of each bus was a board indicating where the bus was going and the time it was due to leave. The street was filled with coffee shops and small open-fronted cafés, whose trade depended on those travelling on the buses. Street vendors set up their stalls in the street, selling bread, sandwiches and iced drinks for people to take on their journey. Small boys ran round trying to sell sunglasses. Little girls wandered from one bus to another with trays of cakes to sell.

Petrusky street was constantly blocked with traffic. Buses used to turn round in the middle of the street in an attempt to park. Usually the bus driver owned the bus as well and employed three or four boys to keep the bus clean and in good repair. At night they slept either inside the bus or on top of the roof because the bus would be looted if left empty. With the boys sleeping on the buses at night, Petrusky street attracted the girls who came to work as prostitutes. The coffee shops open during the day became bars at night.

People filled the buses, three persons to one seat. They could take whatever they liked with them providing they paid a small fee. They took their Hondas, bicycles and furniture which the boys tied on to the roof of the bus. One boy would stand at either end of the bus, calling through the door to passing Hondas and cars to clear the street. The drivers drove very fast. During the long trips through the countryside the boys would sit together on the roof of the bus. They were wind-blown and sun-tanned and enjoyed every minute of the trip. They climbed with ease from the roof to the inside of the bus through one of the open windows and never seemed to slip, even at high speeds. There were no bus stops in the country and villagers would wait at the side of the road, ready to hail and halt the bus.

I visited various refugee camps with a group of Protestant Vietnamese women involved in charitable work. The first camp I visited was about thirty miles from Saigon, on the coast road to Vung Tau. It stood on the site of a children's village which had housed up to a thousand children. Then, because of some suspected political involvement, the village had been wiped out by the Viet Cong and many of the children had died. Now the empty site was occupied by about two thousand Montanards who had been driven from their own villages by continuous clashes between the Communist troops and the South Vietnamese army. The Montanards were Vietnamese Indians who lived in the jungle areas of the Central Highlands of Vietnam. As a race they were very different to the Vietnamese and rather looked down upon on account of their primitive way of living and the dark colour of their skin.

We left Saigon in small groups, each group travelling in a minibus, and took tins of milk, fish and U.S. army biscuits to give to the refugees. Leaving the city, we crossed the bridge over the Mekong river to reach the highway. The highway was full of fast-moving traffic. Army trucks and jeeps, tankers, fruit and vegetable lorries coming to Saigon and a few private cars sped along throwing up the dust behind them. From the top of the bridge, which was heavily guarded by soldiers, I could see the surrounding countryside. It looked flat and bare, with just a faint outline of hills discernible in the distance, towards Vung Tau. Small flat-roofed villages and factories were scattered just off the roadside, with the occasional rice paddy between them. Children were tending cows and oxen on the sparse grass growing along the verges. Helicopters circled overhead.

We continued along the highway until we reached Bien Hoa, where we turned off to the right past Long Binh, the huge U.S. army base. The countryside was more open here and we drove through several rubber plantations. The trees were planted in rows, with a groove cut out in the bark of the tree for the rubber to collect and empty into an upturned coconut shell. Every bridge we passed was patrolled by soldiers. On either side of each bridge were look-out towers, surrounded by bunkers and barbed wire. In the middle of the bridge was a spotlight facing the river, so that the soldiers could keep watch during the night for any Viet Cong who might try to blow up the bridge.

We continued along the road until we came to a dirt track which led across the countryside to the refugee camp. The dust from the road blew up and we had to close the windows. As soon as we arrived at the camp the Montanard people gathered round us. They were very lean and dark-skinned, their black hair falling over their faces and almost covering their eyes. Ragged children with distended stomachs played in the dust, naked and barefooted. The women wore long skirts and many held a baby sucking at their breasts. The men wore shorts and a few just wore loin cloths.

The camp was very large, the people living in different quarters, each with a village leader. The buildings were similar to English farmyard barns used for storing hay. Each dwelling had been erected in makeshift fashion out of corrugated iron and about ten to fifteen families lived in each. There was nothing inside but the dust on the ground. The Montanards' only possessions were the very clothes they were wearing. The Americans had given them coconut mats to sleep on and a few large pots and pans for cooking. The people collected fallen wood and cooked over open wooden fires. They ate mostly rice, with just a little dried fish. There was no sanitation and the people defecated in the nearby fields. There was no water supply and the nearest river was a couple of miles away. The people walked to the river to bathe each day but it was too far to carry water back to the camp for drinking and cooking. Every day a few fire engines would come from Saigon to bring the villagers water.

At the far end of the camp was a building used as a clinic and sick bay. Two Vietnamese girls, both trained nurses, worked and lived here. The nurses had hardly any medicines and the few they did have were already outdated. The Americans had donated several bottles of dextrose and saline for intravenous infusion, but there was not enough to go round. Most of the medicine bottles were already half empty and covered in dust. A dressings tray lay on a shelf but even the gauze and cotton swabs were dusty. They still had to be used because there was nothing else. There were no beds for the children and they and the babies had to lie down on on the floor, on the coconut mats. At night, the children had no protection from mosquitoes as they slept and there were many recurrent cases of malaria. Very young babies, already suffering from malnutrition, often died.

Large numbers of refugees wandered aimlessly round the countryside because of the continued assaults on their villages. Often the A.R.V.N. soldiers would take refuge in a nearby village during a battle they knew they were losing and the Viet Cong would therefore attack the village to drive out the A.R.V.N. soldiers. Sometimes the Communists merely wanted the land round the village. Continuous fighting, destruction of the village and fear would eventually force the inhabitants to leave. They would abandon their burning homes at the last possible minute, scarcely giving themselves time to escape. They took only bare necessities, rice, a few cooking pots, a small kerosene stove and a mat to sleep on at night. If they had pigs and chickens they would put them in their cart as well.

The refugees walked the countryside until their shoes wore through and their feet were covered in blisters. Often they had no water to drink, especially during the dry season, and little or no food to eat. Many died during their long trek to reach safety. The village chief or priest would lead the fleeing refugees and the army usually relocated them to another area considered 'safe'. In spite of their suffering and losses they would work hard to build another village. They toiled during the heat and humidity of the day, digging the dry land to build wells; they chopped down trees from the nearest woods for their new homes. Their work was not often rewarded as fresh outbreaks of fighting continued to spread and they would be forced to leave once more. Many refugees had built three or four new resettlement villages.

Various organizations based in Saigon, such as the International Red Cross, UNICEF, World Vision and the American USAID (United States Agency for International Development) developed programmes to assist the refugees in resettlement villages and to supply them with food, medicine and clothes. Inevitably, everything had first to be cleared by the Ministry of Social Welfare. Aid sent to help the refugees did not always reach them. Many goods were stolen and later sold in the market. Sometimes trucks were not available to carry supplies to the camps or the soldiers were reluctant to drive into contested areas. Often the roads were impassable because of heavy fighting and the bombing of bridges. Delays of this kind meant that loads of foodstuffs rotted in storage and had to be thrown away.

People returning to Saigon from the country brought back differing stories. In January 1973 there was talk of a cease fire which never came. When the Communists violated a proposed cease fire President Thieu would speak to the people and try to encourage them by saying they would fight to the last bullet. On every holiday and national day in Saigon Thieu would order each household to fly two South Vietnamese flags to the Communists' one flag. Thieu was disliked by the South Vietnamese and the Communists. It was said amongst the South Vietnamese that since Thieu was becoming rich from the war and the American presence in Vietnam he did not really try to end the fighting. It was also said that corruption flourished under Thieu as he profited from it himself. The gold and diamond rings on his hand alone were supposed to be worth over one million piasters. We also heard rumours about the number of Viet Cong apparently infiltrating into Saigon every day. They were supposed to be in our own police force and army, or working as teachers and students.

Everyone in South Vietnam had to hold an I.D. card by their seventeenth birthday. Every day and during the night, the police and soldiers made house to house searches for anyone who might be trying to avoid military service, or for anyone not holding an I.D. card. If anyone tried to run away or escape over the roof the soldiers would shoot them as Viet Cong suspects. Young men without I.D. cards were either thrown into jail as political suspects or made to go into the army. Any soldiers who were caught after having deserted from the army were arrested and then sent to Quang Tri, on the DMZ (demilitarized zone), to act as runners to the regular soldiers. Usually deserters had their heads shaved and were not even allowed to carry a gun. During combat they always died first, and many were not yet twenty years old. Anyone who admitted to being a Communist during interrogation was shot by the firing squad.

It was quite an honour for a South Vietnamese soldier to kill a Viet Cong and he was often rewarded with a medal. Some soldiers kept a souvenir of the dead Viet Cong they had shot, such as one of his teeth, which they would pull out themselves. The Viet Cong were really hated. After an assault in the country their dead bodies would be pulled out into the middle of the street or left in the centre of the market place for everyone to see. Known Viet Cong sympathisers in a village were sometimes executed in public, their heads cut off and suspended on the top of a pole.

Whenever I met other Americans in Saigon I always talked to them about the problem of refugees and homeless people and asked them if there was any way in which they might like to help. I also approached the Australian army just before they pulled out and they gave us the remainder of their sleeping blankets. The blankets were so big that we cut them in half and made two. I went to the Third Field U.S. army hospital to ask for medicines and whilst I was there I met an American who was shortly leaving

Saigon. He told me that they had about one hundred boxes of 'C' rations that they would not be using and he promised to let us have them. Each 'C' ration box contained about twenty-four tins of food and also cigarettes. Once we received a whole shipment of cornflakes sent by air from Hawaii which we also distributed amongst the refugees. Sometimes the women would bring along religious books and give them to the refugees and soldiers we met along the roadside. Even the soldiers accepted them thankfully.

In February we went to visit a resettlement village about one hundred kilometres to the south of Saigon. The village was near My Tho, a small town on the Mekong river, and the gateway to the Mekong Delta. The Mekong is the third largest river in Asia. It floods the valleys of the Delta, providing a rich and fertile soil. At least two crops of rice are grown a year, offering the largest export of rice in the world. A ferry transports both military and civilian traffic across the river onto the south-bound road. The countryside on either side of the highway was beautiful. Miles of patchwork rice paddies stretched out before us, lush and green. On the horizon the blue sky reached down to touch the green fields, illuminated in the sunshine. Tall trees heavy with coconuts swayed gently in the wind. There were flowers everywhere. Swollen streams and winding rivers meandered between the rice paddies. Huge buffalo waded through the paddies, with small muddy-looking boys riding on their backs.

Tiny villages were scattered over the countryside, built up above the rice paddies on mud banks to prevent flooding during the rainy season. The houses were made out of bamboo wood and had thatched straw roofs. Men and women were working in the paddies, standing up to their knees in water, planting out the rice. Old men were ploughing the land with an ox steadily pulling the plough. The country people wore scarves wrapped round their heads under large coolie hats.

It was hot and there was no shade in the Delta. The highway was long and full of heavy traffic. Women and young girls had set up stalls along the roadside and were selling freshly cut pineapples. They were deliciously sweet and full of juice. The bridges across the rivers were still heavily guarded by soldiers and you were not allowed to stop on a bridge. Tiny fishing boats drifted down the river, against a background of palm trees and tall reeds.

As we approached My Tho we could hear gunshots and the

sound of rockets exploding ahead of us. In several places along the highway I noticed tankers hidden behind a clump of trees. It looked as if they were expecting trouble. Huge army trucks rattled past us, in both directions. They were either transporting soldiers or filled with boxes of ammunition. There were so many soldiers in each truck that they had to stand. They had thin, drawn faces and their uniforms were torn and muddy.

On reaching My Tho we turned into the main street. We had to drive through the town because the resettlement village was on the other side. On entering the main street we were forced to stop. At the end of the street we could see planes diving through the air, bombing an area close to the village. Having come such a long way we didn't want to turn back without first delivering the food to the refugees who needed it so desperately. We therefore waited with everyone else until the fighting had ceased and the road was reopened.

I could not believe we were so near an air raid. I watched with amazement as the planes climbed into the air, twisted, and then suddenly turned and dived with such intensity that I wondered if they would be able to ascend again. During the dives we could see the bombs dropping swiftly through the air and then exploding, sending up clouds of black smoke. The vibrations of the explosions shook and rattled the corrugated iron roofs on the buildings. A few windows were blown out, sending glass shattering to the ground. Shutters and doors swung open.

I never felt afraid. I just wished I could have been nearer the fighting so that I could have brought medical help to the injured. I noticed that the people standing beside us were not really frightened. The children had been dismissed early from school because of the fighting and even they just stood in the street to watch. We waited for about an hour and a half before the fighting ceased and then drove through My Tho and out into the country. The smoke from the explosions formed heavy black clouds above us. A few trees and thatched houses were burning, the people standing outside and watching. The resettlement village was not far away. The village chief told us that the Viet Cong were hiding out behind the woods opposite their village. I looked over to the woods, which were not far away. The Viet Cong were probably watching us now.

The village was well-planned and the refugees had worked hard to build it. The houses were built of wood and were tiny.

They were spaced evenly apart with small trees and flowers growing between them. Each family had a house but there was nothing inside except a single mat on the floor to sleep on. There were small windows built in two opposite walls but it was still hot inside. The floors were rough and needed constant sweeping because of the dust. The refugees had dug their own wells and carried water to the fields they had cultivated behind the village. They were hoping to build a pipeline to feed the fields if they could obtain the necessary materials. They tried to make use of everything round them. The women made baskets and hats from the bamboo wood and the men carved models and made smoking-pipes which they could sell in the market. They were so happy to receive the 'C' rations and the cornflakes we had brought for them.

We drove further into the countryside to visit five hundred soldiers and their families who were living in a disused U.S. army barracks. As we approached the barracks we saw several tankers hidden behind the trees, watched by soldiers armed with machine guns and hand grenades. The soldiers who lived in the barracks seemed just as poor as the refugees. They were so badly paid they could barely afford to buy enough food for themselves and their families. The barracks were very old and looked empty and desolate. The walls were riddled with bullet holes. The soldiers grew their own crops behind the barracks. They had no running water or electricity and had to draw water from the well and burn oil lamps. When we gave them the cornflakes they opened the packets and started eating them straight away.

Before Mrs Beach returned to England we visited other orphanages in Saigon. Most of them were run by either Catholic sisters or Buddhist nuns and the conditions were horrifying. One of the worst was in the district of Go Vap, about three miles outside Saigon. The mortality rate was very high and it was believed that about forty babies died there every month. The buildings looked rather like a prison—just large bare rooms filled with children. When the Americans had surplus foodstuffs to donate they would give them to Go Vap first since it was the largest orphanage and housed five to six hundred children. The Mother Superior, known as Sister Lucy, thrived in a world of corruption and used to keep the things given for the children herself. Her office was equipped with U.S. tables and chairs and air conditioning, she also had a refrigerator full of food and a television set.

She sold what she did not want in the market and had bought a new car with the money she had saved. Although the orphanage housed more children than it could care for, Sister Lucy never permitted any adoptions.

All the orphanages were dirty and overrun by rats. The children were neglected and many never went to school. When they grew up they could not read or write and it was difficult for them to find employment. The handicapped children were often hidden away in a back room, as if they were something to be ashamed of. In Go Vap the handicapped children were housed in an annex in the country. Two sisters looked after about fifty of these children who spent most of their lives lying on the floor in their own excrement, covered in flies and staring at the blank walls. Those who survived these conditions grew up mentally retarded. They never saw the outside world and were probably not even aware that one existed. They never experienced love or affection. They were deprived of everything a normal child takes for granted. Their lot was worse than an animal's and sometimes it was a relief for the child to die. Two French doctors from the Grall hospital in Saigon eventually visited Go Vap and completely redecorated it. The walls were painted in bright colours, and the empty rooms were filled with pictures, potted plants and flowers. Live birds hung from the ceiling in bird cages. The doctors instructed the women to clean the buildings and the mortality rate slowly improved.

When children have been neglected for so long it is hard to nurse them back to health. Mrs Beach visited an orphanage in Bien Hoa and found three handicapped children who were close to death. She brought them back to the house with her and I nursed them. They smelt so bad that even when I washed them the smell remained. Not only were their bodies covered in sores and infections, but the inside of their mouths as well. Their breath smelt and their teeth were rotten, either black with decay or yellow from lack of cleaning. Their gums and tongue were infected, their throats red and swollen. I could not clean their mouths because at the slightest touch they would bleed. It was too painful for the children to either eat or drink. At first I could only feed them on small doses of water with sugar added. Later I fed them on diluted milk and gradually started them on small amounts of solids. Sometimes the children could not hold their feeds and would either vomit or have continuous diarrhoea. They were so thin and under-nourished that their bones had never had a chance to develop properly.

There was an old people's home in Saigon called Phu My. It was situated on Tin Nghe street which led out from Saigon towards the Bien Hoa highway. There was a rubbish dump outside the home that lined the walls from one end of the street to the other. Phu My housed one thousand old men and women who had nowhere else to go. They also had over two hundred orphaned children and about thirty children suffering from polio. The Mother Superior, Sister Rose, was French and spoke fluent Vietnamese. She was a large woman of about sixty with grey hair hidden under her veil. She was very strict and rarely smiled. She worked hard and conscientiously and expected her fellow Sisters to follow her example. The Sisters were very kind to the inmates but it was impossible for them to give adequate care to so many.

The very old men who were senile and tended to wander out into the busy street were often shackled to their beds. The mentally insane were locked away in a back room which was unfurnished except for a single bed secured to the floor. The windows were barred. Even the mentally retarded children had to be shackled to their beds because there was no one available to look for them if they wandered off. The men lived in a huge hall filled with rows of small iron beds, very close to each other. There were four halls of this kind, each hall containing about two hundred beds. Some of the men were very sick or dying, some unconscious. They lay on wooden boards, often with no clothes on, and flies settled on their open sores. In the middle of the room I saw an old priest standing over the bed of a very sick man who moved restlessly on his bed, unable to relieve himself of the pain. His skin was pale and pinched. Another emaciated old man held a fan over him to try to cool him. The priest prayed that he would not have to suffer too long.

The old men who could walk came over to welcome us. I gave them the cigarettes I had, which despite their weakness and frailty they almost fought over. I went off to buy some more cigarettes and handed them round. The children who were kept shackled to their beds were kept in the same room as the old men. The room was hot and stuffy and smelt of urine. The old men were dirty from lack of washing for there was no water or electricity and water had to be drawn from a well outside in the courtyard. Inside the room it was quite dark, except for a single oil lamp burning on a small table in the middle.

The men walked round on the stone floors without any shoes on. They fell over and bumped their heads or broke their bones. They were cared for by Sister Elly who was tiny and quite old. She moved quickly and silently, handing out medicines, giving injections, helping someone take a drink, or calling the priest to come and say the last rites. She had hardly any medicines and those she did have were all out-dated. Behind Phu My was a piece of waste land used as a cemetery. There were scarcely any gravestones as few could afford one.

In the mornings the men who were able to walk went across to the well, drew the water themselves and washed. Those who could not walk did not wash unless someone carried them some water in a bowl. They ate out of the same containers and the food came round in a communal bowl. They ate chiefly the stodgy red rice which was cheaper to buy and filled them up and occasionally some dried fish and a spoonful of very weak vegetable soup if there was enough to go around.

The children received more care than the old men. The Americans had built a small swimming pool for the polio children. The older girls who lived in the orphanage would go into the swimming pool with these children and show them how to use their limbs. The Americans had also built a small physiotherapy room for the handicapped children, equipped with parallel bars and steps to climb. All the children had been to the National Rehabilitation Centre and were fitted with calipers and shoes which they wore throughout the day.

Sister Rose did not take advantage of her position. She made use of everything given to her to help others. She allowed the older girls to use sewing-machines to make clothes for the children. She planted vegetables and fruit trees in the spare land around the cemetery and between the buildings. She also kept pigs and chickens. The grounds of the home were clean and neatly planted with trees and flower beds. There was a chapel in the grounds where the Sisters worshipped every day and the old people were encouraged to go to church if they wished.

Towards the end of November 1972, Mrs Beach finally obtained the passports and exit visas necessary for the group of polio children to visit England for treatment. During her absence I was to continue working in the orphanage and also look after the house. Helen and Marion, the two extra nurses, arrived in Saigon shortly after her departure at the end of November. They soon settled in and enjoyed working with the children. We would spend the evenings together, walking round the city trying to remember the names of the streets, wandering through the markets, drinking coffee and testing Vietnamese food from one of the stalls or small cafès.

One of the most popular Vietnamese foods was 'Pho', a delicious bowl of soup made from noodles, vegetables and thin slices of beef. Small fresh mint leaves, hot red peppers, nuoc mam and a slice of lemon were added to it. People would eat 'Pho' especially when the weather turned a little cooler, usually in the mornings before they went to work. The street outside the 'Pho' shop would be lined with Hondas. Small street boys would watch the Hondas, wait for someone to leave the shop and then rush in and finish any left-over soup.

Just before Christmas 1972 Mrs Beach returned to Saigon with Barbara, the trained nurse and midwife who was to take over as team leader. Christmas in Saigon passed by very quietly as the most important time of the year for the Vietnamese is Tet, the Chinese Lunar New Year. The date of Tet varied according to when the new moon was expected during the end of January and beginning of February. Christmas was more like an ordinary Sunday. Many people still went to work and even the market places remained open. People would decorate their homes with brightly coloured paper lanterns and huge Christmas stars and those who could afford to would buy a Christmas tree, fairy lights and even a chicken to take home and cook. On Christmas Eve people liked to dress up and go out. There were firework displays to welcome the festive season. Curfew was lifted for the occasion until about one o'clock. Most people liked to go to midnight Mass and all the Catholic churches would be open and alight with the soft glow of candles burning inside. We decorated the orphanage and Mrs Beach cooked a chicken and Christmas pudding which she had brought back from England.

The Vietnamese began to prepare for Tet about one month before. Side stalls were erected around the main Saigon market place, selling the traditional Tet coconut and banana sweets, flowers and flowering branches, fruit and cooked rice. This was either sweet and filled with bananas or savoury and filled with meat. The mixture was wrapped in banana leaves to keep it fresh. Loud speakers were put up round the market place playing music recorded from the local Vietnamese radio station.

Tet usually lasted for three or four days and in some parts of the country for up to two weeks or more. No one went out to work and the market places closed. The hospitals seemed to empty and many of the patients would go home for most of the staff left too. Houses were filled with flowers and enough food was prepared to last throughout the holiday, for it was the custom not to cook during Tet. Everyone liked to dress up in new clothes. Even the street children would save what little money they had collected to buy themselves a new shirt or a new pair of pants.

Tet was a family reunion, a spring festival, a national holiday, and everyone's birthday. The Vietnamese did not celebrate each individual's birthday but everyone was one year older at Tet. It was the time to pay homage to ancestors, visit family and friends and observe traditions. When visiting a traditional Vietnamese family during Tet, it was the custom to pay your respects to their ancestors before greeting the family. In a Buddhist family a photograph of the ancestors would be placed on a small altar, together with fresh flowers and fruit, candles and incense. The family would prepare a special dish of food and offer it to their ancestors, lighting the candles and burning the incense on the altar before eating the food themselves.

Tet was also the time to correct faults and forget past mistakes. People always tried to have all their debts paid by Tet so that they could start the New Year afresh. During Tet people thought very carefully about whom they would visit, believing that if they should meet with an unworthy or dishonest person it would bring them bad luck throughout the following year. Everyone wanted to associate with well-respected and well-liked people who would bring good luck. During Tet you were not allowed to lose your temper or display ill feeling for fear of doing so all the year round.

Shortly after the Tet holiday was over I decided to leave the Ockenden Venture. I had thought about this for some time now. As I found my way around the city I began to understand the Vietnamese way of life and could see clearly the problems which faced the people. In some parts of the city conditions were even worse than those of the orphanage. I also felt that although we had three more nurses to complete our team, we were not really enlarging our work programme. I felt we should be working more closely with the Vietnamese people, preparing them to take over from us, so that we could move on to something else. After all, we would not always be there to do the work for them. I always felt that foreigners working in Saigon were too distant from the Vietnamese. They lived in their own houses, worked at an orphanage or child care centre during the day, and then returned to their own homes in the evenings. No one seemed to be in intimate contact with the Vietnamese and few foreigners ever ventured into the poorer areas of Saigon. I now wanted to find out what happened to the children who lived on the streets and to help them as best I could.

CHAPTER 4

Just before I decided to leave the orphanage I met Father Hoang, a Roman Catholic priest and the director of the Streetboys Project. The Streetboys Project was founded by a young American journalist called Dick Hughes who had come to Vietnam in 1968 as a young free lance correspondent. He came to report on the war but his mind was distracted by the street children—thousands of them. Children not yet in their teens were pimps and pick pockets, professional thieves, knife fighters. Boys with polio crawled in the gutters; boys in their teens were heroin and morphine addicts. The children often went hungry when they could not make a living off the street. When they were sick they received no medical attention. More often than not they were picked up by the police and thrown into jail as vagrants. The war and society's indifference to them had stripped these children of their very being. Some had lost all confidence in humanity. Others had forgotten who they were, what they had suffered. . . .

Near the big market place Dick found many small boys who gathered there to sleep each night. Sometimes the children asked him in his own language what his name was, what he was doing and when he would return home. As time went on their relationship grew. One night Dick asked several of the boys to share his house and gradually the number increased. He wanted a place where the boys could find the basic requirements of life: sleep, food, water for washing, clothing, and most important, the right to be a person. The boys never lived in luxury and they had to share the household chores. Friday night movies were added, then an occasional picnic. Dick believed that when the boys stuck to him out of love, when there were few clothes, few conveniences and facilities, and little money, the project would be sound. Once the boys trusted him everything else would follow: schooling, discipline, work, dignity and the difficult search back into themselves in an attempt to compensate for what they had lost and to find some happiness.

There were many problems. Most of the boys were sick and needed treatment, so Dick found doctors and dentists who volunteered their services. It was also unbelievably difficult to obtain the necessary papers for a boy to be sent to a school to learn a trade. At first Dick received money for his project from people in Saigon or perhaps from friends in the States who sent a few dollars. Most of the time it was a dollar here and a dollar there. The Saigon companies of Esso and Shell and Foremost Dairies also contributed. Although there were forty-four voluntary agencies in Vietnam only a few offered to help. At one stage Dick even cashed in his return ticket to the States to meet the bills of the hostel.

Dick eventually set up five houses for boys, four in Saigon and one in Da Nang. From the outset Dick let his Vietnamese friends have direct contact with the children. He devoted himself to a second, yet vital plan: to campaign for help from abroad. Many donations arrived and permitted a continuous organization. In each home or 'family' there was a maximum of twenty boys, with a father of the family or an older brother to act as house leader and a woman to run the household.

I went with Father Hoang to visit the four homes in Saigon and also the new technical centre. The first home was Co Bac, the welcoming house. The home was open to all street boys who could go there whenever they wished. Some of the boys would choose to stay and later move on to one of the other homes; some would just go when they needed a little help, food and shelter or just someone to talk to. Many boys who left would later return.

The second home we visited was called Hope 5. There were twenty-two boys living in this family, aged from eight to twelve years old. Father Hoang had been to court with the boys to obtain their birth certificates, the first legal paper they had ever owned and of which they were extremely proud. They were the same as other children now for without a birth certificate or I.D. card they had no hope of leading a useful, stable life. All the boys went to a community school in the neighbourhood and were encouraged to do some kind of vocational training.

Hope 6 was situated in the same vicinity as Hope 5, but on the other side of the river, stretching into the open country. It was really the Project farm. The twelve boys here raised pigs and chickens and dug their own ponds to keep fish and ducks. They grew fruit trees and planted their own fruit and vegetables. The boys earned themselves a small salary of 200 piasters a day. They were also asked to join an agricultural co-operation where they would deposit 500 piasters per week as their own capital. They received training in farming and animal husbandry.

The last home we visited was called Truong Minh Ky and this housed the older boys. These boys, aged between fifteen and seventeen, would go to the technical centre and learn a trade either in Honda or refrigerator repair or in photo-developing. Others attended high school and studied for their exams. One boy had learnt to speak fluent English. Truong Minh Ky was the most difficult home because the boys realised what lay ahead—enlistment for military service.

The homes were small, simply furnished with the bare necessities, yet comfortable. I could feel the family atmosphere, the sense of belonging, of having an identity. There was only one strict rule: no smoking. The house leader would keep a personal file on each boy. Owing to the war many boys became separated from their families. If a parent or relative was thought to be alive the house leader tried to find them in order to assess the family situation. One boy had been separated from his family during a rocket attack on their village, when his home was burned down. Several years later he returned to his village and entered his parents' newly-built house on the same spot. He saw his picture on the family altar and his parents thought their son had come back from the dead.

Father Hoang was a fine man whom I admired very much. He was in his forties, a little plump but still very nice looking. Although he was Vietnamese he was often thought to be Korean or Chinese. Father Hoang was a well-educated man and had also travelled abroad. He had studied in French and spoke both English and French fluently. He was very popular and the boys really loved him. He was so easy to get on with, so kind and patient, and always calm. I could not work with Dick for the Streetboys Project because the homes for the boys were run by Vietnamese staff only but I wanted to work closely with Father Hoang and share in his involvement with the street children.

Any foreigner who wished to stay and work in South Vietnam

had to be sponsored by an organization which already had a contract and was registered with the Ministry of Social Welfare in Saigon. After the withdrawal of most American troops from Vietnam, the Third Field Army hospital had been turned over to the Seventh Day Adventist Church. The hospital was run by a team of qualified doctors and nurses sent over by their church in the States. Most of the Vietnamese medical staff who worked in the hospital were of the same religion. There was a chapel in the grounds of the hospital and the main Seventh Day Adventist church was about two miles away.

I decided to apply for a job at this hospital and was interviewed by Miss Oldham, the director of nurses. Her office was spotless and she herself had a clean, well-scrubbed appearance. I sat down before her, dressed in my Vietnamese clothes and open sandals, and casually lit a cigarette. She looked quite shocked and I wondered what I had done wrong. Miss Oldham asked me if I knew about the Adventist church. I hadn't even heard of it until I came to the hospital but I told her I thought it was like the Protestant church. She started to tell me about their beliefs and their principles, how they lived their lives in this world in preparation for their second life in the next. They believed in keeping their mind and soul pure, ready to be accepted by Christ. They looked after their bodies because their body was given to them by God and really belonged to Him and was part of Him. They never ate meat or fish because these foods were considered unclean. They believed that the rivers were contaminated by waste products which the fish fed on, making them unfit for consumption. They *never drank* tea or coffee since stimulants were not considered necessary for a healthy body. They *never drank* alcohol or smoked.

At first I did not believe Miss Oldham and thought she was joking. I couldn't help laughing at what she told me. Father Hoang was waiting for me outside and when I told him about the Adventists he wondered if I still wanted to work there. Daunted as I was, I had already given in my notice to the Ockenden Venture and the following day I collected my few belongings and moved to the hospital. I lived with the other Vietnamese nurses in a large dormitory which was partitioned into smaller rooms. We each had a single U.S. bed and an old used U.S. army locker. I spent very little time in the dormitory because when I wasn't working I was on the streets with the children. Most of the other girls spoke English. There was only one problem: cigarettes were forbidden and I always had to smoke in the lavatory.

The hospital was now mostly filled with Vietnamese patients, although there was still one ward reserved for Americans. The American nurses working there were all very kind and tried to cover each ward in the hospital. There were only local nurses on the Vietnamese ward and I was sent to help them. There was also a children's ward, maternity ward, intensive care unit, private patients' wing, operating theatre and recovery rooms. We also had an out-patients department, X-Ray equipment and a pharmacy. The buildings were clean and fully air conditioned with all the latest equipment flown to Vietnam from the States. It wasn't what I really wanted, but it enabled me to be of use while I decided how best to devote my life to the street children.

The hours at the hospital suited me. We worked for two days followed by two nights every week. We worked twelve hour shifts from 6.30 a.m. to 6.30 p.m. with just half an hour for lunch which was usually rice and soya beans. It was hard work but the system at least gave me time to work with Father Hoang on my free days. The Vietnamese ward was a mixed ward, with the men on one side and the women on the other. We treated about fifty patients at a time. Nursing in Vietnam was completely different to nursing in England. Owing to the shortage of qualified doctors, the nurses had very little time for general nursing care of the patient. Here patients received more care than in a Government hospital because there was a trained staff, but treatment was expensive and only the more wealthy Vietnamese could afford to be admitted.

When a patient was admitted to one of the six Government hospitals the whole family would usually go in to look after him. Many of the basic tasks the nurses performed would have been done by a qualified doctor in England. Most of the Vietnamese nurses were very skilled because they had had so much experience. Nurses would administer intravenous infusions and blood transfusions themselves. They would learn how to put in sutures, to remove foreign bodies and to cauterize broken blood vessels to prevent life-threatening conditions. They would do virtually everything except operate.

There was very little wastage in a Government hospital due to the shortage of supplies. Most of the medicines were French and the equipment American. Nothing was thrown away. Disposable syringes and needles were sterilized and used again. Catheter sets, enema tubing, even transfusion equipment was washed out and used again without even being sterilized. Most of the hospitals had poor sanitation. You had to squat down to use the toilets, which proved difficult for the very sick patients. There were no bathrooms, only broken sink units scattered throughout the hospital, and no hot water.

The wards were packed with patients and their families. Two patients would share the same bed, lying at opposite ends. No linen was provided, just a plastic sheet over the mattress which wasn't even wiped over between patients. All through the ward drip bottles would be hanging from the ceiling, tied by a dirty bandage or a piece of string. The family or the patient himself would watch the drip, regulate the speed and call the nurse for another bottle to put up.

The floors were dirty; rubbish and used dressings were dropped or swept into the corner. People would put a plastic mat on the floor, lie down and go to sleep. Others would set up a gasoline stove in the corridor or on the balcony and start cooking. Sleeping hammocks and mosquito nets would be put up between the beds. Women would sit on the stairs talking, feeding their babies. Children would be running around playing. Street vendors used to come in from the street carrying baskets of fruit, bread or small cakes. Children sold iced water or ran round with a kettle selling hot water.

Many patients died. Sometimes the doctors and nurses just couldn't cope; sometimes the patient could not afford to buy his medicines and if the hospital could not supply the medicine, he died. Very often patients needed blood but even if the blood was available they could not always afford to buy it. The Vietnamese never donated blood to a hospital, they always sold it. Drug addicts and junkies badly in need of money came in from the street and sold their blood. Infection spread quickly and was a major cause of death. Many dead babies were left on the rubbish heaps in the street. Opposite almost every hospital was a shop which made and sold small wooden coffins all day long.

Vietnamese funerals—for those who could afford them— were very beautiful and could cost anything up to £1,000. White was always worn for mourning, never black. When a wealthy Vietnamese person died his body was washed and dressed in his best ao-dai, in the traditional manner. The body would be placed in a coffin and then returned to the family home, where it would remain for up to three days. The coffins were very elaborate, often hand painted and carved. During this time other members of the family, close friends and neighbours would come and pay their respects. Incense was burnt and a small offering of flowers and fruit made to Buddha. Visitors gave an envelope containing a money note to the family to help cover expenses. They were always offered Chinese tea or a fruit drink. Professional mourners were hired and they would sit outside the house all day chanting and praying. It was considered good luck to pass a funeral procession in the street but bad luck to see a wedding. Pregnant women were not allowed to attend weddings or funerals.

The hearse had more the appearance of an elaborate carriage. It was very decorative with traditional pictures of dragons, flowers and Buddha both carved and painted on it. The coffin was placed in the middle and in the front of the carriage was a large framed photograph of the dead person, surrounded by candles, burning incense and flowers. The mourners walked behind the hearse and were dressed in long white robes and white head-cloths which were usually hired or made for the occasion. Friends and neighbours followed in a long procession. A bus or even an army truck would be hired to transport the people home again.

Very old men, young men and boys who died in the street or in jail were taken to the cemetery either by the police or the refuse collectors. Their bodies were left in the mortuary until the boys who worked in the cemetery buried them. The bodies were put on a table if there was room or just left on the floor. The mortuary had no refrigeration service. The only way to keep a body in reasonable condition was to pay the boys who worked there enough money to keep running out to buy blocks of ice. The smell of the mortuary made you physically sick and passers-by would hold a handkerchief over their nose and mouth. Often the door was left open and you could look in. There were usually four or five naked bodies inside, crawling with maggots. Rats would chew the flesh and tear it off. It was a nightmarish scene. When homeless people or those without identification papers were buried they didn't even have a coffin. Their bodies were carried out in a coconut mat, dropped into the grave and then covered with earth. There was no gravestone, not even a wooden cross. After the burial only the cows and horses returned, trampling

Tuyet, Father Hoang, Mai and Chao (*from left to right*) in the courtyard of Te Ban prison with other girls from Le Lai

Girls in their cell in Te Ban, with Tuyet and Mai in the front row (*third and fourth from the left*)

Liz's home for girls. No, Van and Hoa are standing in a row (*second, third and fourth from left*) and Cu Ly, Lien and tiny Thanh are kneeling in front of them

Younger brothers and sisters of the girls in Liz's home and children from Le Lai

Boys outside their cell in Te Ban

No and Lien distributing fruit to the older women prisoners in Te Ban

Beggars outside the cathedral in Saigon

A small street boy with a huge bag of rubbish

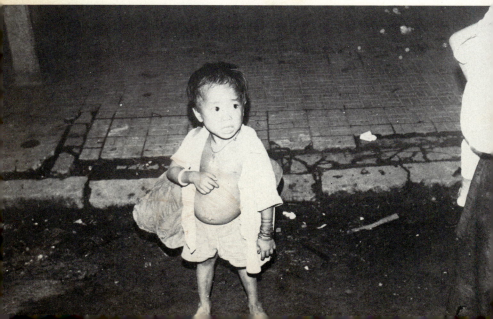

over the uneven earth looking for a patch of grass on which to graze. Flowers were rarely left on a grave because someone would always come and steal them and sell them to someone else.

The boys who worked in the cemetery were only street boys themselves, barely in their teens. They dug the graves and buried the dead, sometimes burying boys not much older than they were. In return they were given their food and lodging. They lived in a small house overlooking the cemetery but only returned there to sleep at night. During the hottest hours of the day the boys would stretch out on one of the graves under the trees and go to sleep. They played football in the driveway, undisturbed by their surroundings.

This was part of my world. Sometimes I felt there was no escape from the filth and poverty, the heartbreak and the deep, deep suffering, but despite my sorrow at what I saw I just felt continually frustrated that I couldn't do more. I worked for about eighteen hours each day and developed a very close friendship with Father Hoang. He was always ready to listen to me, to be there when I needed someone to talk to. He used to worry about me, telling me that I worked too hard, slept too little and didn't eat enough.

I also had a very close girlfriend called Tima whom I met at the orphanage just before I left. She could no longer afford to support her two children after her American boyfriend had returned to the States. Her mother was Vietnamese and her father was Indian. She lived in her mother's house with her children for her father had returned to India when she was still a child. Tima was very poor and we sought Father Hoang's help. He found her a job as a cook in one of the homes for older boys. She was a very kind girl and spoke quite good English, but she was inclined to be extremely possessive towards me and was jealous of my other friends.

When I worked with the street children in the evenings Tima used to come with me and translate. Sometimes when I stayed too late on the streets to return to the hospital before curfew, I would stay at Tima's house. She lived in a very poor, overcrowded area of Cholon. During the Tet offensive of 1968 the houses in this district had been completely destroyed. They had been rebuilt and resembled tenement flats, each consisting of two small rooms. Tima's mother was a very fat lady who sold onions and carrots in the market. With the money she made she bought jade earrings and rings which all Vietnamese women liked to wear. The women cared far more about their long painted finger nails and their jewellery than they did about clothes.

Tima's house was crowded with people—her own family and her two children as well as other friends and relatives. Sometimes we could hardly find space enough on the floor to lie down and go to sleep. We all slept on the floor with our clothes on because the police often made house checks during the night. Everyone was very kind and I loved staying there. It was a very noisy area and sometimes we could hardly sleep at night. The neighbours used to beat their children; the man drank too much and there were many street fights; Hondas raced up and down outside. There were rats everywhere and they ran over us while we slept.

It was Tima who gave me my Vietnamese name, Co Nam. As soon as I finished my work in the evenings she would come and meet me. I would change out of my white dress into my Vietnamese clothes, and we would go down to Saigon market place. We travelled on the lambretta buses because the fare only cost 30 piasters each and I needed to save all the money I could to buy soup for the street boys living round the market place.

I met these boys the very first time we ate in the market place. They were waiting for us to finish eating so that they could grab any left-overs. I invited them to eat with us and they brought their younger brothers and sisters over. Some were carrying small babies whom their mothers had sent out with them to beg. Soon this little group of children invited their friends along and every night we would eat together crowded round one of the tiny stalls. However hungry the children were they would always share the food with each other. I loved them dearly.

I saved my small monthly salary from the hospital to buy soup for the children. Although the soup was cheap we had many little mouths to feed and I wrote to my family and friends in England asking them to send me money. One night I didn't have enough money to buy the soup. I gathered all my European clothes together and took them to the clothes market on Ham Nghi street. I sold my six dresses, my jeans, T-shirts and shoes and then went to the market place to eat. I didn't care about clothes any more, I only cared about the children. I now only had two pairs of black satin pants and two shirts that had been well washed and had started to fray. Yet I felt completely accepted by the Vietnamese and that was all that mattered.

After our meal in the market place Tima and I would go to work in Saigon hospital. The hospital was very near the market and about the poorest and most crowded hospital in the city. I just went in and started helping the doctors and nurses. They never said anything but were pleased to have help. Sometimes I forgot about the curfew and we would have to walk home. The police would stop us in the street and tell us to go home quickly to avoid being arrested.

Saigon hospital was the emergency hospital, but there was never any emergency equipment available, for anything that was donated was sold in the market. Inside the hospital was a large entrance hall which was supposed to be the emergency room. It contained six stretchers supported on wooden stands. In the evenings there were only two Vietnamese nurses and perhaps a couple of medical students to help the doctors cope with all the emergencies. Usually the doctors would go home at about 4.30 p.m. in the afternoon.

When the nurses were very busy and there was no doctor on duty, patients requiring immediate treatment had to wait for so long that they often died before a nurse even reached them. Quite young people were brought to the hospital having taken an overdose of tranquillizers or sleeping pills. If the nurses were already pumping out another boy or girl the patients would have to wait—and while they waited they died. Many more patients died in the emergency room than survived. When the stretchers were full patients would be left on the floor. No one noticed if they stopped breathing. There was no suction available if they began to vomit and choke. If a patient died he was left where he was until one of the porters came to remove the body. Drug addicts and junkies came in to look for a place to sleep at night.

Soldiers and civilians were admitted with gunshot wounds, but soldiers were also frequently brought in after fighting in drunken brawls. When the Vietnamese people had a fight they seemed bent on killing each other. They would try and hit their opponent with a brick or a heavy lump of wood or smash a bottle over their heads. Some of the soldiers came in saturated with blood, but still tried to carry on fighting. I remember one soldier who came in with a knife wound in his stomach and half his guts coming out. He was so angry that he tried to hold in his stomach with one hand and hit his opponent with the other. Eventually the police had to handcuff him. The police would bring in their own prisoners as well—perhaps they had beaten them up once too often. Not wanting a death on their hands they brought them to the hospital often unconscious but still in handcuffs, and dumped them on the floor.

At night there would be one nurse on duty in the wards. In every office there was a bed and after 10 p.m. the nurse would lock the door and go to sleep. Intravenous infusions were taken down at night and put up again the next morning, unless a member of the patient's family was able to look after it. If the patients were very sick during the night one of the relatives would call the nurse. Sometimes she would be fast asleep and wouldn't wake up, or else she just wouldn't bother. Patients could be left crying out all night in pain before they died.

Working in Saigon hospital was depressing because I saw so many patients die who could have been saved. One night a middle-aged man was brought in by his family after he had taken an overdose of sleeping pills. He was still conscious but he had to wait so long to have his stomach pumped out that he began to lose consciousness. When he was pumped out he started to be sick and inhaled most of the vomit back into his lungs. He required immediate suction; there was none available. He began to turn blue as he slowly choked. There was no oxygen. I turned him on his side and using my hand and a towel tried to clean the vomit out of his mouth. Suddenly his heart stopped beating. I applied cardiac massage and his heart started beating again. We rushed him up to the second floor operating theatre where there was supposed to be some equipment. The drug cupboard was locked and someone had gone home with the keys. We put a drip into his arm, gave him some oxygen and applied continuous suction. For three hours I stayed with him, trying to save him, but he died.

Very old people who didn't have any money were left on a stretcher or a wooden camp bed in the corridor. Even if there were beds to spare patients had to pay for them. These poor creatures lay in draughts either naked or in clothes soaked through with urine. Very often they were covered in their own excrement which dirtied the beds and the floor. The smell was appalling and no one would go near them, not even the nurses. No one bothered to feed them or even offer them a drink. They just faded away. I remember one old man who had just come in from the street. He tried to walk down the stone steps to the toilet and fell down and fractured his skull. One of the porters lifted him back to his bed and left him there. Blood swelled up inside his head and started to trickle out of his ear, dripping on to floor. No one came to help or comfort him and he died from a brain haemorrhage.

Even Father Hoang was upset by the conditions in the hospital and gave me some old used clothes that had been sent over from the States for the refugees. Tima and I would wash the very old patients each evening and change their clothes. Their own were so filthy that we had to throw them away. Those who came in from the street were covered in head and body lice. Sometimes we would spend a couple of hours picking the head lice out of their hair. We used to take milk to the old people. Their mouths were crusted and dry, their teeth black and rotten. The nurses didn't like us doing this because the patients only urinated afterwards and there was no one to clean it up. The smell was so foul that we were often sick ourselves. On some nights I could scarcely face going inside. The stench was so terrible, the people so pitiful and there seemed so little we could do to help them.

One morning I went into the hospital early to visit a young woman who was dying. Inside the emergency room I saw four men with masks over their faces ready to move a dead body. They opened the door to a small room which they used as a mortuary and pulled out a boy of about twenty, very dirty, almost black. I wondered why he had died so young. They started to kick him and I couldn't understand why they were kicking him if he was dead. They continued kicking him until he suddenly woke up and moved his arm. I couldn't believe it. He wasn't dead at all and yet they had put him in the mortuary. Next they pulled out an old man who really was dead. He had been dead for about two days and the smell of his body was nauseating. The young boy was a drug addict and someone had brought him in to the hospital the night before after finding him in the street. The medical staff, not knowing what to do with him, had put him in the mortuary. I thought this was unforgiveable. What would have happened if he had woken up in the night and turned over on to a dead man? If this was the kind of treatment carried out in a hospital, I began to wonder what happened in the prisons.

Father Hoang was afraid that experiences such as these were too much for me. I became very thin but I refused to relax. Sometimes I would donate blood to the hospital for a patient who was too poor to buy any. One week I donated blood twice in two different hospitals, first for a soldier who had tried to commit suicide by shooting himself through the face and then for a young girl who developed a huge stomach abscess after surgery. Following this my own resistance to infection became very low and I contracted a mild case of hepatitis and jaundice. My eyes and skin looked yellow and I couldn't eat anything without being sick. I went to see a Vietnamese doctor and because of my sickness he treated me for pregnancy. Vitamin and iron pills didn't really help me much but after two weeks in bed I soon recovered. Not long afterwards I felt something crawling down the side of my face and discovered it was a little black insect. Tima looked through my hair and I was full of head lice. Every evening in her home she would wash my hair and she and her mother would spend an hour or so picking out all the lice. After about one week I was clear. I went to the hairdresser and had my hair cut short.

One day Father Hoang took me to Vung Tau, a small village on the coast of Saigon to meet Father Qui, who also ran homes for streetboys. In Vung Tau the boys had built small wooden homes on the side of the mountain. The setting was so quiet and peaceful, the only sound being that of the wind blowing through the trees or the sound of the waves on the ocean gently lapping against the shore. I felt it must have been a very lonely life for the boys at first, away from the bright lights of the city, but they all seemed very happy. All of them went to a school about two miles away and every day they walked there and back. In the evenings they would swim, play football, or just sit playing the guitar and singing songs.

Father Qui was so humble himself, wearing a long black habit, frayed and full of holes, and broken sandals. He was a very thin man and his hair was turning grey with worry and old age. His own house was full of refugee families and yet he had little money of his own. He encouraged everyone to work and the boys grew their own fruit and vegetables and had built their own fishing boat. They also had a Honda repair service and kept their own chickens and ducks and pigs. Father Qui shared whatever he had but sometimes they could only afford to eat rice with potatoes mixed into it.

Father Qui also ran an orphanage which housed about two

hundred children who were cared for by Catholic sisters. The building itself was incredibly derelict. All the doors and shutters were broken and flapped in the wind. The floor was broken and parts of the roof were falling in. Plaster was peeling off the walls. Small, painfully thin children stood shivering with hardly any clothes on. A few of the older children were sick with malaria and lay outside in the corridor covered with rags and newspapers to keep them warm. They only ate twice a day, usually just rice with nothing added.

After my visit I returned to this orphanage every week on my nights off with Tima. We bought fish and vegetables in Vung Tau market so that the sisters could make hot soup for the children. On the warmer days we took the older children swimming. Whenever I ran out of money I asked Miss Oldham or one of the American doctors working at the hospital to help. Tima and I would get up at 4 a.m. and leave on the first bus at 5 a.m. The journey took about three hours.

I loved Vung Tau. It was a small, quaint fishing village. There were still many unmade roads and transport was by horse and cart. The mountains reaching down to the sea were very beautiful. The slopes were green, full of tall palm trees and flowers. Vung Tau also attracted the Americans. The sea was warm and there were miles of long sandy beaches. Several hotels had been built looking towards the sea above the town. They were fully air conditioned, with night clubs and bars. Many of the girls who worked in the bars in Saigon came to Vung Tau because there was less chance of being arrested as prostitutes. Vung Tau's main industry was fishing. I loved to wander round the fish market and watch the boats go out to sea and return with their catch. The fish were unloaded into wooden crates and covered in blocks of ice before being sent off to the Saigon markets. On one of the mountains was a beautiful statue of Buddha, gleaming brilliant white in the sunshine. The view from the mountainside made you feel you were in paradise.

I felt very privileged when Father Hoang introduced me to Dick Hughes. He was about the most handsome man I have ever seen. He had been an actor in the States but had given up his career to stay and help the children. I loved Dick for the wonderful person he was. He was quiet and reserved, and never lost his temper. He worked hard, sometimes writing letters all night long to raise funds. He loved the boys and most of the boys on the street knew him. They used to call him 'Anh Dick' which means 'brother Dick'.

Sometimes Father Hoang took Dick and me out to a restaurant for a meal. Father Hoang was grateful to us for helping his people and he tried to support us in every way he could. Sometimes we went to the pictures. There were several cinemas in Saigon. French and American films were the favourite and also the Chinese Kung Fu films. The children used to play Kung Fu in the streets. Vietnamese television showed only plays and the news but never films. During the American occupation the Vietnamese loved to watch the American television station for the U.S. forces. Their favourite cinema films were *Love Story* and *Doctor Zhivago*.

Father Hoang tried to visit each of the homes every day and I went with him. If the boys were sick I would look after them. Some of the older, more difficult boys lived in Father Hoang's own house. They needed to be with someone whom they could love and respect and usually reformed after living with Father Hoang. They began to go to Father Hoang's church every day and planted out his garden with flower beds and small trees.

There was one boy called Qui who lived with Father Hoang. Qui had been Dick's first boy in the Project and had been a street boy for most of his life, leaving his home when he was very young because he never got on with his father. Qui made his living from shining shoes and had later turned to stealing. After frequent periods in jail he turned to drugs. When Dick met him he was so high from opium injections that he was totally unaware of anyone or anything round him. Dick took Qui to hospital and looked after him for ten days, making sure that no one brought him any drugs. Qui then went to live with Dick. He learned to speak good English and was always very volatile. Sometimes he would become violently angry and break everything in sight including windows and telephones.

Qui was twenty-one and now lived with Father Hoang whom he loved more than his own father and to whom he was very loyal. But he could not leave behind all his old street habits. He no longer took opium but like most of the older boys, he took sleeping pills to forget when he became depressed. Sometimes the boys took up to twenty or thirty sleeping pills and Father Hoang would usually just let them sleep it off. They could buy as many pills as they liked in the Pharmacy without a prescription and they usually bought Tranquinal.

At times the boys became restless and angry with each other. Sometimes they would have an ordinary fist fight, sometimes a knife fight. Qui always kept a knife on him, but usually used it as a warning to the other boys to leave him alone. He also had a couple of hand grenades, two guns and a flare which he had obtained from a friend in the army. He kept them hidden and was always afraid that Father Hoang might find out. Qui was the most difficult boy and the most daring; he liked the other boys to think of him as their leader, and to respect him. His moods changed quickly. One evening he would plan to get even with someone who had upset him, the next day he would tell the boys about faith and religion and how they should all listen to Father Hoang and go to church.

Father Hoang took everything that was sent over from the States for the Streetboys Project to his house. Qui would work hard making up boxes ready to be distributed to the homes. Sometimes things were stolen but Father Hoang never became angry. He told the boys that everything he owned belonged to them and that if they continued to steal they were really stealing from each other. Every day the poor people in Father Hoang's parish came to ask for help. During his absence the boys would help the people, give them a few clothes, school books for their children and medicines when they were sick. They all needed responsibility.

There was another priest living in the house called Father Chau. Father Chau did not approve of Father Hoang's close relationship with the boys and looked upon them with suspicion and mistrust. Whenever he went out during the day he locked and bolted his door and even bought a padlock. The boys knew how Father Chau felt about them and tried to stay out of his way. It was believed that Father Chau even kept a rifle in case one of the boys should try to enter his room at night.

I developed a very close relationship with Qui who used to call me 'Chi Nam' meaning 'older sister'. He would tell me all about himself, his family, his life on the streets. He described Te Ban, the children's jail. I was so horrified at his account of the conditions that I realised I had to see for myself and help. My visit convinced me of the direction of my future work.

CHAPTER 5

Te Ban was the centre of forced education. The police had launched a campaign—'Lam dep thanh pho'—to clean up the city streets in an attempt to boost Saigon as a tourist attraction. Their 'cleaning up' meant collecting all the street children and homeless people and putting them in jail. Children taken to Te Ban were not supposed to be held there for more than forty-eight hours, but sometimes the police forgot about them and they remained for as long as two months. Nearly all the street children had been put in Te Ban at some stage of their life. I knew of one boy who had been taken to the centre one hundred times.

Te Ban was only a small jail, consisting of four cells, each holding about one hundred persons. The first cell was for the children. Innocent children whose only crime was that of being homeless were locked inside it. The cell only had one toilet in the far corner and smelt of urine. There were no washing facilities and most of the children were covered in scabies. There was nothing inside the cells apart from large concrete blocks to sleep on and rats ran over the floor.

The children were very thin and their clothes were torn and dirty. Some of the boys, handicapped from polio, lay on the floor in a corner of the room. One eight-year-old boy was totally blind and some were only five years old. Many had lost an arm or a leg in a mine explosion. Most of the children had shaved off each other's hair to rid themselves of head lice. One boy had cut his hands and arms with a razor when locked in solitary confinement. The solitary confinement room was known as the 'dark room' and feared by everyone because of the rats and the ghosts they believed to be there.

All the police carried heavy wooden canes with which they would beat the boys. The boys were made to turn their knuckles down on the concrete and the police would beat the palms of their hands, tearing off the skin and leaving them sore and bleeding. Another punishment was to make the boys walk up and down the courtyard on their knees during the middle of the day when it was very hot. They were often beaten round their heads and their bodies were covered in huge red marks which sometimes bled. Many of the boys had tattoos on their arms. They read in English 'Who loves me' or 'When I die, who will cry for me'. The boys used to call themselves 'Bui-Doi' which in English means 'Dust of Life'. They Thought of Themselves as The dust blown from street to street in The wind.

The next cell held all the women. Most of them were very old and had been arrested for sleeping in the streets. Some were sick with fevers and malaria; others suffered from leprosy and I noticed that their fingers were almost eaten away. There were also young mothers who had been arrested for begging in the street with their babies. When the police brought the mothers to jail they had to bring their babies and children with them, because there was no one else to look after them. Two or three of the women were mentally insane. They stripped off all their clothes and walked round naked. They never washed and were full of head and body lice. The police would hit them and they just laughed.

Some of the younger girls were only in their teens and had been arrested as prostitutes. They were charming and most of them spoke some English which they had picked up from their American customers. They asked me my name and why I had come. They told me why they had been arrested and how the police treated them in jail. The girls were very pretty and sometimes the police wanted to sleep with them. If they refused they were either hit or kept in jail. One girl was only fifteen years old and already pregnant. They asked me when I would come back to visit them.

The third cell held all the teenage boys and young men, many of whom were opium addicts. A doctor used to visit the jail every every morning and would hand out tranquillizers to the addicts, a few vitamin pills, something to stop diarrhoea, and aspirins. The boys would crush these pills, mix them with water and make injections into their veins. They only had one needle and a syringe which everyone used. Their arms were covered with needle marks and abscesses because the needle was dirty.

Drugs could be brought into the jail from outside. Visitors

were allowed in once a week and they would bring in drugs hidden in a loaf of bread. If the boys had enough money they would pay one of the police to go out and buy sleeping pills. The police were so poor themselves they would agree.

Some of the boys lay flat on their backs, completely unconscious from the drugs. They breathed heavily, their eyes still half open and rolled back, and foamed at the mouth. Yet they looked so young, barely sixteen or seventeen years old. They were naked because they burned their clothes to make a fire so that they could boil water to mix the drugs. Their bones stuck out through their flesh and their arms and legs were covered in scratches and boils. Many of the boys had inflicted knife wounds on themselves through sheer misery and the feeling of hopelessness. Many of the older boys were ex-soldiers, some of whom had lost both legs or arms. The army paid them no money once they were redundant and it was impossible for them to find employment. In desperation they turned to opium and anti-depressants as their only way out.

In the last cell were the very old men, and even they were hit by the police. Due to the overcrowded conditions they easily contracted tuberculosis. Their cell smelt revolting; there was urine all over the floor. Some of the men were dying from neglect and starvation. When they were sick they did not have the strength to go to the end of the cell block to eat and no one brought them any food or drink.

Next to their cell was a large eating hall filled with long wooden benches and tables. Although the Government gave the jail enough money for the people to eat properly, it was never spent. The women who worked in the kitchen only bought the cheapest rice, the poorest fish which was so salty and so full of bones that it could hardly be eaten, and a few vegetables for soup. They divided the money they didn't spend between themselves. Some of the old men helped to prepare the food, make up the fires and wash the bowls. The fish was boiled without being cleaned or scaled. The girls told me that when they ate the fish they developed a rash and their whole body itched and so they lived on rice alone.

I was horrified at what I saw. When I first went to Te Ban my eyes filled with tears of indignation and sorrow. I felt a great lump rise in my throat and I could barely talk. I wanted to cry for everyone there, but I couldn't in front of them. Not when they suffered so much and still smiled so bravely. I kept asking myself what these people had done to deserve such a terrible existence. Who had the right to judge these innocent people, to lock them up, to offer them a life of such abject misery? When I saw the policeman beat the children I could feel my hands sweat and my heart beat. I wanted to tear the stick out of the policeman's hand and strike him. But had I done so I would never have been allowed to return and would not have been able to help the children.

A group of Vietnamese social workers worked in the jail. Every morning the girls would arrive for work dressed in beautiful ao-dais, their hair done and their make-up carefully applied. They worked in an office filled with flowers behind the cell block but never went near the cells. They only helped 'good' boys and recommended punishments for their considered 'bad' boys. I was introduced to them on my first visit to the jail but never went to see them again.

Every week I returned to Te Ban with Father Hoang. We took clothes and soap for the boys and medicines for the doctors to distribute. If we had distributed these ourselves and one of the staff, resentful of the work we were doing, had seen us, we could have been blamed for any death which occurred. I continued working at the Adventist hospital and in Saigon hospital in the evenings. As Tima and I went to Vung Tau every week to buy fish for the orphanage children there, I decided to buy more fish to bring back to Saigon for the boys in jail. We would cook about 30 kilos of fish in Tima's house and Father Hoang would then drive us to the jail. I still went down to the market place to buy soup for the street boys and met more and more people living on the streets.

When I first started taking food into the jail everyone fought for it. More prisoners ended up being hit by the police than they did eating. The only way to distribute the food was to go from one cell to the next giving something to each person. We started to buy bread and put the fish inside so that everyone had a sandwich. We went to the market and bought one hundred loaves of bread, cutting each one into four in order to feed all the prisoners.

I wrote letters to everyone in England I could think of asking for financial aid. I asked Miss Oldham and the other doctors and nurses at the Adventist hospital to help. Even the kitchen staff saved all the left-over food for me to take to the jail. When I could afford to, we bought tins of milk for the very old sick men who couldn't eat and fruit and sweets for the children. I always gave something to the police as well in an effort to establish some kind of relationship with them, so that we could all work together to help the children. Occasionally I bought them a bottle of whisky. Our relationship did improve and they became more lenient towards the children. As the children grew accustomed to us, they no longer fought over the food because they knew there would be enough to go round. The police no longer needed to use their sticks. Eventually they didn't even bother to accompany us and just gave us the key to go in and out of the cells as we wished.

Father Hoang used to ask the boys where they lived so that we could try to contact their family. If parents came to collect a child who promised to go home and not back to the streets, the police would set him free. Some of the boys with no families left the prison to live in one of Father Hoang's homes. One of my happiest moments was to watch a boy leave the jail. I was allowed to take the very sick to Saigon hospital. The doctors allowed us free medical care because I had worked there so often. When the patients had recovered we would try to reunite them with a relative or friend.

I remember one old man in jail with white hair and a long white beard. He told Father Hoang he lived under the bridge near the jail and we were given permission to drive him home. Father Hoang and I sat in the front of the car and Qui sat in the back to look after him. When we left the jail the old man told Father Hoang that he really lived in Bien Hoa. By the time we reached Bien Hoa the old man had urinated all over the back seat and all over Qui. We drove round for about an hour and a half, hoping he might recognise his home but he couldn't remember where he lived. It was a very hot day and the inside of the car began to smell. Eventually we had to return to Saigon and take him back to the jail as we couldn't just leave him in the street. The police laughed when they saw us. I think the old man just wanted a ride.

Children were still occasionally locked up in the dark room and one day we found a seven-year-old boy who had been placed there by the court. His father had died and his mother was in hospital expecting a baby. The little boy had to stay at home to support his younger brothers and sisters. He had stolen a watch from the market in order to buy food. Father Hoang had him moved out and put with the other boys. He was so afraid when he came out of the dark room that his whole body shook. He walked along with his arms folded around himself for protection. Father Hoang asked his cousin who was a lawyer to follow the boy through court and a week later he was released.

Then I met a boy called Cu Lang in the dark room. He was only fourteen and had been put there after one of the other boys had thrown boiling water over him. He had second degree burns which were weeping and infected due to the filth in the jail. I took him to the Adventist hospital and he was admitted to the ward where I worked. The next day he had his burns debridged and dressed under a general anaesthetic. He was also full of worms and had head lice. As he recovered he started to help the other patients in the ward. Every morning he would wake up early to help the older patients get up and would push them in a wheel chair to the toilet. Two weeks later he left the hospital completely cured.

We were not always successful. There were some we didn't reach in time . . . I thought one boy had contracted malaria and asked to take him to the hospital. The police said he was a drug addict and would not permit him to leave. He lay in a corner of the cell covered in an old blanket and shaking feverishly. I gave him some milk but during the next few days I was so busy that I didn't have time to return. I was doing extra night duty at the hospital because seven cases of typhoid fever had been admitted. When I returned to the jail I couldn't find the sick boy. The police told us he had gone home but I didn't believe them. One of the boys finally told me he had died.

I felt empty inside. I could feel the blood drain from my face and I suddenly felt very cold. My hands shook and I wanted to be sick. Where was his body? The boys told me that no one had fed him since I had given him the milk and that he had died the day before. I had been one day too late. I felt it was all my fault. The refuse cleaners had taken away his body on the back of their cart. Who was he? His name was Nguyen Van Long, known by his friends as Phuong and he was fourteen years old.

I asked Father Hoang what action we should take. He sadly replied there was nothing we could do. He didn't want me to look for his body but I insisted on going to the cemetery on Le Van Duyet street. It was the largest cemetery in Saigon and almost all homeless people and street boys were buried there. It was in the district of Chi Hoa, near to Chi Hoa prison. One of the boys working in the cemetery had known Nguyen Van Long on the streets and had recognised his body. They hadn't yet buried him and told us to come back in the afternoon. Before leaving we ordered a small headstone. It was a very simple one, with just his name and 'Bui-Doi' written on it. 'Nguyen Van Long, Dust of Life'.

That afternoon Dick, Father Hoang and I returned to the cemetery. The boys had found an old wooden coffin and the headstone was ready. They lifted Nguyen Van Long's body out of the mortuary wrapped in a coconut mat and placed it in the coffin. I was shocked when I looked at his body. I just muttered God's name quietly to myself and tears streamed down my face. Father Hoang put a handkerchief into my hand. Dick stood by my side and put on his dark glasses to hide his own tears. I could not believe it was the same boy I had met in the jail just a week before. One side of his face was crawling with maggots which had eaten away his flesh. His eyes were still open but they had lost their colour. His body was filthy and looked old and yellow; his hair was matted and bloodstained.

The boys put the lid on the coffin and hammered nails into it. I placed a wreath of flowers on top and we followed the boys through the graveyard. It was September, towards the end of the rainy season, and the muddy water that flooded the cemetery came well over our knees. I took off my shoes and rolled up my trousers. The stench was horrible as I slid through the slippery mud. The boys had already dug the grave and had to bail out the water before putting down the coffin. The grave was not quite large enough and the coffin got stuck half-way down. The boys jumped up and down on top of it to push it to the bottom. We burned incense and lit two candles. We put incense on the surrounding graves. No one said anything. We stood round the grave, silently, solemnly. Father Hoang gave the boys some money for their work.

I wanted to be alone, I was too upset to talk to anyone. I returned to the hospital and spent an hour in the shower scrubbing the mud off my feet and legs. Even my nails were caked with mud and I could still feel the smell of death. I washed all my clothes. It was early evening and I went to bed. I couldn't sleep, I kept thinking about Nguyen Van Long. And I thought about God. Why should an innocent child bear so much hardship and suffering? Nguyen Van Long was the victim of a cruel environment, an example of man's inhumanity to man. Eventually I got up and went out to a small café outside the hospital. I sat alone until curfew, drowning my sorrows with beer.

I also wanted to visit Chi Hoa prison which housed about nine thousand prisoners, including two thousand boys in their teens and nine hundred smaller children. No one was allowed into Chi Hoa because of security precautions. The authorities were afraid someone might write about the conditions in the newspaper. About twenty American prisoners were held in Chi Hoa, mainly on charges of theft, and every Saturday morning one of the American doctors from the hospital would visit them. I asked the doctor if I could go with him and he agreed.

Chi Hoa was a huge red brick building that had been built by the French. High walls surrounded it on the outside. Having been searched by the police you passed through the main gate into an outer courtyard. Here there was a smaller building leading off the main prison where the prisoners were allowed to meet their visitors. To enter the inner courtyard which was directly outside the prison you had to pass through another gate and tell the police where you were going. They could refuse you admission.

Once inside the inner courtyard the American doctor went to visit the American prisoners. I stood alone outside this huge building which looked so bleak and forbidding. Several police vans drew up carrying men of all ages and boys who could not have been more than ten years old. As they walked past I noticed they were all handcuffed in pairs. Saturday morning was one of the days they went to court. I still didn't know how I was going to get inside. I went over to the police standing just inside the prison and asked to see the prison governor. The police telephoned the governor who agreed to see me and I followed one of the policemen upstairs to an office on the top floor. I felt nervous now and didn't know what I was going to say to him.

The prison was run by Lieutenant-Colonel Tran Van Hai who had received his military training in Texas. Colonel Hai loved women. He asked me to sit down and offered me tea or coffee to drink and cigarettes. I asked him for one of the American cigars he was smoking, a packet of which lay on his desk. Colonel Hai was astonished that I smoked cigars; I told him I smoked them all the time. For the next two hours Colonel Hai turned on the charm. He loved my Vietnamese clothes and thought I would look beautiful in an ao-dai which he wanted to buy for me. He was pleased I liked Vietnamese food and suggested I should go out to dinner with him as he knew all the best restaurants. Whenever he stopped talking to sip his tea or smoke I asked him questions first about himself and then about the prison and the boys who were held there. Then I told Colonel Hai I would love him to show me round.

He escorted me through the main part of the prison. Prison officers stood to attention and saluted Colonel Hai, running ahead of him to unlock doors and let us through. We walked through long dark passage ways behind the cells out into another courtyard in the centre of the prison building. All the cells overlooked the yard. They were built three storeys high and I could see they were crammed with people. The cells looked as if they were smaller and more crowded than those at Te Ban. People stood looking out between the bars all the way round. In the middle of the courtyard was a high wall with a watch tower dividing the yard into two parts. There were rows of barbed wire everywhere.

Conditions at Chi Hoa were far worse than at Te Ban. The prisoners were only fed two bowls of rice a day, whereas at Te Ban the boys could eat as much rice as they wanted. Sickness was rife. So many people suffered from scabies and skin diseases that they were all put in a cell together. I was amazed they were alive at all and I realized later that many did die. The guards looked cruel and carried heavy leather whips. As we entered the boys' cell the children stood up with their hands at their side, looking worried and afraid. One little boy was only five years old; he had stolen 200 piasters. Another boy was only seven years old; he had stolen two metres of cloth in the market. They had no protection against the mosquitoes or the cold at night and many were dying of malaria. Boys were often placed in Chi Hoa by the court before their trial. Many were quite innocent but could remain in prison for several months before being called before the court and released.

We went over to the hospital which was behind the main prison. In reality it was just a smaller cell block where they kept all the sick, old and young. There were no beds; the prisoners lay on the floor. Some were covered with old blankets, others curled themselves up in a coconut mat to keep warm, some had nothing. Medicines and medical equipment were allocated to Chi Hoa but everything was sold. There was little the two doctors working there could do. The whole place looked more like a prisoner of war camp than a hospital.

I left Chi Hoa promising to return. Colonel Hai instructed his driver to drive me home in his jeep. He told me to contact him if I wished to return and asked me if I wanted to work in the hospital. I would have loved to, but I don't think the Saigon authorities would have approved. I did return to Chi Hoa about a week later, with Dick and Father Hoang. We bought five hundred loaves of bread, one hundred tins of milk, a thousand bananas and two barrels of soap flakes. We distributed the food ourselves amongst the young boys and the sick in the hospital. I returned to Chi Hoa on several occasions but there was never anything we could do to really help the boys. We couldn't take anyone out because the prisoners had been placed there by the court.

Most of the boys and a few of the girls I met in Te Ban jail lived in or near Le Lai street, an area of Saigon that was known as the 'drug area'. There was a small alley between Le Lai and Vo Tanh street where almost any kind of drugs—opium, heroin, speed, barbiturates and tranquillizers—could be bought. On either side of the alley way were smaller alleys leading to tiny wooden houses about the size of a single room. Nearly all the people living in this area dealt in drugs. Drug addicts who did not live in one of the houses lived and slept in the street.

I had heard about Le Lai and wanted to go there. Dick and Father Hoang advised me not to go because some of the addicts were desperate for money and were known to have attacked foreigners. However, I was still determined to see the area for myself and one evening I went alone. I walked along Le Lai street and through the alley. It was dark except for a few oil lamps burning on tables set outside the coffee shops. I was aware of the people watching me, their eyes following my every step. I felt as if someone lurking in the shadows might jump on me at any minute.

Most of the addicts used opium which they prepared themselves for injection. It looked black when they injected it. Opium sold for 200 piasters per 1cc. Some of the addicts took it three or four times a day in quantities of about 2–3 ccs a time. This could cost them up to 2000 piasters a day. Most of the girl addicts earned their money by working as prostitutes. The boys resorted to stealing, working as pimps or pushing drugs. The opium came from the 'Golden Triangle' between Laos, Burma and Thailand. Most of it was flown into Vietnam (with the encouragement of the French and later the Americans). It was processed into heroin in Saigon by merchants who had to give a huge rake-off to the police. Both the French and Americans found that this was the best way to finance and keep efficient the Saigon police.

A little way up the valley I saw an old man sitting with a needle and syringe in his hand. A small group of boys crouched on the ground around him with their sleeves rolled up, ready to choose a vein. I watched the old man injecting the black opium into the boys. His only light was that of a small oil lamp on a table next to him. Each boy paid him before he gave the injection and he used the same needle and syringe for everyone. I went over to join the little group and squatted down beside them.

One of the addicts turned and stared at me. He looked surprised and grinned. 'Hey Co Nam, you know me—Te Ban.' I heard the other boys murmur 'It's Co Nam'. Some of the old men and other addicts sitting sleepily in the alley looked up and smiled as they recognised me. They asked me if I wanted to 'shoot up'. The old man offered to 'shoot' for me and said I didn't have to pay. Another boy rolled up my sleeve, starting to look for a vein. I told them I didn't want to 'shoot up'. One of the girls approached and told me I would feel good. I would walk on air and everything would be beautiful.

I sat down in the alley with the young addicts. The girl, who spoke English very well, was called Mai. She bought me a couple of cigarettes and a glass of coffee. We started to talk. Mai had eaten nothing all day and didn't even want any coffee. She told me she took sleeping pills because she felt so sad about her life. She was slim and wore a pair of tight blue trousers and a yellow shirt. Her hair was long but falling out in places. She wore heavy make-up and had long painted nails. She told me she had heard about me, 'a girl that looked American who was called Co Nam'. The other girls whom I had met in the jail had told Mai about me. She herself had been in Te Ban many times and also in Tu Duc, the women's prison. She tried to stay on sleeping pills but sometimes she had to have an injection of opium, to forget ... She usually worked as a prostitute in the evenings, but tonight she had slept.

Before I left Le Lai I promised Mai I would come back the next day and I returned the following afternoon. Mai was still in the same place, still in the same clothes and still wearing the same make-up. She was sitting on a stool leaning against the wall outside the coffee shop. Her head kept dropping as she dozed. She had taken twenty sleeping pills. Some of the boys asked me if I had any money because they were hungry. I was afraid they would spend it on drugs so I ordered some food for them and some coffee for Mai. I helped Mai drink the coffee, most of which she spilled. I got her a plate of food and encouraged her to eat something. She invited me to eat with her and we shared what we had.

I began to pass by Le Lai street when I left Saigon hospital in the evenings. Sometimes it was quite late at night and I would see people sleeping in the street. It was so sad to witness their poverty, their hardship and silent suffering. Women who came into Saigon to sell opium brought their children with them. These children grew up amongst the addicts and using drugs came as naturally to them as learning to read and write. I knew a little seven-year-old boy whose mother came every day to Le Lai street to sell opium she had brought in from the country. I used to see him smoking it in the evening. He looked sleepy and bleary-eyed and kept falling over as he walked along the street.

I started to go to Le Lai during the day to buy food for some of the girls and boys living there. I always stayed to eat with them and we would have long talks together. I asked Father Hoang to give me some clothes for those who had just come out of jail. I used to buy shoes for the children who didn't have any and take medicines to the old men when they were sick.

If Mai wasn't working I would always meet her on Le Lai. She would either be sitting sadly in the café or sleeping in the street. Sometimes she had taken so many sleeping pills that she didn't even recognise me. One day I couldn't find her and discovered that the police had taken her to jail. The next day I went to Te Ban and found Mai with some of the other girls. They had all been working in Tu Do street the night before and the police had arrested them for soliciting. The girls pleaded with me to get them out of jail. But where could I take them? How could I look after them? Father Hoang and I discussed the problem. We obviously needed a home for girls and I became more and more determined to open one.

I met the girls on Le Lai street on the evening they were released and they were already preparing to go to work. They hadn't even eaten. That same evening I met Jacqueline, a very attractive half negro, half Vietnamese girl who had two pimps working with her as escorts. She had taken Judo lessons from the man who trained President Thieu's bodyguards and even the police were wary of her. Some of Father Hoang's boys remembered Jacky from their days on the streets and had seen her fight three Americans at once. Even Qui knew Jacky and stayed away from her.

Jacky was strong. People were afraid of her and did anything she wanted. She was a beautiful girl when she made herself up and found work easily. She was happy-go-lucky and cheerful. Her English was very good and she never stopped talking and telling jokes. Her pockets were always full of sweets for the children and she would look after the addicts. She would obtain drugs when they needed them; she would hold them down when they were rolling about in agony in an attempt to quieten them.

Jacky rarely used opium. She used to get 'speed' from the Americans and inject large doses into her veins. She needed to keep going, to keep talking, to go out and have a good time. The speed helped her; with this she could stay awake for days on end. Early every evening I would see Jacky prepare for work. She would sit in the street with an assortment of wigs, make-up and well-worn clothes strewn round her. She used to go to work in short 'hot pants', a low-necked shirt and high-heeled-shoes that she could hardly walk in. She always wore a wig, bright red lipstick and heavy eye shadow with long black false eyelashes. Her pimps would escort her down the street, one on either side of her, to steady her as she tried to balance on her shoes. I became good friends with Jacky soon after our first meeting. She told me to call her if I was ever in trouble, but I never had any cause to do so.

Mai also grew very close to me. She would always call me 'Chi Nam' and introduced her friends, Hom, Tuyet and Chao to me. Hom and Tuyet were sisters but Mai and Hom always worked together. Hom was pretty and had a gentle personality. She was always popular with the Vietnamese boys and even Qui was in love with her. Tuyet was attractive too, but was much more aggressive by temperament. She had grown up on the street and had sold flowers and peanuts to the Americans as a child. She was well able to take care of herself and had spent eighteen months in Tu Duc prison after a knife fight with another girl whom she had stabbed in the leg. Tuyet made most of her money by stealing. She didn't like working as a prostitute because she had a Vietnamese boyfriend. Her boyfriend was an opium addict and unable to work himself but Tuyet still loved him and gave him all her money. She already had one baby by an American and Jacky's mother looked after it.

Chao worked on her own. Her father was Cambodian and had remarried after her mother's death. Chao's father and stepmother were good to her and loved her. But when the Americans came to Saigon Chao couldn't keep away from them. She loved sex and hung round the bars every night. Her father would beat her when she came home and eventually she left her parents and went to live on Le Lai street. She soon became addicted to opium. Although she was a beautiful girl she neglected her looks and having lived at home she could not cope with street life.

I became increasingly involved with these girls and their problems and knew that I could not help them constructively unless I could offer them a family environment. I still dreamed of founding my own home.

CHAPTER 6

In November 1973 Father Hoang had to go to Da Nang to visit two homes for street boys and I went with him. Da Nang is about six hundred miles north of Saigon. Due to outbreaks of fighting in the countryside we could not go by road, so we flew there in a Boeing 727 on an Air Vietnam flight. It was the rainy season and as we landed in Da Nang we could see the floods below us. We stayed in the home of a Vietnamese woman who supervised the finances of the two homes.

Da Nang was in many ways similar to Saigon. It is a much smaller city but still very overcrowded and well known for its night life, for the American presence had attracted the girls to the bars. We saw many small boys at work in the streets. Most of them were walking round selling bread, their voices rising above the noise of the traffic and the crowds of people. Others were watching cars, shining shoes or walking the streets with a large sack thrown across their backs collecting the rubbish. We bought bread from the boys and gave it to the children who were sitting in the empty market place or wandering down by the riverside looking for a place to sleep for the night. We stayed out until just before the curfew. I could still hear the boys as I lay in bed that night. Their sad voices echoed through the quiet city streets, as they called in vain for people to come and buy their bread.

The next morning we could hear noise in the distance, the sound of gunfire and small arms. Helicopters circled overhead. We returned to the street and bought hot soup for all the street boys we saw. Then we went to visit a well-known hillside on the outskirts of the city called the Marble Mountain which was full of caves. We went by jeep and the boys came with us. The countryside was beautiful but very desolate. It was flooded in most parts for the land along the roadside was very flat. We could see the mountains rising in the distance. In one of the villages we passed through the people had found a dead Viet Cong and put his body in the market place for everyone to see.

The next day Father Hoang and I went to Hue, which had been the capital of Vietnam before the French occupation in about 1850. We left very early in the morning and travelled in an old Peugeot used as a taxi. The mountains we drove over were more beautiful than I could ever have imagined. They were heavily wooded and stretched for miles into the distance. The roads were narrow and winding and the driver drove very fast, throwing us from one side of the car to the other. On the other side of the mountains was the sea; small hamlets were scattered along the coastline. Many of the telegraph poles on the road near Hue had come down because of recent fighting in the area. A few of the bridges had been blown up and were still under repair.

Hue was a beautiful city, well kept and clean and not over-crowded like most other cities. We went to see a priest who was a friend of Father Hoang's. He was busy filling three trucks that were taking food and relief supplies to the refugees who had fled from Quang Tri. I asked Father Hoang if we could go with them. He told us it could be dangerous but I still wanted to go. Soldiers were driving the trucks up to Quang Tri in case there was an ambush. We drove along in pouring rain and in some places we passed through about three to four feet of water which came right over our jeep. People were moving all along the roadside, walking barefooted through the mud, many travelling southwards to a safer area to live. About two to three hours later we came to a resettlement village on the border of the province of Quang Tri. The sky was dull and grey and it was still raining. The countryside was flat, bleak and waterlogged. It looked rather like a huge lake.

The refugees were led by a priest who lived in the ruins of a very small house that had been bombed. He told us that three Viet Cong had been found dead in his house after the fighting. Sometimes, he said, he felt he could still smell the bodies. The soldiers distributed the food to the refugees. Many of the women were carrying a baby in one arm and a rifle in the other. They lived very near to the 17th parallel which divides North and South Vietnam and were constantly afraid of attack. Civilians were not usually allowed into this area because of constant clashes between the South Vietnamese army and the Communist troops. The priest whom we met at the village drove us on to Quang Tri city by jeep. He was also a Major in the army. Three of his soldiers came with us and another jeep followed with about six more soldiers. They were constantly on the lookout for enemy snipers.

It had stopped raining now, the clouds had started to disappear and the sun was coming out. The major drove quickly; he looked nervous and anxious and kept his eyes straight on the road ahead of him. Everyone was tense, no one spoke. We were coming into an area where about 40,000 people including civilians had once died. There was not the slightest sign of life. When the people had fled Quang Tri during the offensive in early 1972, they had dropped everything and run for their lives down this very road, never to return. A railway line had once run along the side of the road but this had been completely blown up. Pieces of railway track were strewn on the ground, carriages lay upturned or on their side, some suspended in the air. Helicopters and jet fighters lay scattered over the land, their nose end pointing into the ground. Along the roadside were piles of tin cans, used ammunition boxes, tin helmets and used war arms. Tankers lay upturned or on their side, smashed to pieces. This futile destruction caused by war was heartbreaking to see. Even the land had turned to a white sand and nothing grew there any longer. Not a bird flew in the sky; not a single blade of grass grew by the roadside. Everything looked dead for miles around.

Before we entered the city the soldiers told us not to walk amongst the ruins because there were still many unexploded terrorist bombs made of plastic. We drove through the remains of the city up to the river. This was as far as we could go—the 17th parallel. We looked across the river Thanh Han which divides North and South Vietnam and could see the red flags flying and peasants working in the fields. It was dangerous to be there and I did just wonder if one of the Viet Cong on the opposite bank would see my yellow hair and try to shoot, thinking I was an American. On our side of the river the red and yellow South Vietnamese flags were flying. There were many young A.R.V.N. soldiers standing along the river bank, their M.16s pointing towards the North. I thought how brave they were to stand there, almost a direct target for the Viet Cong.

As I looked at the ruins in front of me I could not believe that this had once been a city. Piles of rubble were all that remained of houses, schools and churches. Not one building remained intact. I looked closely at the ruins. There was not a square inch of wall without a bullet hole through it. Street after street was the same. No dogs walked amongst the ruins; no chickens pecked in the dust. The city was silent, dead, completely devastated by war. It was like being in a ghost town and I was relieved to return to Saigon.

I had to work at the Adventist hospital over Christmas 1973. On Christmas Eve, after a long day at the hospital, I changed into an ao-dai and rushed over to Father Hoang's church for the midnight Mass. The church was full and most of the boys from the homes attended the service. Father Hoang had prepared a Christmas dinner in his house for some of the other priests after the Mass, and he invited me to stay. The next morning I had to leave his house at 5 a.m. in time to return to the hospital for work at 6.30 a.m.

Immediately after Christmas the police started on another campaign to 'clean up the city'. They drove round the streets picking up all the street boys and returning them to Te Ban. As the numbers in Te Ban increased, sickness spread even more quickly. I took bread, milk and fruit to the inmates about three times a week. We took the sick to the hospital. Some of the boys came to stay in one of Father Hoang's homes and we tried to return others to their own families. Within the first week Mai, Chao, Hom and Tuyet were all back in Te Ban. Mai became depressed and very thin because she refused to eat; Chao was also sick. It was upsetting to see these charming girls in such surroundings. Had they been given the chance to change their way of life, they would have done.

We had to open a home for the girls. It was the only way we could help them to lead a normal life. The girls were about my age and some were even older, with babies of their own. We started to look round for a suitable house and for someone who could live with the girls and look after them. I thought that I should take care of the younger street girls who were not already involved in a world of drugs and prostitution but that an older, more experienced person should look after the older girls.

On 20 January, 1974, just three days before Tet, everyone was released as usual from Te Ban. As the people left Father Hoang and I gave them an envelope containing a new money note—the custom during Tet. Most people kept their money note but some used it as a fare into Saigon. They didn't know where they were going or what they were going to eat that night.

Later that day I went to Le Lai street where I met up with many people who had just been released from Te Ban. It was Tet, they were free and everyone was happy. We sat round one of the tables outside the coffeee shop, drinking coffe and smoking 'Capstan' cigarettes. All the 'Bui-Doi' smoked Capstan and I joined them. I met Mai and Hom who were just getting ready to go to work on Tu Do street. I loved these people as my friends, as my own brothers and sisters.

The next day, 21 January, just two days before Tet, a tragedy occurred. Some of the children just released from Te Ban were playing in the square outside the market place; a few were sleeping. A group of soldiers had gathered close by. Suddenly, one of the soldiers dropped a hand grenade. We never knew if it was an accident or if he had committed suicide. Fourteen children were injured and five died. One of the girls who died was called 'Cuc'. We had first met her in Te Ban a few months before. She was only fifteen years old and five months pregnant.

We visited the children in Saigon hospital. Most of them knew and recognised us. It was terrible to see them lying there, injured and unable to do anything for themselves. For the next few days I stayed in the hospital with them and Father Hoang brought us what we needed. I continued to work at the hospital over Tet itself because there was only one nurse left in the emergency room. The rest of the staff had gone home for the holiday. We were kept busy with one emergency case after another because most of the other hospitals had closed.

In February 1974, I opened the first home for girls in Saigon. We had tried to find someone to run the home but no one seemed to be interested. Everyone was keen to help the boys but no one wanted to help the girls. I didn't know how I would cope with the older girls because I knew it would be hard for them to break their old habits. I wanted to run the home on a similar basis to that of the street boys' homes, with about eight to ten girls living together like one ordinary family. We found a house near the district of Cholon, about half a mile from the city centre. It belonged to a Vietnamese man called Mr Hieu who was very interested in developing the scout movement throughout South Vietnam and he had also started a home for street boys called

'Nghia Sinh'. Our house was very close to 'Nghia Sinh' and he told us to come to him if we ever needed help. We only rented the house and Father Hoang paid him a year's rent in advance. Dick Hughes very kindly offered to support us financially.

Father Hoang suggested we should name the house 'Cuc' in remembrance of the girl who had been killed in the hand grenade explosion. I thought it would bring bad luck to the house if we named it after someone who had just died, especially since our aim was to bring a new life to the girls. I wanted to call the home after the famous Hai Ba Trung sisters who rode through Saigon on elephants in A.D. 40 and led the Vietnamese people to fight against the Chinese. We had a little name board made which we put up outside the house. It read: 'The Girls Project, Gia-Dinh Hai Ba Trung, Hy Vong 7' which in English means 'The Girls Project, Hai Ba Trung family, Hope 7'.

It was a small house built of brick with a corrugated iron roof and one large room downstairs. We had a wooden partition built which divided the room into two. At the back of the house was a tiny kitchen with nothing but a small sink. There was just one small room upstairs and the bathroom was under the stairs. Inside the bathroom was a toilet, a small wash basin and a shower tap. We had electricity and the house was fitted out with lights and a ceiling fan. The walls were white washed and had blue shutters at the windows.

We lived in a very poor, overcrowded area of Saigon which few foreigners ever visited. Our house was one of a row of houses in a narrow lane off Tran Binh Trong street. Opposite the lane, on the other side of this street, was a large building used by the police for administration and criminal investigation purposes. At the top of the street was Hung Vuong street which led into the centre of Cholon. About two hundred yards down Hung Vuong street was the main bus station leading off Petrusky street. It was a very busy, noisy area with plenty of bars in the adjoining streets. Opposite our home was a house built out of wood and corrugated iron which held about ten very poor families. At night there was not enough room for everyone to sleep inside the house so most of the children would sleep outside in the lane.

Children played in the lane all day long and street vendors came to sell their produce. Rubbish was dumped in huge piles and the children urinated outside. Many of the poorer houses had no toilets and no water. There was a tap at the top of the lane where the women did their washing and the men would collect buckets of water for household use.

When Father Hoang first took me to the home my neighbours thought I was an American in Vietnamese clothes. I didn't want them to think of me as an American; I wanted them to think of me as one of them. The house was very dirty and I wanted to clean it before the girls moved in. I found an old dirty bucket, filled it with water and went outside to clean the lane in front of the house. Everyone was watching me. I took off my shoes and rolled up my trousers as I washed the paintwork and swept away the rubbish. Father Hoang heard the onlookers say that I couldn't be an American because if I was, I would have someone to work for me. Some of them thought I had an American father and a Vietnamese mother. Father Hoang drove me to the Adventist hospital to collect my clothes. I was to continue working at the hospital but would live in the home.

Father Hoang sent one of his boys over to stay with me on my first night at the home. His name was Qui Nor (little Qui). Qui Nor and I went over to a small cafè in the street and ate 'Pho'. Some of my neighbours followed me and were surprised to see I could eat Vietnamese food. I slept on the floor with all my clothes on, in front of the window. Some of the women looked through the window and asked Qui Nor why I wasn't sleeping in a bed. Was I comfortable on the floor? Why had I come to live here and where was my furniture? They had never seen an American live and dress in this way. When Qui Nor explained to them that I was 'Anh' meaning English and not 'My' meaning American, they were even more puzzled. They had never heard of England and later asked me what part of the States England was in!

The next day we visited one of the American-owned warehouses along the Bien Hoa highway. Most of the Americans had pulled out by now and their surplus goods were being distributed to the orphanages and foreign charities. We told them about the girls' home and they gave us six chests of drawers, two large office tables and two swing chairs. My neighbours were relieved to see I had some possessions and rushed out to help unload the lorry. Qui visited me that evening and brought me a little dog which the boys at Hope 6 had given him. We called him Nixon.

Dick had been talking to the American Women's Club about my home to see if they could help. The next day they visited me and decided to donate a gas cooker and a refrigerator. Father Hoang and I then went to Te Ban and asked Mai, Chao, Hom and Tuyet if they would like to come and live with me. The police agreed to release them and arranged for us to return the next day. We brought out one other girl called 'Thanh' who had lived in the Ockenden Venture orphanage. She was a very well-built girl and had cross eyes. We also invited one very old woman called 'Ba Muoi' to come and live with us. She was a marvellous person and the girls liked her. She had been in Te Ban ever since my first visit because she had no home of her own.

The girls were elated at the thought of leaving Te Ban and were determined never to return. We bought some soup and rolls for lunch and Father Hoang stayed to share our first meal, which we ate in a circle on the floor. We then sorted through the piles of boys' clothes at Father Hoang's house, looking for something suitable for the girls to wear. All my clothes were either too old or full of holes. We also prepared a box of soap and towels, toothpaste and tooth brushes to take back to the home. Before the market closed that evening we went to buy pots and pans, rice bowls, chopsticks and a few drinking glasses. The girls also bought some flowers to put in the home.

That evening we had our first meeting. We never had any very strict rules and the few rules we did have, the girls made up themselves. One rule was not to use drugs or to take anything from someone else without asking. Everyone had to be quiet after the curfew so as not to disturb those who wanted to sleep. The housework was to be shared and everyone had to help keep the house tidy. The girls decided to take it in turns to go to the market and do the cooking. Another rule that the girls agreed on entirely by themselves was not to have boyfriends in the home. I wanted the girls to run the home in the way they wished. After all, it was their home and I would live there like an 'older sister' ready to help them whenever they needed me.

The next day Mai and Hom got up early and went to the market to buy enough food for the day. We had invited Father Hoang to have lunch with us and the girls spent all morning preparing a very special Vietnamese dish. Ong Nam, Father Hoang's driver, delivered a sack of rice. I took Chao to see one of the doctors at the Adventist hospital. Miss Oldham had told the doctors that I had just opened a home for girls and they had agreed to give us free medical treatment. Chao was afraid she had venereal disease. She had scarcely been sleeping at night because she was so worried and felt so uncomfortable. A quick examination showed she only had an infection and after a short course of antibiotics it soon cleared up.

The girls kept themselves very clean and spent hours in the shower every day washing their hair and trying to rid themselves of the old smell of Te Ban. All the girls had huge head lice which they used to comb out of their hair. They had altered the clothes we had brought from Father Hoang's house to fit them and they washed and changed these garments every day.

Our neighbours in the lane accepted the girls spontaneously. Women would come into the home and help the girls sew their clothes. They introduced us to a dentist. One of the women used to cut and manicure nails and she came to do the girls' nails and paint them different colours. Mai insisted that I should have my own nails manicured.

We lived a long way from the Adventist hospital and as I travelled on the lambretta buses it used to take more than an hour to get there. I had to get up at 4.30 a.m. and leave the home at 5 a.m. The girls were alone all day but they needed to be trusted and to have responsibility and I did not worry about them. Sometimes Father Hoang would visit the home during the day to see that everything was all right. If the girls knew he was coming they would cook me some food for lunch and ask Father Hoang to drive them to the hospital. In the evening, the girls would always wait for me to return home so that we could eat together.

Every night we would hold a meeting in English and discuss everything from the running of the home and our relationship together, to the girls' own lives, their worries and problems. The girls were very open and very honest but it was only after we had lived together for some time that they really began to confide in me. Sometimes I would stay up all night listening to them.

The memory of the old street life haunted the girls and sometimes they drank Bac-Xi-Dai—a very strong Vietnamese whisky, almost 90% proof—to blur the memory; sometimes the drink would help, but more often than not it made them feel worse and they would be tempted to use drugs. The girls tried very hard to stay away from their old habits. They knew that both Father Hoang and I loved and cared for them and they didn't want to upset us. They were afraid of hurting us after we had tried to help them. They did all they could to help me and always wanted me to be happy. When I came home from work in the evenings they would always have the rice cooked and small dishes of meat or fish prepared. They also washed, ironed and mended my clothes.

One day Mai asked Father Hoang to give them some money so that they could buy material to make me a new pair of black pants and a few shirts. They asked one of the women in the lane to sew the clothes, using the measurements from one of my old shirts. They wanted to surprise me and kept this a secret. The pants they had made were so tight that I couldn't wear them and I had to give them to Mai. The shirt was a very low cut one and I couldn't wear that either. But the thought was there.

At the week-end, if Ong Nam was free, he would come to the house and drive us out into the country or to one of the markets. Sometimes we would go to the farm at Hope 6 and take a picnic. The girls would spend hours getting ready, changing their clothes and combing their hair. They liked to look pretty; they were searching for happiness, but—most of all—for someone to love them.

The girls asked me if they could go to the Vietnamese American Association to learn sewing and attend English classes. With the help of the American Women's Club, the girls were taken to the Association, introduced to their teachers and helped to enroll. Father Hoang gave us a sewing-machine as a gift from the boys' project. The American women gave us some material and the girls started to make their own clothes at home.

Sometimes the girls wanted to come with me to Te Ban, but I was reluctant to let them. I tried to prevent them from becoming involved with the streets again or from making too close a contact with some of their old friends. One day they helped me distribute the bread and milk to the prisoners and at first everything went smoothly. The police and the people in jail could not believe the change in the girls. Then some of the girls' former friends started to ask them to bring in drugs. When the girls refused they were accused of no longer caring about their friends. Quite a few arguments broke out and eventually the girls stopped visiting Te Ban.

In the early spring of 1974 the American nurses working at the hospital had a pay rise. Miss Oldham also increased my salary from 25 dollars to 100 dollars per month. As soon as I was paid I took the girls to the market and bought them new shoes. They went to the hairdresser's to have their hair cut and shaped and on Sunday afternoons we went to the cinema together.

We all loved our dog, Nixon, but he suddenly became ill and kept vomiting worms. He seemed full of worms and two days later he died. The girls decided to bury him before I returned home. Mai and Hom put Nixon in a box and took it to a patch of soft ground outside the police station. After they had dug a hole and buried Nixon, the police inquired what they were doing and made them dig the box up again. They were afraid the girls were planting explosives to blow up the police station and insisted that Nixon be left on the rubbish heap in the street.

During the first few weeks at the home everything went well. The girls were happy and enthusiastic. They shared the household chores and took it in turns to go to the market. They were very tired and slept a lot. They were also hungry and never stopped eating. They enjoyed going out to school and made themselves plenty of new clothes. In the evenings we would sit and talk together or go into one of our neighbour's homes to watch television.

Mai was still losing her hair. She could pull out whole handfuls at a time and was terrified that she would eventually lose it all. We took her to the doctor who gave her massive vitamin doses. The girls had tattoos on their arms. They felt embarrassed when they went out wearing short-sleeved shirts, and would cover their tattoos with plaster. The girls tried to remove them but it was impossible to do so safely. They would either cut or scrape them off with a sharp knife and this caused a lot of bleeding. Infection would set in and always left behind a scar.

The old woman, Ba Muoi, still lived with us. We used to think of her as our grandmother. The girls used to joke, saying they would find her a husband so that we could have a grandfather. Although we all loved Ba Muoi, no one liked to sleep next to her at night because she always urinated on the floor. At first we thought Nixon was the culprit, but after Nixon had died the floor was still wet in the mornings and we knew it was Ba Muoi. But I was in favour of Ba Muoi living with us. I wanted to create a family atmosphere for the girls and felt it would be better to mix the age groups, to have an older person, perhaps some children, and of course, some animals, rather than just have a group of girls of the same age.

It wasn't long before the people in Te Ban knew about the

girls' home and where we lived. When they were released from jail many used to pass by the home, partly because they were curious, but usually to ask for some kind of help. Many of the drug addicts and some of the old men who lived in Le Lai street brought their children to me for safekeeping. The girls welcomed the children into the home because they wanted something better for them. But although the girls liked the children, they didn't like any adults coming to the home from Te Ban or Le Lai. It reminded them too much of their own pasts, which they now wanted to put behind them.

At first, only about four or five children came to the home. The girls loved and cared for them as if they were younger brothers and sisters. They would wash and cook for the children, look after them when they were sick. They used to make new clothes on the sewing-machine and dress the children up. There was a small infant school at the end of our lane which the children began to attend. We also bought another dog called Lucky.

The girls wanted to keep baby chickens and ducks and built a little hutch just inside the kitchen. But at night, while we were asleep, the rats came and ate the baby birds and we lost them all. The next time we went to the market the girls bought some fully grown chickens and ducks and this time we kept them in the bathroom. The bathroom was tiny and there was nothing for the chickens to perch on except the toilet seat. Eventually they became so accustomed to us that when we used the toilet we would have to sit on the edge of the seat and the chickens would sit next to us. The ducks were happy, especially when we took a shower. Everyone enjoyed the animals and I wanted the girls to be happy.

Some of the children were very shy and reserved when they first came to the home. Our puppy Lucky loved to chase up and down the lane after them. The children enjoyed playing with her so much that they forgot about their shyness. They could cuddle her and express their feelings of love more easily with an animal than a person. They used to fight over who slept next to her at night. Later, one of the boys from 'Nghia Sinh' came to the home and brought us another puppy. She was just a ball of white fluff and we called her 'Yoko'.

I was extremely contented living with the girls and learnt a great deal from them. They taught me to be completely unselfish, to be patient and to really appreciate something when I had it.

Sometimes I wouldn't be able to find my shoes; one of the other girls would be wearing them, so I would have to wear someone else's. If I went out anywhere with Father Hoang the girls would give me one of their shirts to wear, and when I came home they would probably be wearing mine.

When I went out with the girls they would always walk along holding my hand. Vietnamese men would embrace each other in the street. They were never thought of as homosexual, it was just a natural thing to do. When we went to sleep at night we all lay down together. The girls often threw their arms and legs across each other. The children snuggled against us during the night because they needed security. Even the ducks and chickens became so tame that when we awoke in the morning they too would be asleep on our blankets. When the children slept next to me they always gave me head lice. I never felt annoyed and we would sit in the lane picking them out of our hair. Most of my neighbours would be doing the same. We seemed to become involved in each other's problems and best of all we loved and cared for each other. Our way of life was very simple—yet beautiful. When you are poor and live amongst the poor you realise the importance of friendship and people's need for each other.

CHAPTER 7

Sometimes I compared my present way of life to my existence in England. I felt I was lucky to have been able to adapt so quickly to such a great change. Even my thinking changed and I began to think more like a Vietnamese than a European. I missed my own family and at first I missed my mother's fruit cake. But I never missed anything else and I never felt I had made a great sacrifice in going out to Vietnam. I loved the country and I enjoyed working hard and helping the people—that was my happiness. What meant most to me was the giving and receiving of love. Material things were of little importance to us; we were important to each other.

People used to ask me how I could live like a Vietnamese. I always wore Vietnamese clothes and ate exactly the same food as they did. When I was in England I loathed the sight of dead fish or fish heads. In Vietnam we used to buy fish heads to make soup and would pick every piece of fish off the heads to eat. The only part I didn't eat was their eyes. When meat was too expensive to buy we would eat cooked blood. I ate frogs' legs, snails, eels and even lights which in England are only given to dogs.

I have always suffered from migraine and every six months or so I would have a migraine headache and be forced to lie down all day. The girls used to cook me a pig's brain to eat because they believed it cured headaches. Another treatment for headaches was to stick scented white tape on either side of the forehead. Whenever we were sick with a fever we used 'Chinese medicine'. This consisted of mentholated oil which was applied to the skin and scraped with a coin until blood appeared under the skin but did not actually break through the surface. It was supposed to drive out the fever. Another theory was that this rather painful treatment would make you forget about the pain you already had. Whenever I was sick the girls used to do this to me and I was sore and bruised for several days afterwards. The Vietnamese believed that much of their sickness was caused by wind, and they would always wear sweaters on a windy day, although it was usually quite warm.

The American women would invite me to their homes for a meal to try to feed me up but I never went. I would have gone if I could have taken all my girls with me. They bought me fresh fruit and canned fruit juices from the American P.X. because they thought I needed the extra vitamins, but I used to give them all away to the girls.

One day Jacqueline decided to visit the home. She came early in the morning after she had been out all night. My neighbours' eyes nearly popped out of their heads when they saw her arrive. She wobbled down the lane in her high-heeled shoes, hot pants which were so short that they were half way round her hips, and clinging sweater. She was laughing and smiling to herself and talking to the children playing in the lane. She asked our neighbours where 'Co Nam' lived, saying she was my sister. She came into the home, exchanged greetings with everyone, and sat down exhausted in one of the chairs. First she removed her wig—to the amazement of the children. Then her shoes came off, her false eyelashes and finally her make-up. Jacky squeezed into a pair of Chao's pants, saying she was off to the market to buy something special for us to eat.

After sleeping in the afternoon Jacky began to get ready for work. We had to tell her that she couldn't live in the home and continue to work on the streets. The men in the lane would call the girls prostitutes, especially when they were drunk. Jacky told us herself that she knew she couldn't stay in the home. She felt she had been on the streets for too long and that it was too late for her to make the break. Street life was the only life she knew and she would always return to it. She brought her children to the home and stayed for one week before returning to Le Lai. Sometimes I would meet her in the street, usually near Le Lai, and we would talk over a cup of coffee; sometimes I would meet her in the jail.

Although the girls seemed contented in the home, I suspected that the day would come when one of them would decide to leave. I noticed they were sometimes very restless and uneasy in the evenings. When I asked what was worrying them they said it was something they couldn't tell me about. Then, late one evening just before we went to sleep, Mai and Hom asked me if they could go out to buy some cigarettes. I gave them a packet but after we had turned out the lights they still slipped out. I waited for them to come back, but when they didn't return Chao and I decided to go and look for them.

It was almost curfew time when we found Mai and Hom down on Tu Do street. They were standing outside one of the bars with two men. The girls had returned to Le Lai to change their clothes and put on their make-up. Mai was wearing a pair of black and orange trousers and a white shirt. She had put on long, black false eyelashes and had painted her lips with bright red lipstick. Hom was dressed in a pair of red velvet trousers and a white sweater. When Mai saw me she started to cry. I told her everything would be all right, and that they should come home now. I thought the two men standing with the girls had tried to pick them up, but it turned out they were plain clothes policemen.

Mai and Hom told us they had been arrested for soliciting in the street and were waiting for the police car to arrive to take them to jail. Within the next five minutes the car arrived. As they sped off down the street Chao and I ran after them, to reach the police station before curfew. Several other girls and a small group of street boys were also at the station. Someone was calling my name. I turned round to see who it was and saw Jacky. She had taken too many sleeping pills that day and had not realised what had happened until she woke up in jail. I was surprised to see her looking so cheerful. She said she had been in jail so many times before that it no longer made any difference to her.

Mai and Hom were already being finger-printed. They looked ashamed and just stood there with their eyes fixed on the ground. I felt so sorry for them. The police kept calling them prostitutes and asked them why they slept with the Americans and not the Vietnamese. Chao and I asked to see the police chief to explain to him about the girls' home in the hope of obtaining their release. He told us that Mai and Hom had been arrested several times before for prostitution and that this time they would be sent to Tu Duc prison for women for six to twelve months. He also told us that if we did not go home he would have us arrested for violating the curfew.

Chao and I had to walk home. The next morning we woke up

early to go and see Father Hoang, whose cousin was a woman lawyer called Loan. She was a very beautiful young woman and an extremely successful lawyer. Loan spoke to the police who told her that the girls could not be released because they were already entered in the book to appear in court. If they were released now and their names scratched from the book, someone would accuse the police of accepting a pay-off.

When the girls appeared in court Loan presented them and explained their case. She spoke of our home and of how we were trying to help girls like Mai and Hom. Loan asked the judge to release the girls, pleading that they just happened to be in the area of Tu Do street when they were recognised by a policeman. The young judge called Loan over to him. He had always fancied Loan, even though he knew she was already married. He told her he would release the girls if she promised to meet him afterwards. Loan reluctantly agreed in order to prevent the girls being sent to Tu Duc.

When Mai and Hom left the court they asked me how I could ever accept them into the home again. I explained that as we tried to live together like one family, we should love and help each other through the difficult as well as the easy times. I told them that the home was really theirs and that they were free to return at any time. The next day Hom decided to leave again but Mai remained with us.

After this incident I decided to see the Mayor of Saigon, General Do Kien Nhieu. I needed to obtain some kind of official paper which would recognise the work I was doing in the home, so as to avoid such collisions with the police. The girls ironed my long black ao-dai and black satin pants before I set off, saying that if I made a good impression on him I would probably get the papers. Mai also dressed carefully and came with me. Father Hoang drove us to the City Hall and waited outside in the car.

General Do Kien Nhieu was extremely helpful. I was reminded of my interview with Colonel Hai at Chi Hoa for he was just as charming, offering me tea or coffee to drink and cigarettes to smoke. He spoke English very well and listened carefully as I told him about the girls' home, explaining the sort of problems we expected to face and my reasons for needing his help. I told him of my involvement with the street children, my work in Te Ban and Saigon hospital and how we went out on the streets at night to make direct contact with homeless families.

He seemed very impressed and said he would give me his full support. He called his secretary and dictated two papers to be typed. When the papers were ready he signed and stamped them with his official signature before handing them to me. The first paper gave us permission to open the girls' home and to continue to bring assistance to girls and children who were either homeless or from very poor families. The second paper stated that I could go anywhere at any time, even after the hours of curfew, and that full assistance was to be given to me in whatever I undertook to do. I left his office with a sense of triumph and felt relieved that my work was now officially recognised.

Sometimes objects would disappear from the home. At first we didn't really take much notice but one morning we woke up to find the radio missing. We hunted everywhere for it but no one could find it and we realised it had been stolen. During our nightly meetings together we made lists of the things that had disappeared, but no one ever seemed to know anything about them.

Tuyet had told us that she couldn't sleep without the radio and she used to go to sleep listening to it. We thought it rather strange that she had gone to sleep without it on the night it had disappeared and had said nothing. Then Tuyet started to go out a lot during the day, especially when I wasn't there. When I was working at the hospital or was out with Father Hoang, Tuyet would often go out and come back just before me. She never said anything to me but the other girls noticed. When I asked Tuyet where she went during the day, she would say she had been to the market or had gone for a walk.

One evening I returned home to find everything missing. The cassette and camera had gone, and also some money. I asked the girls where Tuyet was and she had apparently been out all day. I had a feeling I would probably find her on Le Lai street and went straight there. People told me that she had been there earlier, trying to sell a camera and a cassette.

When Tuyet returned to the home she was very quiet. I questioned her about the missing objects but she still denied all knowledge of their whereabouts. We sat down and talked together, and although she didn't actually admit to taking them, she did tell me that sometimes she couldn't help stealing. The next morning Tuyet left the home and returned to live on Le Lai. I still saw her about but she was usually high on sleeping pills.

She became very thin and looked very depressed. She continued to live with her boyfriend and she had to steal to supply him with drugs and medicine. I told her that she could always return to the home if she wished and that we were there if she needed help.

I realised from the outset that we would not be able to help every girl who came to live with us. I never felt we had failed when a girl left the home to return to the street. But I used to feel sorry for them and always tried to visit or contact them so that they knew that we still loved and cared for them. There was always a chance that they might wish to return. I was never discouraged by the various thefts because material things were unimportant and could always be replaced. But I did feel I should try to find out why the girls were compelled to steal.

By mid-March only Mai, Chao, Thanh and a few of the children from Le Lai were still living in the home. The old woman, Ba Muoi, had left to try and find her family again. Thanh had fallen in love with Qui and used to keep his photograph by her at night. Qui couldn't believe Thanh loved him and neither could Mai or Chao. Thanh was so big and Qui was so small and skinny. The girls used to laugh at Thanh and tease her. She continually became upset and eventually decided to leave the home as well. I think she went to live in Go Vap orphanage and some months later we met her again, in Te Ban.

'Yen' arrived shortly afterwards. She had been an old girlfriend of Qui's and he had asked me to bring her into the home. Yen was only sixteen years old and already three months pregnant. She came from a very large family and lived near Hope 5. Her mother and father were still alive and she was the oldest of ten children. Her father was sick and unable to work and her mother worked in the market to try to support the family. She had left home to live with her boyfriend and now he had gone into the army, not realising that Yen was pregnant. She was very thin and had at one time taken opium. Her arms were scarred with needle marks and tattoos, some of which she had tried to scrape off.

Yen settled quickly into the home and worked hard. She enjoyed going to the market and doing the cooking and she also looked after the younger children. She didn't speak any English and either Mai or Chao would translate for us. At first Yen didn't tell us about her baby and it was only after we realised she was putting on weight that we discussed the situation. The following Sunday we asked Ong Nam to drive us to Yen's home in order to tell her parents of her condition. Mai and Chao wanted to come as well and we brought the children with us for a ride out. Her house was a wooden shed which the family had built themselves, with a cement floor and no windows. Her mother and father, her ten brothers and sisters, and also her grandparents all lived in the one large room. Yen's oldest brother had been arrested for stealing and was in Chi Hoa prison.

We sat down with Yen's mother and told her about the baby and Mai explained about the girls' home. Her mother smiled and agreed to let Yen stay with us. Then she asked Mai to say that she herself was pregnant again, and could we help her because she was very poor. When we returned to the home that evening six of Yen's brothers and sisters came with us. I took Yen to see one of the doctors at the Adventist hospital for a check up. We found out that she had venereal disease and that the baby was growing upside down in her womb. Yen was transferred to the Vietnamese maternity hospital and had to go there three times a week for treatment. Her venereal disease soon cleared up and she had a trouble free pregnancy. Several girls came into the home through Yen and all adapted quickly to their new life.

The American Women's Club donated two more sewing machines to the home and asked the girls to sew small cot sheets and baby blankets for distribution to the various orphanages. They offered to pay the girls a little pocket money in return for their work. The girls sewed all day and even during the night, taking it in turns to use the machines. They were given a week in which to finish the work but it was usually completed the next day. Mai and Chao worked hard and saved their money to drink coffee in the evenings. I was concerned about them but they assured me they were only going to the coffee shop and they always came home again.

The next girl who came to us was called 'No'. She had heard about the home through Yen. Her parents had died and she lived with her married sister and their younger brothers and sisters in a tiny ramshackle wooden house in the centre of Cholon. No sold fish in the market during the day and worked in a bar in the evenings to earn enough money to support her family. Although she wanted to come and live in the home she was worried about leaving her family, so we invited the children to come as well. Her young brother, 'Cu Ly', was in fact old enough to go into the boys' project, but I didn't want to divide the family and so they all came to live with me. When they arrived at the home they were literally dressed in rags. The youngest boy, 'Thanh', was only three years old. He was suffering from malnutrition and was so underdeveloped that he could not even walk.

I continued to write letters to people asking for money for the home and we gradually saved up enough to buy a sofa and two easy chairs, a couple of tables and a few stools. Father Hoang gave us a television set. The home at last looked like a real home —and we were a real family. The number of girls coming into the home continued to increase and we had rather more girls and children than I had expected. At night when we went to sleep, we had to push all the furniture to the side of the room to make enough space for everyone. Some of the girls slept on the table tops and on the chairs. On some nights it was so hot inside that I took a blanket and went to sleep outside in the lane where it was cooler. There were so many of us that we had to start eating in two sittings because we did not have enough bowls and spoons to go round.

'Lien' and her two children came to the home in April. Lien had been living with an American G.I. who had stayed behind after the U.S. army had withdrawn. He loved Lien and their two children but Lien had refused to return to the States with him because she still had an elderly mother alive. Her eldest daughter, Kim Chi, was seven years old and her youngest daughter, Bach Tuyet, was just five. Bach Tuyet was very fair and although she was cross-eyed people used to think she was my daughter because we looked so alike. Lien spoke good English and was very kind and patient. I entrusted the running of the home to her in my absence and she was a great help to me.

A group of girls who had been living and working in the bars round the bus station on Petrusky street came to the home. Many of them had regular boyfriends who would hire them out in the evening to sleep with their friends and then pocket the proceeds. Sometimes the boys came to the home to try and take the girls back again. They usually came in a group and were high on sleeping pills. I used to feel very protective towards the girls and refused to allow the boys into the home. I would stand in the doorway with my arms outstretched and if the boys tried to enter I would give them one hard shove. Chao and No, my two strongest girls, always stood behind me and the boys usually got the message and left us alone.

I noticed that many street boys and girls inflicted wounds upon themselves. Usually they would slash their arm with a sharp knife; not over the veins on their wrists but on the outer arm. Sometimes my girls would do this and there would be blood everywhere. They always refused to go to the hospital to have stitches put in and I would have to bandage their wounds and look after them myself. Wounds like this took a couple of weeks and sometimes months to heal and always left a scar.

My twenty-second birthday, in May 1974, was the happiest birthday of my life. I decided to have a party in jail for all the boys in Te Ban. I also invited the girls and the children from the home, Dick and Father Hoang. We bought a magnificent roasted pig decorated with flowers and all the trimmings. Lien and Chao had ordered a four tier iced cake and in the morning Ong Nam drove them to collect it. Father Hoang drove Mai and me to the market and we bought one hundred and twenty loaves of bread, bottles of fruit drinks for the boys, and a bottle of whisky for the police. I also brought along two hundred No. 6 cigarettes, sent by my brother from England, to give all the boys a smoke.

The girls and I spent the whole morning bringing all the food to the home and preparing for the party. We then changed into our best clothes, ready to be driven to Te Ban by Father Hoang and Ong Nam. Lien brought the cassette and some tapes of the Beatles and The Rolling Stones. The boys in Te Ban were so excited to see us that they clapped their hands and shouted when we arrived. We all had a drink with the police and then arranged the food in the food hall, which was slightly cleaner than the cells, setting it out on the tables with the cake and the pig in the middle. When the police brought in the boys from their cells they gaped in astonishment at the feast.

I gave one of the older boys a huge carving knife and told them they were to eat everything. The boys cut the pig and ate until they were full. The girls mixed the fruit drinks and I cut the first piece of cake which I gave to the chief of the jail as a token of our friendship. Then I gave the cake to the boys and they demolished it all. The whisky we had drunk earlier had gone to our heads and when Lien put on the cassette we started to dance. All the boys clapped their hands and moved in time to the music. For the first time Te Ban was full of laughter and joy. It was a party I shall never forget.

The next day it was raining hard and was cold and windy. That afternoon, Lien and I saw a tiny little boy huddled in one of the doorways off Le Lai. He was soaked to the skin and shivering from the cold. He looked so pale and anaemic and was terribly thin. We asked him what his name was and what he was doing there. He was called Qui and he had come to beg for a little food or money to support his mother who lived under one of the stalls in the market. We invited him to come back to the home with us so that he could eat and change into some dry clothes.

When he came out of the doorway I noticed that most of his hair had fallen out and that he was covered in scabies. His sores had opened due to constant scratching and were oozing pus. Some of the customers eating in the restaurant told me not to touch him in case I became infected myself. Lien called a cyclo and we got in, with Qui sitting between us. When we arrived home we washed him thoroughly with soap and gave him some clean clothes to wear. Chao was cooking that day and she brought him a bowl of rice with meat and vegetables. He was starving and ate three bowls-ful. After he had finished we called another cyclo and went to look for his mother. He lived a long way away, on the opposite side of the city, and everyday he used to walk to Le Lai to beg.

It was pelting with rain as we slid through the mud across the market place looking for his mother. We found her sitting under one of the empty stalls. She had lost both her legs in a mine explosion and started to cry when she saw us. She told Lien that Qui was her only surviving son. Qui pointed to the sores on his body and told us that his brothers and sisters had been covered with the same kind of sores—even on their mouth and eyes—before they died. His mother thankfully accepted our offer to have him in our home, and we then began to visit her each week to give her enough money for food. During his first few days at the home Qui became very ill with asthma and one night we had to rush him to the hospital. I think he would have died if we hadn't met him. I thanked God that He had led us to him. It was another birthday present.

Reports continued to flow into Saigon about fresh outbreaks of fighting in the isolated regions of the Delta. It was the rainy season and sometimes all the lights would be cut during the storms, and for a minute everyone would think the Viet Cong were coming. The girls would rush over and bolt the doors and pile up the furniture in front of them. Late one afternoon in June we were sitting quietly at home. It was raining hard and the sky was grey and forbidding. Some of the girls were sleeping, others were reading. Suddenly we heard an army truck draw up outside in the lane and we could hear a lot of shouting. Inside the truck was a crude wooden coffin with the South Vietnamese flag over it, symbolising a soldier killed in action. The soldier must have lived somewhere in the neighbourhood, and the people stood watching in silence, wondering whose son it was.

The dead soldier was thirty-three years old. His mother was a dear old woman who lived in a tiny house on the corner of the lane. When they carried the coffin into her home she broke down and cried. She went into her kitchen and took a large knife with which to stab herself, but one of the younger sons managed to stop her. All that night the girls took it in turns to sit with the family and boil kettles of water to make tea for the mourners who came to visit the coffin.

The next night we went to sleep as usual. It was still raining outside with occasional thunder. The strange sound of funeral music drifted down the lane from the home of the dead soldier. I fell asleep, but soon woke up again as Chao screamed. I jumped up to put on the light, thinking she had had a bad dream. Chao looked very strange and pale. I called her but she didn't hear me. Lien started to slap her face but she never flinched. Suddenly her body became rigid and her fists were clenched tightly together. She started to have a fit, the convulsions being so violent that we could hardly hold her. Lien rushed into the kitchen to grab a spoon to push between her teeth so that she couldn't bite or swallow her tongue. At first we couldn't open her teeth and she started to froth at the mouth, completely losing consciousness.

The other girls were afraid and started to cry, thinking that Chao was going to die. By this time, the old woman who lived in the house opposite had rushed in to help. She started to rub green and brown Chinese medicine on to Chao's skin, until we could see the blood appear just below the surface. Chao's fit ceased and she woke up feeling very tired, and quite unaware of what had happened. We tried to sleep again but Chao had five more fits that night and Lien and I sat up with her.

The next day I told Father Hoang what had happened. We

decided to buy a small crucifix of Jesus on the cross to put on the wall over Chao as she slept. We also bought a small cross and chain for Chao to wear round her neck. Lien went to the market to buy a chicken to offer to Buddha, and the girls burned incense in the home. They believed that if they could please Buddha, he would drive away the evil spirits.

Father Hoang and I returned to Te Ban in the afternoon to distribute the bread and milk to those still held there. Mai and No came to help because I was feeling so tired. In the evening I had to get ready to go on night duty. I took a shower, hoping this would make me feel better, but when I looked in the mirror I thought how pale I was. Suddenly I felt very sick and dizzy; the room started to spin round and I fainted. The girls caught me as I fell. The Chinese medicine they gave to me soon woke me up again. That night I slept next to Chao and she continued to have fits. I took her to the doctor the following day but he couldn't find anything wrong with her and gave her some sedatives. We all thought the fits were caused by some kind of emotional problem.

Chao told me that when she was a prostitute on Tu Do street an old man from Cambodia who was said to be a witch had told some of the girls that if they gave him something of their own which they treasured, he could bring them everlasting success and happiness. The girls believed him and gave him money when he asked for it. Soon Chao was visiting the old man every month. He had told her that he held some kind of spell over her and that if she refused to visit or pay him, he would curse her with ill health and bad luck until she died.

Chao had not been to visit the old man for some time now, but the memory of his words was playing on her mind. She believed the curse was coming true, that her fits were due to the illness that would befall her, and that soon she would die. I told Chao that this couldn't possibly be true; that no man could hold such power over someone else, except God Himself. Every day I took Chao out with me and tried to involve her in as many activities as possible. I wanted her to forget the old man from Cambodia. A few weeks later her convulsions stopped.

Nearly all the girls in the home used to wake up in the night at one time or another in the grip of a nightmare. Strangely, they nearly always had the same dream. They used to see a white haired old man walking through the home, dressed in a long white coat. He would approach the girl and call her to wake up and go with him. The girls would wake up screaming, white with fright. All the Vietnamese believed in ghosts because of the number of people who had died in the war. During the Tet offensive of 1968 many people had died in the area in which we lived. Our neighbours told us that our house had been destroyed and later rebuilt. They said all the people in it had been killed and were buried under the house. I am convinced this is why the girls believed in ghosts.

By mid-summer 1974, I had thirty girls and children living in the home (we originally intended to have ten) and still more kept coming. Father Hoang suggested we should open another house. We thought about buying the house next door and knocking the two houses into one. Then, in mid-July I received a letter from my older brother Dave asking me to return home as quickly as possible as my mother was very ill. I had to wait for two days to obtain an exit visa and then left Saigon for England. My mother was in hospital in London and died ten days after my arrival. I stayed with my brothers Dave and Jim for two months before returning to Saigon. I had to go back. I couldn't disappoint the girls, the children and the boys in Te Ban—not when I knew how much they loved and trusted me. Father Hoang had written to me in England. Apparently Loan had gone into the home to look after the girls but they had refused to speak to her. Chao had left, saying that if she couldn't live with 'Co Nam' her older sister, she would rather return to the streets. When I arrived at the airport all the girls, Dick and Father Hoang were waiting to meet me. It was a happy reunion and the girls had decorated the house with flowers to welcome me back. I felt I had come home.

CHAPTER 8

During my absence in England Father Hoang had bought the house next door and the two houses had been knocked into one. The second house was similar in size and shape to the first with a large room downstairs, a simple kitchen and one smaller room upstairs. No one slept very much on the first night of my return. We stayed up talking together for most of the night. The girls told me what they had been doing and what they had done to Loan when she came to the house. Father Hoang admitted that no one had been able to control the girls while I had been away, and that if I had not returned he would have closed the home. The girls had gone out at all hours and had neglected their household duties. I did notice on my return how well 'lived in' the home looked. The following day we got up early, pushed all the furniture into the lane and cleaned both houses.

Most of the girls living in the home were of the Buddhist faith. We decided to make a little altar of remembrance to my mother, as was the custom. Every day the girls bought flowers and fruit in the market and put them on the altar as an offering. They lit candles and burnt incense. The girls looked upon my mother as their own and we placed a large photograph of her on the altar.

Father Hoang suggested we should open a sewing factory and sew the military uniforms for the South Vietnamese army. We needed a contract with them first, and Loan set to work to obtain one. If we had our own factory, all the girls could work and we could give some kind of employment to the other poor people living in the lane. We needed an income to help us become more self sufficient and to enable us to carry on our work. Every evening the girls and I took food to Saigon hospital. We used to make rice soup, with vegetables and meat, for the most needy patients and the very old. We would go by bus, transporting the soup in saucepans and kettles. It was very rewarding for me to see the girls helping those who were less fortunate than they were.

My relationship with the girls grew warm and close. I thought of them as sisters and we lived really happily together. Vietnamese social workers from the Ministry of Social Welfare would occasionally visit the home. At first they could not accept the girls and asked me how I could bring myself to live with prostitutes. I could not understand their attitude and deplored it. The girls were not prostitutes but people who needed help and who were warm-hearted and understanding.

All our neighbours accepted the girls and would often leave their children in the home for the girls to look after while they went to work. They would come to the home and ask for some rice if they did not have enough to eat. Sick people who did not have enough money to go to the doctor or to buy medicine also asked us to help them. The girls used to watch me administer medicines, dress wounds and treat fevers. They soon learned to do these things themselves. When they met some of their old friends in the streets or in the market place, they used to tell them about their home and their 'family'. They were proud to say they no longer needed to use drugs. They had found themselves; their life had a meaning. They had learnt to care again, for themselves and for each other.

When Chao knew I had returned to Saigon, she came back to the home. Unfortunately she had started to take opium injections which sometimes made her quite violent. Every day Chao insisted on going to the market. Although I always gave her enough money she never bought enough food and we found out later that she only spent 500 of the 2000 piasters I gave her and used the rest of the money to buy injections of opium. Then she started to invite the other girls to accompany her and tried to encourage them to use drugs. When they refused Chao became afraid that they would tell me about it, and she would hit them. Eventually we had to ask her to leave the home and she returned to the streets.

I always felt sorry for Chao. Sometimes, when I was out with Lien or Mai, we would see her. Chao made a very bad prostitute and none of the other girls would work with her. Using drugs, she completely neglected her looks and would dress up in short hot pants and short-sleeved sweaters which exposed all her scars from needle marks. She became quite slim because she spent all her money on opium and didn't bother about eating. Then her body started to swell due to ill health and infection caused by using dirty needles. She returned several times to Te Ban and was finally sent to Tu Duc.

Mai missed Chao very much because they had always been good friends. She started to visit her mother again, who lived on the army base just inside the airport. Mai's mother had never loved or cared for her and in fact they hardly knew each other. Her stepfather refused to speak to her and she became so upset that she began to take sleeping pills again. She would take up to ten pills at a time and increased the number to twenty. She then started to return to Le Lai and eventually left the home to resume her life with Jacky, Tuyet, Hom and Chao. We often used to see her out at night but unlike Chao she was extremely successful as a prostitute. She knew how to dress and look attractive and she always made a lot of money from the Americans. She still came to visit the home and often shared her earnings with the girls and children. Much to my regret we could not persuade her to return to us.

Loan at last completed her contract with the South Vietnamese army. They agreed to give us ten more sewing machines and to supply the girls with 10,000 military uniforms every month. These uniforms were already cut and just needed to be sewn. We opened the factory in a street quite near the home leading towards Cholon. A group of Chinese girls who were trained machinists started the factory for us and my own girls were to take over after they had finished their courses at the Vietnamese American Association. The Chinese girls worked hard and were soon producing more than the given amount every month. We paid them a small monthly salary based on the number of uniforms each girl had sewn. The rest of the money went towards the running costs of the home and the rent for the factory. I now had fifty girls and children living in the house and by the end of the first year over one hundred girls had passed through my hands.

On 6 November, 1974, Yen gave birth to her baby. Everyone was thrilled and we all rushed up to the hospital to visit her. She had a beautiful little girl weighing 2.4 kilos and we called her 'Peanut' for short. Then, to everyone's surprise our dog Lucky gave birth to three premature pups. No one knew she was even pregnant, and I don't think Lucky knew either. To our great sorrow all the pups died soon after birth.

Christmas was drawing near and I visited Father Hoang in order to discuss a Christmas programme for the home, the boys in Te Ban, and the people on the streets. While I was there Qui came in looking distraught. He had just had a blazing row with another boy and had wanted to fight him, refraining from doing so in order not to upset Father Hoang. Qui suddenly left the room and shortly afterwards we heard him scream. We rushed out to see what had happened. He had cut off his little finger with a knife. His finger lay on the floor and there was blood everywhere. Qui said if he hadn't cut himself he would have cut the other boy. I applied a dressing to the little stump and bandaged his hand. He had cut straight through the bone. Father Hoang picked up the finger and kept it in a screw top jar. At first Qui refused to go to the hospital, but he finally agreed a few days later when the pain continued and signs of infection began to show.

Qui had to change into a gown to go into surgery for a local anaesthetic. He handed me his knife and a flare to hold for him. I didn't know what to do with the flare, and was afraid it would explode. Qui assured me it wouldn't and told me to hide them in my trousers. If anyone had seen them, he would probably have been arrested. I waited outside the surgery, too frightened to move. Inside, I could hear Qui swearing and cursing every time the doctor hurt him. The doctor cut away the remaining bone and stitched up the end of his finger.

Qui stayed with us for a few days in the girls' home while his finger healed. He used to say he loved me like his sister, and tried to do all he could to help me, but then he would suddenly start throwing knives around, and this terrified the girls, especially when I wasn't there.

I stopped working at the Adventist hospital at the end of 1974 and spent all my time with the girls, helping as many poor and needy people as possible. We continued going to Te Ban with bread and milk for everyone there and each night we took the soup to Saigon hospital. The girls would make the very old people as comfortable as they could and help to feed them. They also brought them clean clothes.

We met a boy called 'Phuoc' on the streets. He was fifteen years old and suffering from diabetes. His mother had brought him to Saigon hospital for treatment and begged in the streets to pay his hospital bills. One day she disappeared and Phuoc, although still ill, was discharged from the hospital because he could not pay to stay there. He began living on the streets and looking for his mother.

When we met Phuoc his feet and legs were so swollen that he could hardly walk. We took him back to Saigon hospital and when he was discharged he came to live in the girls' home. I gave him injections of Insulin every day until he no longer needed them and he then went into the boys' home. He suddenly returned to the streets and when we eventually found him he was almost in a coma. We returned him to Saigon hospital again and paid for him to stay there. Every day the girls visited him and cooked him special food but he died three days after leaving the hospital. His death was a cruel blow to us all.

We met a girl called Mai whom we found begging on the steps outside Saigon hospital and invited her to come and live in the home with us. Although she wanted to, she was embarrassed by the extensive napalm burns that scarred her face and body. We planned to take her to the Barsky Unit for skin grafting and meanwhile took her food and clean clothes each day. Then she became sick with a fever. Her condition deteriorated. Her throat and neck became so swollen and her breathing so difficult that she could no longer eat. We stayed with her in hospital and buried her when she died, writing her name on the grave and the name of the girls' home below.

So many of the people and children we met on the streets were in need of immediate help. We found an old man who had been hit by a car and left in the street to die. We reached him just before he lost consciousness and he told us what had happened. He hadn't eaten for five days and was painfully thin. The police rushed us to the hospital with him, the siren blowing all the way. We could see the blood swelling his head and running out of his ear. He died from a fractured skull, three broken ribs, one broken arm and a broken leg.

The girls worked hard and became really involved in helping these people. Soon they were able to go out by themselves. The police allowed them into Te Ban and they worked in Saigon hospital. On some days we did not arrive home until well past curfew. The other girls would have coffee and hot food waiting for us. I no longer felt that I was running the home but that we were sharing it as friends.

Three girls went to the orphanage at Vung Tau to help look after the children and lived very frugally. Sometimes there wasn't enough food to eat and they didn't get paid. At the week-ends I would give them their bus fare to return to my home, but they usually stayed in Vung Tau and spent the money on the children. The girls gave of themselves unselfishly and asked for nothing in return. They were content to improve the lot of people less fortunate than themselves and any success we had was a source of great satisfaction.

Yen and her friends preferred to stay in the home. They would share the household chores and supervise the younger girls or newcomers. They each had a measure of responsibility and knew that I trusted them. One of the girls completely took over the kitchen. She went to the market every day, did all the cooking herself and kept the kitchen immaculate.

At the week-ends we would all go to the cinema or take the children to the zoo. Sometimes Ong Nam would drive us out to the country. The girls would spend hours getting ready, changing their clothes and putting on their make-up. One day we went swimming in a river to the south west of Saigon and jumped in with our clothes on. When we got out of the river we found that most of us had ripped our pants. No one minded—we were happy.

We also started going to church on Sunday mornings. We would get up at five thirty in the morning to go to the six o'clock Mass. Some of the girls had never been to church before, and when the collection came round I gave each girl about 20 piasters to put in the box. They asked me if this paid for the bread they had eaten at Communion. We continued going to church until one morning, on our way home, some girls working in a bar called the girls from the home prostitutes. My girls rushed home to change their clothes and then returned to the bar, where a big fist fight broke out. I ran down after the girls and joined in the fight. We won, of course, and even gave some of the bar girls' boyfriends black eyes. But after that we had to stop going to church.

Just before Christmas 1974 there were many demonstrations in Saigon against the Thieu regime and government. Sometimes we would go down to watch them and more often than not the girls would join in. Always in the front line, they would march down the street, shouting and waving banners. Whenever an anti-government article was printed, President Thieu would order the police to collect and destroy all newspapers. We would see the police outside the printers bringing piles of newspapers out into the streets and burning them all. The street boys would collect up the undamaged newspapers and, without being seen by the police, would sell them at as high a price as they could.

On Christmas Eve we all went to midnight Mass at Father Hoang's church. The girls dressed carefully in their neatly pressed ao-dais and some of them had saved up to have their hair done. A girl called 'Hoa' spent two hours putting on her make-up. She applied a whole bottle of liquid foundation cream to her face and looked like a painted ghost by the time she had finished. When Hoa looked at herself in the mirror, even she realised how ugly she looked. She had made herself up like a prostitute and was so ashamed at this reminder of her past life that she slashed her arm with a knife. Blood spurted out everywhere and while I bandaged her arm, Lien wiped up the blood. Lien and I stayed to sit and talk with her until it was time to go to church and then we all set off together.

I had many plans for the New Year. Although we were now living in two houses we were still overcrowded. If we could raise enough money we wanted to move to the country, just outside the city. We would then be able to grow our own fruit and vegetables, and save enough money to buy our own livestock. We intended to keep on one of our homes in Saigon to house the girls working at the factory. I was also planning another visit to the Mayor of Saigon, General Do Kien Nhieu, to ask him if we could develop a programme for the boys in Te Ban, hoping eventually to turn it into a boys' centre and not a prison. Father Hoang's dream was to have a boys' town outside Saigon, where the boys could live and grow up away from the streets, the prisons and the police. My own dream was to see all the boys released from Chi Hoa prison.

Then, on the night of 6 January, 1975, the Viet Cong tried to blow up the radar station next to Father Hoang's home and church in the district of Phulam. The girls and I had been woken up that night by the sound of rockets coming in, but we did not know where. The next day Father Hoang took me to see the area round the radar station and held a remembrance service in the street. Some of the homes were still burning and many were completely destroyed; several bodies were lying in the street, covered with corrugated iron.

During the night of 7 January and the early hours of the morning of 8 January, the Viet Cong struck again. This time they captured the whole province of Phuoc Long, about forty miles to the north of Saigon. The city of Phuoc Long had a population of 30,000 people. Rumours came back to Saigon that the city had been completely destroyed by rockets. It was believed that about 8,000 Viet Cong soldiers had taken part in the attack. The province was mostly a rich rubber plantation, and because of the density of the surrounding forest the South Vietnamese army could not advance towards the city, and the people in the city could not escape. Also, because of heavy North Vietnamese ground artillery, South Vietnamese planes could not fly over the area. Thousands of people were thought to have been killed and all cinemas, dancing halls and places of entertainment were closed in Saigon for three days.

On the morning of 9 January, Father Hoang and I drove out to the receiving area for refugees who had managed to escape. When we arrived at the camp only 140 families had succeeded in breaking through. The people had fled in panic and had brought none of their belongings with them. The International Red Cross had sent out rice, tins of meat and fish, water containers and sleeping mats, but Father Hoang and I were the first two people to actually visit the camp from Saigon.

One very old man who was crying told us that his wife and nine children had all been killed during the attack. The women, with tear stained eyes, were hugging their children. A thirteen-year-old boy, sobbing uncontrollably, said he had been working in the fields at the time and had managed to escape, but he feared his mother and father, brothers and sisters had all died. We brought the boy back to Saigon.

The people in Saigon feared another Tet offensive. Demonstrations broke out and everyone was wary and on edge. Security precautions were tightened and anyone failing to produce an identity card was arrested by the police. Father Hoang was concerned about the safety of his eight homes should war break out again. We started to put money into an emergency fund. Because of the new threat of war, villagers and refugees leaving the countryside started to flock into Saigon once more and during the next few months the population increased from three to four million. The soldiers had a stall at the bus station where boys could enrol into the army.

Father Hoang was worried about his older boys. They were

under increasing strain because they were afraid of being drafted into the army. Some had lost their identity cards and dared not go out in case they were arrested. Qui had started to drink again and encouraged the other boys to take sleeping pills. Two new boys began to cook opium in the evenings and injected it themselves. Just before the Tet holiday in February, Father Hoang gave each of his older boys about 5000 piasters so that they could buy new clothes. They lost all the money playing cards in the market place and began to steal again, terrified that Father Hoang would find out.

During this time I was working about twenty hours a day, out on the streets, in Saigon hospital and in Te Ban. At night I would stay up typing letters to raise money. There were so many people we had to help. Prices rose sharply and we even started cooking over a charcoal fire in the home to save money on the gas so that we could buy more rice. I never had enough sleep and didn't bother to eat properly. I drank large quantities of black coffee to stay awake and smoked a great deal. I became very anaemic and lost about a stone and a half in weight. The girls gave me lots of milk to drink and tomatoes to eat, saying they would 'make more blood'. I didn't care about myself—I didn't have the time. I loved the people and my one thought was to help them. I had to keep going. I prayed to God to give me strength and thanked Him for giving me the opportunity to work amongst the poor. Father Hoang used to buy me extra food but I gave it to the people in Saigon hospital.

Then one night I became feverish. My temperature shot up to almost 105 degrees. My body ached all over and I was in too much pain to move. My throat became sore and swollen and breathing exhausted me. I felt so tired and only wanted to sleep. I remembered Mai, the girl who had died in Saigon hospital, and I wondered if the same thing was happening to me. If I was going to die, I didn't want to die in the home, and I asked the girls to take me to Saigon hospital, where I would be amongst my friends. They wanted to take me to the Adventist hospital, but I didn't want to spend so much money on myself when we needed that money for the poor.

The girls took me to Saigon hospital just before the curfew. Father Hoang rushed over to see me and wanted to move me again, but I insisted on staying where I was. That night Lien stayed with me. One of the nurses put a drip in my arm and gave me some injections. I have no idea what they were. She also gave me about ten tablets and told me to take one every four hours. Later, we found out they were sleeping pills. As I slept that night, I was vaguely aware of screams coming from the police station next to the hospital. In the early morning, I was awoken by the music coming across on the loud speakers from the market place.

Mai came to visit me and slept on my bed all day until it was time for her to go to work in the evening. Qui and some of Father Hoang's boys came in and brought me some more sleeping pills. Qui advised me to swallow five at a time! The next day I did feel better and decided it was time to leave. Lien helped me to remove the drip from my arm and we went home. The girls were busy cleaning the two houses in preparation for Tet. Some of our neighbours were painting the fronts of their houses. People were buying flowers and flowering branches to decorate their homes. I still worked but felt very weak for some time afterwards.

Many of the boys had been released from Te Ban and Chi Hoa over the Tet holiday and they were all back on the streets. Father Hoang and I bought 100 kilos of specially prepared rice, 30 kilos of meat and 30 kilos of soya bean. This was enough to feed about 1200 people. The American Women's Association also donated some food to us. We sent a box of provisions to each of the boys' homes and made up boxes to give to our neighbours. We also took food to the street boys who worked in Chi Hoa cemetery. One of the American women gave us a huge turkey but it refused all food and the girls were afraid that it would become too thin to eat. We killed it, chopped it up into small pieces and boiled it. What meat there was tasted good. The American women also gave us several rolls of material which we had made up into ao-dais and new pants. We all made our pants very 'hippy' with wide bell bottoms and kept them to wear during the festivities.

During the first three days of Tet the girls and I spent practically all the time on the streets. We filled Ong Nam's van with the rice we had prepared and went out to distribute it to all the poor people, children and beggars we could find. We covered virtually every street in Saigon and the girls took it in turns to hand round the food. One old man cried when we gave him the rice because he was so happy to have been remembered by someone over Tet.

Much to everyone's surprise and great delight, Yen's boyfriend appeared at the home during Tet. He had been away in the army for almost a year and had just returned. Yen, not having heard from him for so long, had thought he was dead. She was overjoyed to see him again and show him his daughter. We visited two of Father Hoang's boys—both seventeen years old—in hospital. They had gone into the army and had both been injured during the recent fighting. One boy had had his leg blown off and had also lost one eye; the other had lost both his legs. They were so brave, still smiling and quite uncomplaining. It was an uplifting experience to see such courage.

Then, at the end of February, fighting broke out again throughout the South. Father Hoang was now national chaplain for all student groups in South Vietnam and was often called away for meetings. Between 19—24 February he was away in Nha Trang. He spoke at meetings and demonstrations in Saigon, some of which were broken up by the police. I never knew anything about politics but I was aware of Father Hoang's involvement. Sometimes I would go with him to meetings of about five or six student leaders. They would meet in the late afternoon or early evening in some isolated place—a derelict garage or shed—on the outskirts of Saigon. I could not understand much of what was said. On 1 March Father Hoang flew to Europe to raise funds for the project and also to meet with delegates in Paris. I began to hear rumours that a 'third party' was being formed to overthrow Thieu's government. The people simply did not believe that President Thieu was strong enough to prevent a Communist take-over.

On 10 March very heavy fighting broke out in the Western Central Highlands, about two hundred miles to the north east of Saigon. There was a major attack on the provincial capital of Ban Me Thuot, which had a population of 80,000 people. We used to keep the radio on all day in the home and listen to the news every hour on both the American and Vietnamese stations. We heard reports of house to house fighting in Ban Me Thuot, entire families being massacred by the Viet Cong. Then we heard that half the city was already under Communist control.

In Saigon the streets were empty by nine o'clock in the evening and people stayed in their homes. The city was full of soldiers and police, all heavily armed with machine guns and hand grenades. Even when the troops were off duty they did not bother to change their uniforms or remove their weapons. Bunkers and look out posts were rebuilt and strengthened with extra sand bags. Corrugated iron street barricades were reinforced.

The girls and I continued working as usual. We noticed the military convoys entering and leaving the city. Trucks filled with young soldiers sped through the streets, followed by ammunition trucks carrying artillery and army supplies. Ambulances screamed after them, sirens blowing full blast. All this activity made everyone feel uneasy. No one knew what to expect. To live and work in such an atmosphere of alarm was a very real experience. When I saw the soldiers leaving Saigon to fight I wanted to go with them. I kept thinking about the people in Ban Me Thuot. All major highways leading to the Central Highlands were cut and there was not much anyone could do to help. Even the army didn't seem to be getting through.

More girls came into the home. A young girl called Thanh had been sent by her boyfriend to sleep with his best friend—and this friend's girlfriend had beaten her up. When Thanh came into the home she was three months pregnant. At first she was so shy and upset that she could hardly talk to anyone. Lien and I took her to the doctor for a check-up and discovered that her whole body was almost black from bruising and in some places on her back she was bleeding under her skin. Her family had rejected her, but when they saw how we cared for her their atittude changed and she eventually returned to live with them and have her baby.

Another new arrival was Dai. When Dai was seventeen she had lived with an American doctor for a year. The doctor was in his late forties and had died through illness while still in Vietnam. After his death Dai worked as a prostitute for she had a large family to support. She became close friends with another prostitute called Thuy and they both began to take opium. Both girls came to the home for help. Then Thuy discovered the bars around Petrusky street and started to work there. She was very beautiful and it was easy for her to attract custom. Sometimes she would sleep with up to thirty men a day and would return to the home to give Dai some money.

Thuy contracted venereal disease but still continued to work. One night she slept with five men and in the morning gave herself an injection of sleeping pills which she had crushed and mixed with water. She collapsed in the street and died on the way to hospital. Dai was so grieved at the loss of her friend that she became addicted to opium and we sometimes used to meet her in Saigon hospital recovering from an accidental overdose.

I missed Father Hoang while he was away and so did his boys. Some of the boys had enlisted in the army and they would visit us when they were on leave. When the local boys saw them coming down the lane in their uniforms they would jeer and shout at them. One night full scale war broke out in the lane. Father Hoang's boys were outnumbered and ran back to our home to take refuge, the locals in hot pursuit. I couldn't let the local boys come into the home, so I stood outside with my arms outstretched and blocked the door. The boys had armed themselves with huge knives, heavy pieces of wood and iron bars. One of them kicked Yen, who was standing next to me, in the stomach. I was so angry that I hit one of the leaders and he left the home with a bleeding nose and a black eye. We discovered later that he was working for the People's Revolutionary Government. The PRG had been formed under the 'Peace Treaty' of 1973 to administer the parts of South Vietnam agreed as being under National Liberation Front control.

By the end of the third week in March Communist forces had gained eight provincial capitals. Security in Saigon was tighter than ever and curfew began at 10 p.m. instead of midnight. We listened to the radio and heard that an estimated 500,000 refugees were fleeing southwards towards Saigon. The whole of the Central Highlands region was now in Communist hands. It was believed that 250,000 refugees were making their way by foot from the Highlands to the safety of the coastal area of Nha Trang. They had to walk about one hundred miles with their possessions tied onto their backs or loaded in small carts. Many of the older people and the children died on the way, from lack of food and water and from exhaustion. The voluntary agencies in Saigon were busy preparing a refugee aid programme and it was agreed that the receiving area for refugees should be just outside the city.

When I realised the speed with which the Communists were invading the South, I went to the bank and withdrew all the money from my own private account. I also took some money from a joint account I shared with Father Hoang. I knew that sooner or later the Communists would take Saigon and I wanted to be prepared. We bought 500 kilos of rice, tins of milk and fish, cooking oil and nux nam. At Father Hoang's house I prepared boxes of medical supplies and took them back to our home, together with piles of used clothing in case of emergency. The situation in Vietnam was changing from hour to hour and I was beginning to be alarmed. Dick was away in Cambodia and Father Hoang was still in Europe. I felt the weight of my responsibility and prayed for the strength to cope with the dangers which lay ahead.

CHAPTER 9

In mid-March I went to see some of the larger welfare organisations in Saigon to find out what they were doing about the current situation. All available personnel were getting together to make up a medical team which could perhaps be sent up to Nha Trang. I put my name down on the list and hoped I would be asked to go. I waited every day for news. Reports came in that it was too dangerous to send foreigners into the area because of the hostility the people felt towards the Americans. Everyone was in a state of panic. South Vietnamese soldiers were turning round and shooting into the refugees and a priest had been shot.

I was not worried about myself but felt deep concern for the Vietnamese people and the thousands of refugees now wandering through the countryside. I was determined to reach Nha Trang and went to the City Hall to make further inquiries. Nha Trang was 278 miles away and the road was blocked sixty miles from Saigon. I asked for an official paper that would let me through police checkpoints, just in case the road should clear and we were able to go.

The Communists had now reached Tay Ninh city, sixty miles to the north west of Saigon and fifteen miles from the Cambodian border. More reports came in over the radio of refugees travelling along the road from Tay Ninh to Saigon. I therefore decided to go to Tay Ninh, since Nha Trang seemed impossible to reach. Lien and Hoa wanted to come with me and Ong Nam said he would drive us there in Father Hoang's car. We left Saigon at 7 a.m. on 25 March. I wore Vietnamese clothes and covered my hair with a scarf under a coolie hat. I thought that the Viet Cong would shoot me as an American if they saw my fair hair. We filled the car with rice, medical supplies and a few clothes.

Everything was quiet until we came to Cu Chi, about twenty-

Liz helping to treat a young opium addict suffering from malaria in Te Ban

The burial of Mai, the young girl Liz found on the steps of Saigon hospital

Liz working in a refugee camp outside Tay Ninh City shortly before the takeover

Liz giving bread to the refugees from Tay Ninh

Refugees living on the streets of Saigon
just before the takeover

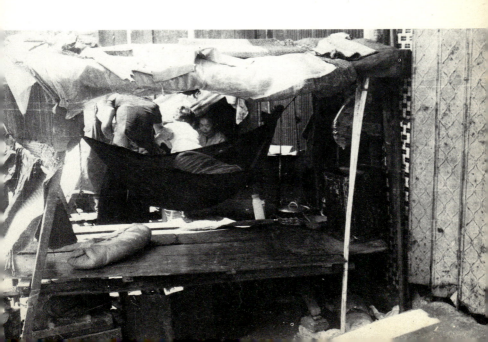

Street children in Danang

Resettlement camp on the border of Quang Tri province. The women are armed with rifles

five miles from Saigon. After Cu Chi we began to hear the distant rumble of rockets exploding and could see the smoke rising in the distance. We didn't pass much traffic except for several convoys of South Vietnamese tankers. All along the roadside were scattered military camps built up behind the trees.

Most of the towns and villages were deserted and had already been rocketed and burned down by the Viet Cong. The last town we passed through was completely empty except for the soldiers who were sitting out in the street drinking beer and getting drunk. All the houses and shops were locked up but many of the windows were broken. It was rather frightening driving through these empty villages, particularly when the rockets sounded very close. I wondered how the soldiers could remain in the streets. Lien was afraid and wanted to turn back, but Ong Nam assured her that the rockets were outgoing and not incoming, so we kept going. We continued driving until we reached a village within twelve miles of Tay Ninh.

Over 2,000 refugees from Tay Ninh had gathered at this point and more were pouring out of the city. They were camping out under their carts or trucks which were filled with their few possessions, their children and their livestock. Some families still had a little rice but others had already run out of food and we gave them some of our rice.

The refugees had no leader, the church was already closed and the priest had left. The people did not know where they were going or what was going to happen. Many said they were waiting to go back to Tay Ninh. As we stood there talking rockets were landing just a few miles away and people continued to run down the street away from the fighting. I asked the soldiers if we could drive to the next village and help bring out the inhabitants.

When we arrived the village had been completely destroyed. Only a few bare remains of the houses were left; everything else was completely burnt out. We could see a number of villagers amongst the debris and we called out to them to come to safety. Some were very old, others were crippled and some were just children. We ran over to help the children into the car, then sped off down the street. We did this about four or five times and eventually everyone had been evacuated except for a few farmers who had lived there all their lives and refused to leave.

The rockets ceased to come in at mid-day and Ong Nam took us to a café for something to eat. I was wondering how the refugees would react to me. They were not hostile, as I might have expected, but kind and thankful that we had come to assist them. In the afternoon we returned to the village to see if the people needed anything. Suddenly, the rockets started to come in again. I could hear them zooming over my head, but couldn't see where they were landing. Then I saw an old man on a bicycle fall to the ground. He was cut on his arm and back. He got up again and just stood there looking at the blood trickling down his arm, unable to move. Then I heard someone else behind me, turned round and saw another man fall. He was wounded in his arm and side. Oh God, I thought, I will be hit next. Lien ran over to me and we both dropped to the ground, with our arms over our heads.

The rockets stopped again and it was quiet, strangely quiet. Ong Nam ran over to help the man who had fallen off his bicycle and Lien and I attended to the other. His arm was bleeding badly and I bandaged it for him, using my head scarf. We hurried them into the car and rushed to the local hospital which was in a town about five miles away, through which we had passed earlier. There were two military doctors in the hospital but they only had a few bandages and some gauze, hardly enough to last them until the end of the day, and no medicine. We gave them most of the medicines and bandages we had brought with us from Saigon, keeping just enough for our own use in an emergency.

On our way back up the street to the village the soldiers on the roadside called out to us. They had been told by fleeing refugees that some children with an ox and cart were approaching the other side of the village, but no one had seen them. There were only four soldiers on that part of the street, and they had no transport of their own. Two of the soldiers climbed into the car with us and held their rifles out of the window. We were going into an area close to where the Viet Cong were hiding out.

Ong Nam drove as quickly as he could. On the other side of the village we could see the ox and cart by the roadside. Ong Nam stopped the car and we ran over to the cart. Soldiers were firing and running for cover in the fields around us, but our one thought was to help the five children we saw lying on the ground. We were too late. All the children were dead. Three of them had taken refuge under the cart; two lay on the roadside. 'Oh God, why the children', were the only words I could say as I picked up a little boy of about three years old, with the top half of his head blown off. The soldiers helped me to carry him to the car. Even they had tears in their eyes as we returned to the cart to recover the bodies of the boy's four brothers and sisters. It was a terrible spectacle. Their tiny bodies were covered in blood and ripped to pieces. One little girl had half her back blown out and lay in a pool of blood. Next to the cart lay their ox, eyes wide open, tongue hanging out, also dead.

The children's grandmother lay injured a little further along the roadside but she was still alive. She was in a state of severe shock and wept over the death of her five young grandchildren. We returned to the hospital and waited while the grandmother was treated for her wounds. The soldiers told us that there was still one old man living in the town who owned a shop that made coffins. We waited for the grandmother and then Ong Nam drove us to the shop, with the five children still in the car. We waited for about two hours while the coffins were made. At one stage we had to abandon the car and bring the grandmother to safety as the rockets began to come in again. We watched the last of the town's residents packing their few possessions into whatever they had. When the coffins were ready we placed the five small bodies inside and returned to the place where the refugees were camping. We found the grandfather of the children; he lifted one of the coffin lids and fainted. There were two surviving older sisters but the children's mother had died and their father had gone into the army and had never returned.

When we returned to Saigon that evening I sat down in the home and suddenly realised how lucky I was to be alive. Why had I escaped injury when two men, one in front of me and one behind, had been wounded? I think God must have been looking after me. The girls in the home were a great support. They had cooked for us and put out a clean change of clothes. But somehow eating was not important. All that mattered was that the girls were alive, safe and well. I just wanted to be with them, to see the children play, to see life and not death. And yet when I saw the refugees fleeing from Tay Ninh I wanted to help them too and share a little of their suffering.

The next day I planned to return with Ong Nam, for I had promised some medicines to the hospital. We also wanted to reach Tay Ninh city itself. I tried to persuade Lien and Hoa not to come this time for I knew it would be dangerous. I told Lien we needed her in the home and she agreed to stay. Hoa said she had an aunt and uncle living near Tay Ninh whom she wanted to find and insisted on coming with me. Early next morning we filled the car with medical supplies, clothes and a sack of rice and set off for Tay Ninh. We delivered the medicines to the hospital and I talked to the doctors. They wanted to visit the countryside between Tay Ninh city and the Cambodian border and needed a nurse to help care for the refugees. I agreed to go with them.

We drove through the devastated villages where the rockets had landed the previous day. Whole buildings were completely destroyed, roof tops were blown off and huge holes were blown through the walls. In one village a rocket had landed in the market place and all the market stalls had burned. And yet the refugees returned to Tay Ninh and the villages nearby and continued to live in the ruins. They had nowhere else to go. Three Viet Cong soldiers had been shot by the A.R.V.N. close to where the five children had died and had been tied up and left out in the street for everyone to see.

We reached Tay Ninh that same day. It was a beautiful city with a large Buddhist temple in the centre. Opposite the temple was another refugee camp. The city was very quiet for many people had left. Only a few rockets exploded in the distance, towards the Cambodian border. We returned to the refugees who were camping outside the city and Hoa looked for her aunt and uncle. We found them, together with the rest of their family, packed into an ox cart. Hoa's cousin had just had a baby and had been living in the countryside as a refugee. We asked her if she wanted to return to Saigon with us but she wanted to stay with her own family and return to their home. In the evening we returned to Saigon and took more medical supplies from Father Hoang's house for our return the next day.

Father Hoang's car would not start in the morning and so I left Saigon on the bus. I felt obliged to return because I had promised to go out to the refugee camp. When the bus reached the other side of Cu Chi we followed a military convoy of trucks and tankers for most of the way to the town with the hospital. Just before the town, in the middle of the countryside, the bus tried to overtake the convoy. We were right in the middle of the convoy when the Viet Cong tried to blow it up. Explosions sounded all round us, but I couldn't see what was happening because of the smoke. I was vaguely aware of soldiers leaping off the trucks and running into the surrounding fields, keeping well down and shooting. The driver of the bus didn't know whether to turn back or keep going. Then two soldiers climbed into the bus and told us to drive through. They stood in the open doorway, shooting their rifles into the air, trying to make our passage safe. We were extremely lucky to get through.

We reached the town and got off the bus. The hospital was about two hundred yards further down the street and we started walking. There was no one around. Then, at one end of the street, I could see the convoy approaching. Rockets started to come in again and as the trucks sped past us I could see the white faces of the soldiers. We must have looked just as frightened. There was nowhere for us to hide and we ran from one building to another, carefully on the look-out for any Viet Cong.

The hospital was situated in the next street, very near a bridge which led over the river towards the Cambodian border. A few rockets landed on the bridge and we watched them explode. Most of the soldiers ran away, but one was so frightened that he couldn't move. He seemed rooted to the spot and some of his friends ran back to help him. We reached the hospital just as a rocket exploded in the same street. Then another rocket blew up the wall just outside the hospital. I could no longer bear to look and Hoa and I rushed in and fell down with our arms over our heads. The hospital was empty. I felt sure we were going to die and I remember hoping that we would be killed by a collapsing roof and not by a rocket blowing us to pieces.

We waited, prayed, and waited. The walls of the hospital shook. The rockets still continued to come in but after five minutes Hoa and I got up off the floor and looked round for somewhere safer to hide. In the end room there was a half-built air raid shelter. We jumped in and sat smoking. We could hear the rockets zooming over our heads and landing in the street behind. This was the street we had just come down. We waited in the shelter for what seemed like hours and prayed. We listened closely to detect where the rockets were exploding. They landed in the street in front of us and in the street behind us, but miraculously nothing touched the hospital. I believe that God must have been watching over us. Eventually the bombardment stopped.

We crept out to view the damage. There was a lot of smoke and some of the buildings were smouldering. Then we saw someone coming down the street. Hoa thought he was a Viet Cong soldier so we ran back to hide in the hospital. We heard someone enter and remained hidden until he had left. We crept out again and saw an old man in the street. He was a cyclo driver and had seen us run into the hospital earlier, and had come to see if we were all right. Some of the A.R.V.N. soldiers reappeared in the streets, having run away when the attack began. Just before midday the two military doctors returned. They had not yet gone to the refugee camp near Tay Ninh because of the fighting but were now preparing to leave. We left in a jeep, with two soldiers to accompany us, and all our medical supplies in the back.

I have never been driven so fast in all my life. We whizzed through the empty streets, skidding round the corners. At one point a rocket suddenly exploded in the street ahead of us. The soldier driving put on the brakes so quickly that we almost turned over. The refugee camp was a long way down a dirt track and in the middle of thick undergrowth. We were covered in dust by the time we arrived. We set up a small table in the middle of the camp and set out the medicines. All the people needing to see the doctor wrote their names down on a piece of paper and the doctor called them out in turn. We treated all the children and old people first. We changed dressings and treated local infections but soon ran out of medicines. In the late afternoon Hoa and I had to return to catch a bus back to Saigon. We were exhausted but again went straight to Father Hoang's house to prepare the medicines for the following day.

We continued to go to the refugee camp outside Tay Ninh until early April. The Communist offensive in the South had intensified beyond anyone's reckoning, leaving the South Vietnamese people bewildered, afraid and angry. Thieu had abandoned the entire Highlands. When South Vietnamese troops had withdrawn from Pleiku we heard that they had left behind seventy jet fighters to be claimed by the Viet Cong.

On 20 March Communist tanks attacked Quang Tri. Government soldiers abandoned their posts and fled to Hue. The Communists then cut the road between Hue and Da Nang, the next city to the South. The soldiers fled to the nearby beaches and waited to be evacuated by sea to Da Nang. Many soldiers deserted the army to try and find their families. Trucks and tankers were abandoned, and the soldiers left with just their rifles.

President Thieu had hoped that the soldiers leaving Hue would join the defence force round Da Nang and that this would strengthen the city's position. However, the soldiers arrived in

Da Nang in a state of panic and confusion, along with thousands of refugees also fleeing from the northern provinces. Many officers had abandoned their soldiers in order to flee from Da Nang to Saigon with their families. Left behind with no leadership and no supplies, the soldiers had turned their guns on the civilians and stolen food and money.

Communist forces attacked Da Nang in the same way as they had attacked Hue, cutting the road further south. South Vietnamese divisions broke up and surrendered, fleeing back into the city. Thousands of people flocked to the airport to be evacuated by plane. Crowds fought to get on the planes as they landed. The soldiers got on first because they started to shoot into the civilians. Then Communist rockets started to explode round the airport and the evacuation had to stop. The people turned and rushed towards the coast to try to escape by sea. Refugees and soldiers piled on to the landing crafts or paid local fishermen to take them out to the American ships waiting off shore. Some people even swam out to the ships. Many had not escaped when Da Nang fell to the Communists on 29 March. The South Vietnamese left behind artillery, tanks and planes.

When the first ship from Da Nang arrived in Saigon the girls and I rushed down to the port to see if we could help in any way. The local police took over the job of unloading everyone and we could only stand by and watch. The ship was filled with about 4,000–5,000 people but they were not the kind of refugees we had expected to see. The first ship to leave Da Nang had brought the more wealthy people who could afford to pay their way or who had the right connections. There was not enough accommodation in Saigon for all these people and they were put up in a warehouse by the port. Many had families or friends in Saigon and later left to live with them.

The next ship from Da Nang was supposed to arrive in Vung Tau. Lien's mother lived at Long Hai, near Vung Tau, and so we drove down to visit her and our three girls at the orphanage. Both the orphanage and Father Qui's own home were filled with refugee families and he was trying to feed them as best he could. Vung Tau itself was packed with refugees and soldiers who camped out along the roadside or just wandered aimlessly around. South Vietnamese naval boats kept coming into the port to unload soldiers and their families. Various other smaller vessels arrived crammed with refugees who had nowhere to go and not enough food to eat. Many of the Marines wandered through the town getting drunk, but they refused to pay for their beer.

On our return to Saigon that evening we were held up for about three hours on the Bien Hoa highway, as someone had tried to bomb the President's palace in Saigon. We assumed it was an assassination attempt by the Viet Cong. Helicopters circled the area and huge traffic jams accumulated, for the Viet Cong were believed to be somewhere between Bien Hoa and Saigon. When we finally reached Saigon we bought a newspaper and read that the President's palace had been bombed by an American A37 jet, flown by a South Vietnamese pilot. It showed the country's disillusionment.

On 9 April the Communists entered Long Khanh province and attacked the town of Xuan Loc, which was only about forty-five miles north east of Saigon. During the night of 9 April they shelled the air base at Bien Hoa. Since the signing of the Paris Peace Accords in January 1973, Hanoi had continuously violated the cease fire. The North Vietnamese had secretly improved their transportation and communication system in South Vietnam and had increased the strength of their troops. After the loss of Phuoc Long and the entire Highlands to Communist forces the fall of Saigon seemed inevitable—at least to me. I had not expected them to advance so quickly, but now that they had I expected Saigon to fall within the next few weeks.

It was not only the rapid advance made by the Communists that surprised and shocked the people, but also the fact that the South Vietnamese army had so easily abandoned their defences and fled. I had become aware of their reluctance to fight during the time we were in Tay Ninh. All the rockets had been incoming while we hid in the hospital and yet the South Vietnamese had not fought back. We had also noticed that many of the soldiers in the Tay Ninh area were either drunk or else high on sleeping pills. Sometimes I felt that the South Vietnamese army did not want to retaliate. The boy soldiers were naturally afraid of the Viet Cong and even more afraid of being killed. I think they would have left the army had they been allowed to do so.

The morale of the people was by now extremely low. They became angry and afraid as chaos and confusion spread throughout South Vietnam. If their President could not fight the war and the officers ran away, what hope of support was there from regular soldiers? Although the people were against Thieu, they feared that the South Vietnamese government would be considerably weakened if he resigned.

Father Hoang had written to me saying he was returning to Vietnam earlier than planned because of all the trouble in the South and that he was bringing my older brother Dave with him. Then I received a letter from the B.B.C. in London confirming that a team of photographers were coming out to make a documentary film about my life and work in Saigon. We had originally planned to make the film at the beginning of May, but because of the present situation in the South the date was brought forward.

Father Hoang and Dave arrived in Saigon on 10 April. I was so relieved to see Father Hoang again because we all needed him at a time like this. It was a wonderful surprise to see Dave. He had read in the English newspapers that the rockets were landing in Saigon, which of course wasn't true. Whenever he had cabled me to find, out my plans for evacuation I had replied: 'Everything Fine, Love Liz'. He had not believed me and had decided to come out and see for himself. Dave wanted to stay in the home with us but Father Hoang and I feared that conditions in the area were not suitable for a newcomer to Saigon. Unfortunately we were proved right. Two days later, Dave became sick with a fever and had to move into the Majestic Hotel.

I discovered that while I had been away at the airport Hoa had stolen all our money, about £50, and run away. One of the younger girls had left with her but returned to the home when she realised that Hoa intended to keep all the money herself. The loss of the money did not upset me but I was distressed that Hoa had left the home. She had had such an unstable upbringing and had lived on the streets practically all her life. She had married a policeman and had returned to the streets after her marriage broke up. Her five children went to live with her husband's mother.

Hoa was still taking opium when she came to us from Te Ban but she made a tremendous effort to change her life and finally stopped using drugs. She had insisted on coming with me to Tay Ninh even though we both risked death. Although I realised that Hoa would one day return to the streets I felt I had lost one of my best friends. We never saw her again but Mai reported that she had spent the money on a watch, neck chain and ring which she had been forced to sell and that she was working as a prostitute once more.

Dave was extremely concerned about what would happen to me in the event of a take-over and wanted me to return to England with him. It had never occurred to me to leave Saigon and I tried to make Dave understand why I had to stay. Firstly, there was my home. When I started the home I told the girls that I loved and cared for them and they believed me. How could I betray their trust in me and suddenly abandon them at a time like this? They didn't understand the war and they still needed me. I almost felt like a mother to them and I could not desert my own children. Secondly, there was Father Hoang. He and I had worked together for about two years now and he had always helped me. I couldn't abandon him or the boys I had come to know so well. And then I remembered Te Ban, Saigon hospital and the children on the streets. I had many reasons for remaining behind.

Dave still feared for my safety and to avoid further arguments I agreed to register with the British Embassy. The Embassy officials told us that if the Communists did take over I would probably be taken for an American, raped and shot. Despite Dave's deep anxiety I still refused to leave. The British Embassy then told me that I had to leave Saigon within three days, and Dave started to enquire about an exit visa for me. I just sat down and cried. An ordinary exit visa could be obtained within two or three days, but I insisted on applying for an exit and re-entry visa which took up to two weeks and this at least gave me more time to think what to do. I decided that in the last resort I could run away and hide somewhere. Even if I was captured by the Communists I would at any rate still be in Vietnam with the people I loved. And if the Communists shot me, at least I would have died for that love.

By the time we left the Embassy that day, 11 April, both the British and the American Embassies had started to burn their papers and documents in case of an evacuation. On the same day, we heard on the radio that President Ford had appealed to Congress for additional military and economic aid to South Vietnam. Thieu believed this would boost the morale of the South Vietnamese army and saw the appeal as his last hope of hanging on to power. Many people in Saigon were waiting for the Americans to intervene and save Saigon at the last minute.

That evening Dave and I met Richard West, the British

journalist who had come to Saigon to interview me for the B.B.C. film. I respected him immediately. He was genuinely interested in Saigon and very fond of the Vietnamese people. We also shared the same liking for Vietnamese beer '33' and gin and tonic. The next day, Tony de Lotbinière, Ivan Sharp and Tony Lego arrived from the B.B.C. in London. We met in the Majestic Hotel overlooking the Mekong river. We started filming the next day but I was sometimes so tired because of my work and all the gin and tonics that I could hardly keep my eyes open. We were also still taking the soup to Saigon hospital and visiting Te Ban after we had finished filming.

During the time the film was being made I was also trying to cope with various problems in the home. Yen's boyfriend had not been to visit her for a few days. She discovered that he had been arrested by the police on the grounds of desertion from the army. Yen asked me to go with her to the district police station to see if he was there. The police chief only agreed to see me after I had produced a photograph of myself and during the interview he asked me to go out with him. Her boyfriend was not at the station so I thanked the chief politely and left. We later discovered that he had been taken to Chi Hoa.

One of my other girls in the home, 'Nguyen', had been worried about the recent fighting and decided to visit her mother who lived in the Mekong Delta. She needed some money for her trip and thought she knew how to make it herself. She went into a photographer's shop and posed in the nude, thinking she could sell the photographs to a magazine. I just happened to go into the shop which was in the next street to our home and saw her photographs on display. Afraid lest someone should recognise Nguyen, I asked the man who owned the shop to give me the photographs. Nguyen had already left her address with the owner who recognised it to be that of the girls' home. I had to pay double the normal price for the photographs and the film. Later Nguyen went to collect the photographs herself and the owner quietly told her that 'Co Nam' already had them. I never mentioned the incident to anyone but privately thought it rather amusing.

On Sunday evening, 13 April, I went to see Father Hoang at his home to discuss my future in Saigon. He suggested that I should register with an international organisation like UNICEF or the Red Cross. At least the Communists would then recognise me as a nurse or a social worker, whereas if I continued to live in the home in Cholon I would probably be mistaken for an American and perhaps shot. I made an appointment with UNICEF for the following morning. Father Hoang also told me that he would have to close the Truong Minh Ky home for older boys. Many of them were taking tranquillisers or opium and had become involved with local gangs in theft and fighting. Father Hoang feared that if we continued to help these boys we might be shot for supporting them.

Qui then upset us all that night by breaking into Ong Nam's house. He threatened to shoot Ong Nam if he tried to call for help, threw all his clothes into a pond, stole his bicycle and ran away. Father Chao called the police and Qui was arrested. I wanted to visit him in jail but Father Hoang told me I had to stop helping boys like Qui, who had already been blamed for stealing ten of our sewing machines. I could not abandon him, whatever his crimes, for I had known him for a long time and felt it my duty to help him.

UNICEF agreed that I could stay with them if there was a take over. I rushed down to the British Embassy to cancel my application for an exit visa, but left my address and Father Hoang's telephone number. The Embassy officials told me that I would be contacted if an evacuation took place. On the news that night, 14 April, President Ford asked all 'non-essential' Americans to leave Vietnam within the next week. The Marines were to be called in to help with the evacuation. Heavy fighting continued around Xuan Loc but government troops still held out. Cambodia was about to fall.

On 15 April, Richard West and I drove to the British Embassy to shoot part of our film. As we drove along Thong Nhut street we saw crowds of people queuing up outside the American Embassy trying to obtain passports and exit visas to leave Vietnam. Not only were Americans leaving, but also Vietnamese who worked for the Americans, civil servants, government officials and businessmen. The wealthy Vietnamese who had sent their children abroad to study were desperately anxious to leave the country, afraid that they might never see their children again if they remained behind. Government soldiers were deserting their units to rejoin their wives and children. Panic at the thought of a blood bath in Saigon mounted.

I returned early to my home after we had finished filming because I wanted to be with the girls during such a worrying time. We listened continuously to the news reports on the radio. The girls were aware of the Communist advance towards the South and of the evacuation of foreigners. They asked me if I was going to leave and when I answered 'no' they smiled at me and I think they understood why. That night the Communists shelled the air base at Bien Hoa, hitting one of the ammunition dumps. We felt the impact of the explosion in Saigon. It made the windows of the Majestic Hotel rattle and Dave and the B.B.C. team were somewhat shaken by the explosion. I wished Dave would return to England.

The next day, 16 April, we continued filming the girls in the home until Father Hoang called to tell us that Congress had voted against sending any more money to be used for military aid in South Vietnam. Money would only be sent for humanitarian purposes and in particular to assist the evacuation of Americans and Vietnamese from Saigon. American dollars were being sold on the black market for terrific prices, from the original 500 piasters to about 5,000 piasters each. Only the rich or those with the right connections were able to leave Saigon now. Passports and exit visas could be bought from corrupt officials at about £3,000 each.

On 17 April, we went to film in Vung Tau which seemed comparatively quiet. I did notice road blocks along the Bien Hoa highway and felt that an attack on the capital was imminent. It was my last day with Dave who was returning to England the following day. I felt extremely ill and returned to Saigon with a temperature of 104 degrees. On Friday, 18 April, we heard that Phnom Penh had fallen and that the Cambodians were welcoming the insurgents; at least their war was over now. Lien and I went to meet Dave at the Majestic Hotel and waited with him until the airport bus arrived. Dave was disappointed to be leaving without me and I was sad to see him go. But at least I knew he would be safe.

CHAPTER 10

We finished filming on 20 April and I resumed my work, although I still felt ill. That evening Father Hoang told me that Thieu could never hold out against the Communists and that unless he resigned and someone stronger took his place, Saigon was sure to fall. We never considered leaving for the children still needed us and, after all, the problem of homeless people would still exist long after the take-over. Father Hoang also wanted to continue his parish work and had promised Dave that he would look after me.

On Monday, 21 April, South Vietnamese troops withdrew from Xuan Loc and after a twelve day battle the Communists entered the deserted town. Their forces were now carefully positioned round Saigon. We heard that they planned to attack the capital unless Thieu stepped down, in which case some kind of negotiations could take place. At this point no one knew whether the war would end in peace talks or in a final bloody battle for Saigon. Members of Thieu's National Advisory Council and the U.S. Ambassador to Saigon, Graham Martin, urged Thieu to resign. At first Thieu refused, saying it would amount to desertion. Then on the afternoon of 21 April, Saigon Radio announced that the President would broadcast an important speech at 7.30 p.m. from the Palace.

I think everyone in Saigon must have listened to Thieu's speech and we all crowded round the radio in the home. Thieu blamed the Americans for everything, saying that they had promised to help South Vietnam in the event of pressure by the Communists and had let him down after constant appeals for help. He then announced his resignation and the appointment of the seventy-one-year old Vice President Tran Van Huong as his successor. Although everyone had half expected Thieu to resign the news still came as something of a shock. Most people initially felt that there was no more hope of a peaceful solution with Huong as President, but it soon became clear that the Communists were not prepared to negotiate unless all members of Thieu's government were replaced. We then began to hear rumours that General Duong Van Minh might take over from Huong. General Minh or 'Big Minh' as he was known, had once been President and after years in exile had returned as a formidable opposition leader.

On 22 April, I was feeling so sick and tired that Tony de Lotbinière insisted on booking me into the Majestic Hotel to rest. I had not slept on a bed for so long that I fell fast asleep until the next morning, when Lien came to visit me. Tony and Richard West came in to say goodbye because they had heard there were no more commercial flights in or out of Saigon for the next three months and had to rush to try and catch the last plane. I was extremely sad to see them go but at the same time felt relieved that they would be out of Saigon by the time the troubles started. Lien and I ordered a large tray of food before returning home. We tucked in to toasted cheese and ham sandwiches, ice cream and orange juice, all things we would not have for a long time to come.

The next day a German girl called Marlies Winkelheide arrived in Saigon, so we knew the airport was still open. The American evacuation was continuing with planes leaving Saigon almost every half hour. Marlies had been raising funds in Germany for the boys' home project and had arrived with extra funds for Father Hoang. Father Hoang told me that Marlies had brought 1,700,000 piasters which he would leave in his home with Father Chau and that I was to use some of the money when in need.

By Friday, 25 April, military activity around Saigon had practically ceased. We were aware of the Communist positions round the capital and knew they could launch a major offensive whenever they liked. Saigon remained quiet and no one knew what was happening. In the afternoon Father Hoang came to our home and suggested that when trouble did start I should move to the French 'Grall' hospital where there was still a team of French doctors working. The girls and I went to Te Ban and Saigon hospital as usual. Now the streets were almost empty by nine o'clock in the evening.

On the morning of 26 April, Ong Nam drove Marlies to the home. Marlies told me that Father Hoang was leaving Saigon for France. She said it had been a quick decision and that Father Hoang was waiting at the airport, hoping to get on one of the planes. Ong Nam was very upset that Father Hoang had left and that afternoon Dick Hughes told me that Father Hoang had taken his family with him. Loan had also left Saigon with her family.

I was still convinced that Father Hoang would return to Saigon. He had promised me he would stay, even if it meant being shot by the Communists, and I had believed him. I asked Dick what he was planning to do and he told me he would also leave if there was to be an evacuation of all remaining foreigners. I returned to the home that evening feeling let down by everyone. I wondered how the Vietnamese could run away from their own country and how foreigners could leave years of work behind them. That same day we heard on Saigon Radio that the National Assembly was trying to decide the country's future and that President Huong was being urged to resign in favour of General Duong Van Minh.

During the night of 26 April, several rockets landed in Saigon. Eight people were killed and twenty-two injured. One rocket fell on the roof of the Majestic Hotel, wrecking a top floor apartment that had been under construction for President Thieu. I thanked God that Dave and the B.B.C. team had already left. Another rocket landed just a few streets away from our house in the slum district of Cholon. The explosion woke us up and when we went outside into the lane we saw black smoke rising from the flames.

The following morning Ong Nam suggested that we should go to the air base to try and retrieve Father Hoang's car, which he believed was still there. Ong Nam didn't think Father Hoang would return to Vietnam, and thought we might as well claim the car; he would sell it and we could split the proceeds. I naturally agreed. He gave me the keys and I went to look for the car, pushing my way through crowds of people making their way out to the airport. It was impossible to continue on foot. The air base was enormous and the roads across it were clogged with people trying to leave. I noticed that the American Marines had come in to help with the evacuation. I asked a Vietnamese man with a Honda to drive me around. We found the car but as soon as I tried to take it away the Vietnamese police demanded to see my papers to prove the car belonged to me. I didn't have any papers and the police categorically refused to release the car, so I had to leave it behind.

As I left the airport and the crowds of people waiting to be evacuated, I thought how pointless the American involvement in Vietnam had been and how pathetic the collapse of the South Vietnamese army and government. I shall never forget the confusion, chaos and panic that spread through Saigon immediately before the take-over. To see terrified men, soldiers, American and Vietnamese officials fleeing to the airport to escape with no thought for those they left behind was something I found hard to accept. If that was their attitude I felt glad they were leaving, but I knew that I could never run away as they were doing, even if it meant I was going to be killed.

Before we returned to the home the girls and I decided we should buy another dog. Yoko was expecting pups in a couple of weeks and our other dog Lulu was still just a puppy. I thought that if the Viet Cong were to take Saigon at night a good dog would at least bark and wake us all up, and we would have a better chance of defending ourselves. We looked for the biggest, meanest-looking dog we could find and ended up with a young mongrel called Ringo. Unfortunately he turned out to be afraid of almost anything that moved. Later, when he became accustomed to us, he spent all day playing with the children and chasing about with our other two dogs. He never barked at anything and the girls began to wonder if he could.

Lien and I went to look for some of the American women who used to visit us in the home. Most of them had already left with their husbands. We met one woman whom I had known for about two years and whose husband had been the head of USAID in Saigon. She told me I should move from the area where I was living because once the South Vietnamese soldiers realised they had lost the war they would probably get drunk and I could easily be raped. Any remaining foreigners still in Vietnam were likely to be held as hostages, to enable others to get out. She promised to contact me if she and her husband were evacuated and said she would put my name down on the American evacuation list. That evening Marlies left Saigon on an Air Vietnam flight to Bangkok, on her return to Germany. I wrote several letters for her to post in Germany, including one to Dave and Jim.

Dick Hughes called at the home to see if we were all right. He told me that the Communists were moving into the outskirts of Bien Hoa, just fifteen miles away from Saigon. There was a twenty-four hour curfew on the town. The road was cut between Vung Tau and Bien Hoa at a place called Long Thanh. The Bien Hoa highway was packed with refugees and soldiers walking back towards the capital. I asked Dick if he still intended to leave and he told me he would if there was a final evacuation. I sat down to think and wished Father Hoang would return, although I was now beginning to doubt if he would.

It was seven o'clock in the evening, almost dark. Grey clouds swept across the sky, threatening and forbidding. The atmosphere was strange, almost uncanny. Even the lane was quiet and the children had stopped playing. For the first time I could sense that the girls and my neighbours were frightened. Everyone was tense; the girls moved quickly and quietly as they worked. It had started to rain, with occasional outbreaks of thunder. Each time we heard thunder we stopped and listened. Was it thunder or was it another rocket exploding? How close were the Communists? Were they planning to massacre everyone when they took over Saigon? Or would they just kill all the foreigners? I didn't know what to expect and wondered what the coming night would bring.

I think we all needed support from each other. We knew the Communists could take Saigon any time they liked. There was nothing to do but wait. It was pouring with rain outside and we put buckets and saucepans down on the floor to collect the water which was leaking into the home. The lights kept failing as they often did during heavy rain, so we turned them off and lit candles. We could still hear the planes entering and leaving Saigon almost every hour as the evacuation continued. It was an eerie feeling knowing that everyone was leaving and that I was staying behind. I decided to call at the British Embassy the next morning just to see what was happening. Before we went to sleep the girls locked the doors and windows and stood a chair up against the door in case the Communists tried to enter during the night. We tied Ringo to the door, hoping that he would bark.

The next morning, 28 April, I awoke early, at about 5 a.m. The girls were still sleeping. I slipped quietly out of the home and listened. It was still dark outside, but most of my neighbours were already up and they stood outside listening. An old woman came over and seemed convinced that we would all be killed when the Communists came in. I told her not to be afraid. They would be sure to kill me first since I was a foreigner. We woke up the other girls and started cooking rice for the children's breakfast. All the schools were closed, so the children stayed at home all day.

At 8.30 a.m. Lien and I went to the British Embassy. We took the bus into the centre of Saigon and walked through the city to Thong Nhut street. Crowds of people were queuing up outside the American Embassy trying to obtain passports and exit visas to leave the country. The queue stretched the whole length of the street and was joined by another queue outside the Ministry of the Interior. Some people had been there all night and were sleeping in parked cars and jeeps with their families.

We pushed through the crowds and when we reached the British Embassy I wondered why that part of the street was so quiet. Then I noticed the British flag had been taken down. I went over to the guards on the gate and asked them to let me in. With a look of amusement they told me the Embassy was closed —the British had been evacuated to Singapore four days ago. At first I didn't believe them and then I started to laugh. What else could I do? The week before, the embassy had sent me a letter saying that in the case of an evacuation they would send me details of where we should meet and what I should take with me. But they had left without even contacting me. At that moment, I thought I was probably the only British person still in Saigon and perhaps no one would ever hear of me again.

I didn't really know what to do so decided to go to the cinema, even though it was only 10 a.m. We pushed our way back through the crowds along the street. Some of the people looked surprised to see me, and wondered why I hadn't yet left. The cinema was packed with South Vietnamese soldiers who were also standing behind the rows and down the aisles. The film was in French with Vietnamese sub-titles so I didn't really understand much. An hour later we heard several explosions outside and returned home.

People were closing their shops and the street vendors were dismantling their stalls. Taxis and cyclos were busy taking everyone home. A twenty-four hour curfew was beginning. Lien and I walked over to Saigon market to take a taxi home. People were clearing up broken glass from the last explosion. It looked as if the rockets had come down on the other side of the Mekong river. Back at the home the children were outside in the lane watching the planes fly overhead, now joined by the South Vietnamese helicopter gunships and transport helicopters. Our neighbours were saying that the Communist troops were moving down the Bien Hoa highway and that fighting had broken out on the outskirts of Saigon.

Yen and No were anxiously waiting for Lien and me to return home. One of the older girls, also called 'Mai', had sold 30 kilos of our rice during the morning because she was afraid that the Communists would ransack our home for food and leave us with nothing to eat. Mai was married to a South Vietnamese soldier and had a little girl who lived with her husband's mother. She apologised for selling the rice but wanted the money to return to her family. Three other girls, also with children and families of their own, decided to leave with her before it was too late. I was sorry to see them go but understood their reasoning.

In the afternoon Yen took her younger brothers and sisters back to her own home, but decided that she and her baby would stay with us. We gave her some rice for her family. No took some rice for her sister but she and her younger brothers and sisters remained with us. Lien and I returned some of the children to their own homes on Le Lai street. Whatever the conditions, I felt it was better for them to be with their families at such a time. We told their parents that we would still try to help them but that we had to reduce the number of girls and children in the home. We had now decreased our numbers by about half, and only twenty-five girls and children remained.

We could not go to Saigon hospital that evening because of the twenty-four hour curfew. Outside we could hear a lot of shooting and prayed it was our own soldiers and not Communist fire. Several rockets landed round the airport and we could easily hear the explosions. At 5 p.m. that afternoon we heard that General 'Big Minh' had taken over the Presidency from Huong. Minh addressed the Viet Cong leaders, calling for a national reconciliation and an immediate ceasefire. The people liked 'Big Minh' and believed that he would either save Saigon or at least come to an agreement with the Communists. Many Vietnamese still thought the Americans would return at the last minute and save everyone. We all feared the consequences of being taken by force.

The following morning, on 29 April, Communist rockets slammed down into the airport sending clouds of black smoke into the city. There was still a twenty-four hour curfew over the city and most people either stayed in their homes or talked in small groups outside in the lane. The streets were deserted except for the police and soldiers. The girls had started to sew Red Cross arm bands for us to wear when we went out, as a protection against Communist or rioting South Vietnamese soldiers. Lien borrowed two Vietnamese-style working shirts from one of the women in the lane and I dressed up like a poor Vietnamese woman. I covered my fair hair with a headscarf and put on a coolie hat. I didn't wash in the days preceeding the take-over in the hope that my skin would look a little darker.

The planes and helicopters were still flying overhead and as the rockets continued to explode round the airport I began to feel worried about the older boys who lived nearby in Truong Minh Ky home. I decided to go and see if they were all right and set off by bicycle. I tucked my I.D. card and passport into the top of my trousers, in case I should be stopped by the South Vietnamese police. As I cycled through the streets I felt oppressed by the comparative silence. There was no one around except groups of South Vietnamese soldiers who were still trying to make radio contact with various parts of the city, especially around the airport. They would suddenly speed off in their trucks and jeeps, heavily armed with machine guns and rifles. They looked somewhat surprised to see me cycling along.

When I turned into the street leading to the airport I was confronted with crowds of people in cars, on the backs of Hondas or just walking, holding onto their children and carrying suitcases. The traffic was moving in both directions. Some people were still trying to reach the airport in the hope of being evacuated, others had moved out of their homes surrounding the airfield as the Communist rocket attack intensified and the airport buildings caught fire.

The airlift had to be called off and a helicopter evacuation began. I had to stop several times along the street as the helicopters circled overhead, lifting the few remaining Americans from the rooftops of their homes. As I approached the airport and turned off the main street towards the boys' home, I realised that the area was deserted and that I was quite alone. Rockets were landing very close by, and the police had warned the inhabitants to leave. I wondered what I would do if I met the Viet Cong. Ten boys were still in the home and had remained behind because they didn't know where else to go. I told them to pack their clothes and move into my second home until things had quietened down. Some of the boys had already started to loot from the empty houses, others had taken sleeping pills and were fast asleep.

Before I took the boys back to my home I went up to the airport to see what was happening there. I called at the Adventist hospital because it was so close to the airfield. I thought they might need help with casualties. I wondered if I could go to the airfield itself in one of their ambulances to help the wounded. I was astonished to find that all the American doctors and nursing staff had already left—only a few Vietnamese nurses had remained behind. As the hospital was run by the Seventh Day Adventist Church I hadn't expected anyone to leave. All casualties were being transferred to one of the government hospitals.

In the hospital courtyard I passed a South Vietnamese pilot trying to wave down one of the helicopters. He agreed to take me to the air base provided we could signal a helicopter, but we didn't manage to do so. In the end we both got on my bicycle and tried to reach the airport by road. Rockets were now coming in all the time and I could see them exploding ahead of us. As they came in closer and set fire to nearby houses, the people started to flee. Mothers were running down the street carrying their babies, their husbands following them with suitcases. The police started to open fire but I couldn't see what they were shooting at. Several bullets whizzed over our heads and once we had to jump off the bike and fall to the ground. It was now impossible to reach the air base. Ahead of us I could see several buildings in flames. Both the police and soldiers shot wildly over people's heads if they failed to stop and show their identity cards. Amidst all the noise and confusion the people began to panic.

I returned to the boys' home and hurriedly prepared to leave. The boys emptied any rifles they had of bullets and fired some distress signals into the air. Then they got hold of their fire extinguisher and sprayed it all over the home and themselves. The house was in an appalling mess but they didn't seem to care. Unbeknown to me then, Father Hoang had already closed the home before leaving Saigon but the boys had continued to live there. Part of their looting was due to the fact that they still needed money for the running costs of the home. Their water and electricity bills were long overdue, and they had run out of rice.

Two boys were too doped by sleeping pills to come and two others wanted to carry on with their looting, so they remained behind. Eight came with me and a boy called 'Hung', just recently released from Chi Hoa, rode me home on the bike. As we cycled along I noticed a cloud of black smoke rising into the sky over Cholon. I was terrified that my home had been destroyed.

Soldiers had brought tanks out near to our home and the police had blocked the area with barricades of barbed wire. They would not allow anyone to pass down the street but I had to reach my home and the girls. I got off the bike, climbed through the barbed wire and started to run down the street. I took off my shoes so that I could run faster. The sun was so hot that the melting tarmac stuck to my feet. I kept thinking that I would be blown to pieces if they started to fire the tanks. I continued running and at last reached the home which was still intact. A rocket had landed near the bus station on Petrusky street and one small aircraft had just been shot down in the street behind our home and had crashed into a tree. This accounted for the smoke I had seen. Luckily the pilot escaped without injury and no one was hurt.

Lien and I started to prepare boxes of bandages and dressings in case of an attack in our area. The markets were now closed because of the curfew and some of the poor people living in the lane came to ask us for rice. We moved into the second house, leaving the boys in the first home. All afternoon the children stayed outside in the lane and watched the planes until darkness fell, enthralled by their shapes and the noise they made. The boys had taken more sleeping pills and were already fast asleep. The girls and I sat outside in the lane with our neighbours. No one did any work. People asked me why I hadn't returned to my own country and seemed convinced that I would be shot by the Viet Cong. I told the girls that if the Viet Cong did come to the home and wanted to arrest me, they would have to let me go. I did not want to threaten their chances of survival by allowing them to hide or protect me.

Clouds gathered across the sky and another storm broke out. We listened to the sound of the thunder, the helicopter gunships circling overhead and the constant boom of Communist rockets exploding in and around the airport. President Minh's last attempts to arrange peace talks had failed. There was nothing we could do but wait. Father Hoang's boys had woken up and were moving round restlessly. We settled the children to sleep early and then sat round the radio listening to the news. At 8 p.m. that evening the whole city was blacked out for just over an hour. We didn't know the cause of the blackout and immediately thought that the Viet Cong had entered Saigon. The streets were silent and nothing moved. Light rain had begun to fall and Lien and I decided to have a look outside. We crept quietly through the shadows keeping close to the buildings, half expecting to confront Viet Cong soldiers, but saw no one. We lit candles in the home and sat down, waiting, listening.

None of us felt like sleeping much so we made endless cups of coffee. At about 10 p.m. we heard a truck draw up in the street outside. Lien and I went outside to investigate, naturally wondering if it was the Viet Cong. Luckily the truck was full of our troops who told us that their officers had deserted their units while trying to defend the airport and not knowing what to do they had decided to withdraw. Their captain was still trying to make radio contact but there was no reply. In the end he gave up and the soldiers just sat down in the street and lit cigarettes. The girls started boiling up saucepans of water to make coffee and we took it out to the soldiers. By this time another truck and several jeeps had arrived with about one hundred soldiers who had all fled from the airport. It was evident that we had lost the war for the soldiers were just quitting and going home. A few of them stayed out in the street all night and let out intermittent blasts of rifle fire. We finally went to sleep at about 3 a.m.

During the night I had listened to the last planes leaving Saigon with Americans on board. I wondered if Dick had been on one of those flights. The last Americans had left by Marine helicopters flown in from the 7th Fleet in the South China Sea. Government officials and pilots had made a last attempt to escape in South Vietnamese helicopters and light planes which tried to land on the American ships. However, many high ranking Vietnamese officials were still in Saigon and were now fleeing to hiding places in the city. People were still trying to leave Vietnam from the port of Vung Tau, in anything from fishing boats to naval vessels. It was their last chance of freedom.

On the morning of 30 April, Communist rockets continued to blast down into the airport. I dressed carefully in Vietnamese clothes and once more covered my hair with a scarf and coolie hat. Whole families were wandering along the streets carrying as many possessions as they could hold. Most of them had moved in from the outskirts of Saigon where heavy fighting had broken out. Most people locked their doors and stayed in their homes, afraid to go out. The strain of this interminable waiting made everyone tense. We knew we were trapped.

At 10 a.m. General Minh announced that he was surrendering to the Communists to prevent further bloodshed, and appealed to both sides for an immediate ceasefire. Throughout the morning more people fled from the suburbs of Saigon into the city centre. South Vietnamese soldiers walked through the streets carrying only their rifles, most of them on their way home. Others sat on top of tankers drinking beer and getting drunk. For them the war was already over.

Ambulances and Red Cross cars moved between the tanks. Even people who knew nothing about medicine or first aid had painted the red cross on their cars and were wearing Red Cross arm bands. Some people even painted a red cross on the door of their home, hoping that they might be left alone. The police in the headquarters opposite our lane started to evacuate the building. Before they left they sold off their rice, split the money between them and bought a crate of beer.

The girls and I stood nervously in the street smoking heavily and watching. We heard that the Communists had started to move into Saigon. The situation still seemed unreal. Just before noon about thirty of the street boys from Te Ban came walking along the street to the home. The police had apparently run away and left them locked up in the cells. Together they had managed to break out and release the other prisoners. They hadn't eaten for about three days and the girls went inside and cooked two lots of rice for them which they ate with tinned fish. They then left and made their way to the city centre.

The next person to come to the home was Qui, who had also just broken out of jail. He and his cell mates had fought desperately to break out, fearing they would either die from starvation or be shot by the Communists. Yen's boyfriend also arrived having escaped from Chi Hoa. Altogether about 10,000 prisoners had broken out after the police abandoned their posts. All this activity made us feel more relaxed. Rockets had ceased to explode around the airport and the realisation that the war was really over was to some extent a strange relief.

In the early afternoon we heard that Communist tanks had already moved into Saigon. The last of the police fled from the headquarters opposite us, throwing off their uniforms so as not to be recognised by the Viet Cong and running home in their short pants. The soldiers stripped off their uniforms, even their boots. They threw away their rifles in the street and deserted their trucks and tanks. 'Thach Sanh', a Cambodian boy who lived with us in the home ran out into the street and dressed up as a policeman. He walked down the lane in an over-sized uniform, big army boots and a steel helmet. Everyone laughed at him but we had to tell him to take off the clothes.

Yen's boyfriend found an M.16 gun and blasted the lock off the gate leading into the police station. Then Father Hoang's boys put on Red Cross arm bands and followed him into the station to start looting. About half the neighbourhood rushed over to join them. People and children ran away with as much as they could carry, using the guns to blow down any locked doors. They stole typewriters, cassettes, radios, televisions, chairs, tables, electric fans, canned foods, rice and even ripped out the telephones.

After Father Hoang's boys and my girls had finished looting the boys went back again to pick up some of the guns. We had about ten rifles, mostly AK-47s and also one M.16 gun which we kept in the home for protection against any house to house fighting that might occur. We decided that if the Viet Cong were going to fight we would retaliate and defend ourselves as best we could. We also had about six hand grenades which the boys hid carefully in my clothes. By now there were crowds of people out in the streets stealing and shooting off the guns they had picked up.

At 3 p.m. we heard people saying that the Viet Cong had reached the market in Cholon and were moving through the city. We waited anxiously. Qui put on the radio. It was a Viet Cong programme being relayed from the local Saigon radio station. We went out into the street and saw the first Communist tanks coming towards us. The Viet Cong soldiers were waving blue and red flags with a yellow star in the middle. I just looked at them, scarcely realising the implications of their arrival. It was an extraordinary sensation.

I waited outside in the lane and watched the soldiers take over the police station opposite us. The red and yellow South Vietnamese flags were torn down and replaced by the red Communist flags. Then some of my neighbours suddenly appeared in the lane carrying rifles and wearing red arm bands. I never realised that they were Communist supporters and members of the PRG. Anh Cuong, the man I had once hit to protect my girls, appeared with a group of local boys and welcomed the soldiers. They turned and smiled at me but I was too astonished to reply.

Next, one of the Viet Cong soldiers walked down the lane and came into the home to ask the girls for a glass of water. Lien told me to wait in the bathroom until he had gone but I did not want to risk her life and decided I must let the soldiers see me. If I was going to be shot, I wanted to be shot out in the street and not in the home. I dressed up as a very poor Vietnamese girl in ill-fitting clothes and went out into the street to empty the rubbish. I had my British passport and I.D. card tucked in the top of my trousers. Before I went out I gave Lien my gold cross and chain and also my mother's wedding ring. I wanted her to have them and not the Viet Cong.

As I walked out I had no idea whether I would be shot or just arrested. I walked barefoot down the lane carrying the rubbish and tried to imagine what a bullet would feel like tearing through me. Nothing happened. I thought they hadn't noticed me. I began to empty the rubbish and all the time was waiting to hear that single rifle shot. Still nothing happened. I returned and stood outside the police station straight in front of the soldiers. They must have seen me now. Then they were staring at me and I looked back at them and waited. They smiled at me and I smiled back. Perhaps they thought I was Vietnamese.

I was surprised at how friendly the Viet Cong soldiers were as they talked happily to the crowds of curious people who had now gathered round them. Some wore baggy jungle-green uniforms, canvas helmets and flat sandals made from rubber car tyres. Others were dressed in black pyjama suits. They all seemed to be of the same rank for there were no badges or stripes on their uniforms.

Then Lien came over and gave me a cigarette and we walked round for a while before returning to the home. Military uniforms, helmets, boots, tin cans, bullets and piles of rubbish were scattered all over the streets. The South Vietnamese tanks had now become playthings for children who climbed all over them, laughing and shouting. The abandoned South Vietnamese trucks and jeeps were completely wrecked. People had taken off the tyres, ripped out the seats and dismantled the engines. Privately owned cars that had been left had also been ripped apart.

When we returned to the home Anh Cuong came over and asked us to surrender the guns the boys had stolen. It had been a peaceful take-over and so we gave back all the guns except for two which we loaded and kept carefully hidden away in case of any trouble. We also kept the hand grenades. Then we went into the home and made ourselves some red arm bands to wear. The boys decided to return to their own home near the airport and after they had gone we discovered that one of them had shot off the lock to the drawer in which we kept our money for the running costs of the home and had stolen it all. I was sad and extremely disappointed that one of Father Hoang's boys should have behaved in such a selfish and dishonest way. I sent Lien to ask Father Chau for more money.

That evening the night sky was filled with fireworks and flares as the Communists celebrated their victory over the 'Liberation of Saigon'. We heard that soldiers had driven their tanks up to the Presidential palace and had arrested General Big Minh.

CHAPTER 11

The next day, Thursday, 1 May, Saigon was calm and peaceful. People who had taken refuge in the city returned to their homes. Everyone went back to work and the markets reopened, although everything was much more expensive. I set off by bicycle for the National Assembly Hall on Tu Do street to try to find a British journalist who could send a message to Dave, but I only saw a French journalist. Communist soldiers were sitting on the steps leading to the Hall smiling at everyone. They rode past in old-fashioned jeeps and North Vietnamese peasant girls dressed in black pyjama suits sat with them, waving to the crowds. The girls had long black hair and wore large gold earrings. On the whole the North Vietnamese girls were fatter than the South Vietnamese, not so attractive and they all wore very drab clothes.

In the afternoon Lien and I took the bus into Saigon. North Vietnamese soldiers were buying watches and radios from the locals who charged them fantastic prices. We walked down to the river front at the end of Tu Do street, passing many wrecked American cars and abandoned South Vietnamese tanks on our way. The South Vietnamese navy had deserted their ships which were now filled with Viet Cong soldiers who despite their youth seemed very disciplined. Orders were given quietly and carried out at once. Lien and I could easily understand how they had won the war.

We called at Saigon hospital on our way home. It was so crowded that patients even occupied the floor space in the entrance hall and intravenous infusions were suspended on string hanging from the ceiling. We went up to the second floor and as I entered the ward I was suddenly confronted by about sixty Viet Cong soldiers. I didn't know this floor had been reserved for them and for a minute I was stunned and rather frightened by their presence.

To our relief the soldiers were warm and friendly and told us we were the first people to visit the ward. It would have been awkward to leave and so we sat down and talked to them. I told the soldiers they were the first Viet Cong I had actually spoken to and to my surprise they shook my hand. Unbeknown to me at the time, I could have been shot for calling them 'Viet Cong', as this was the name given to guerrillas recruited in the South, and should have called them either 'Giai Phong' or 'Bo-Doi', meaning a soldier from the North. For the first few days I could not understand their Northern accent and repeatedly referred to them as 'Ong Viet Cong' but they only laughed.

Most of the soldiers in the ward were severely burned or had gunshot wounds and broken limbs. Some had lost an eye or an ear. Since there were not enough doctors and nurses to ensure adequate treatment and medicines were scarce, many spent the first few days in agony. They never complained and I admired them for their courage. Many of the South Vietnamese patients in the hospital had been injured by explosions, and there were also many attempted suicide cases. People were either afraid of a full scale massacre or felt unable to live under a Communist regime.

For the first few weeks after the take-over, I spent most of the time in the hospital nursing the North Vietnamese soldiers and saw many terrible sights. The soldiers were always considerate and appreciated our efforts on their behalf. They used to call me 'Chi Nam'. Whenever I worked late into the evening the soldiers would invite me to eat with them. They shared whatever they had and would also give me tea and cigarettes. They were given superior meals to the South Vietnamese patients and had some meat and vegetables with their rice.

Immediately after the take-over hundreds of casualties were admitted and our work load was enormous. Soldiers were brought in straight from the field in an appalling condition. The blood had dried and caked onto their skin and was difficult to remove without the aid of soap or cleansing lotions which we did not have. They still wore their army uniforms which were often in shreds, dirty and blood-stained. Dressings and bandages had not been changed and their infected wounds oozed pus which dried hard onto the dressings, making them sore and foul smelling. The hospital did not have enough bandages and gauze to change all the dressings and many wounds were just left to fester. There were few forceps and no antiseptics. I changed the burns' dressings using my fingers and a single pair of plastic forceps. Luckily we had bandages and gauze in the home, and although they were not sterile I still had to use them.

One young soldier called 'Anh Hai' was burned from head to toe and I took five hours to change his dressings when he was first admitted. As I slowly unfolded the bandages from his face, small insects which looked like earwigs crawled out and disappeared up his nose before I could catch them. He could not even open his eyes because his eyelashes were so burnt that they were stuck together. When he did eventually open his eyes he was blind in one and partially blind in the other. Every day I visited him and changed his dressings. All his hair was singed and even his lips were burned. I bought him milk to drink and squeezed fresh oranges for him. At one stage I thought he was going to die but a few weeks later he recovered. It gave me such pleasure to see him get up and walk around.

I nursed another soldier who was lying on a stretcher in the corridor. He was twenty years old. I noticed that the bandages covering his face were saturated with blood and when I removed them realised that he had lost one eye. All I could see was blood and pieces of eyelid floating round in it. He was in unbearable pain and was transferred to another hospital which could provide the correct treatment. The North Vietnamese soldiers tried to help one another as much as they could and seemed concerned about their fellow patients' welfare. In the evenings, if we had finished our work, Lien and I would sit down and talk to them. They would tell us about Hanoi and Haiphong, their homes and families.

On 2 May, I returned to the hospital and when I got off the bus I noticed a crowd of people gathered in the street. Some soldiers had caught a boy of about twenty who had stolen a neck chain from a woman's neck. I could not believe my eyes. They took a knife and slit his throat. I felt sick and cold inside. No one was allowed to go and help him and the boy collapsed in the street and died in a pool of blood. I moved away feeling very frightened. I kept thinking about what I had seen and in the afternoon I returned to see if the body was still there. It was in the same place and the sun had dried the pool of blood round it.

The soldiers had put a notice on him in big red letters for everyone to read as a warning against stealing. That evening, one of my girls told me she had witnessed a similar scene in Cholon. She had seen a woman steal money from the pocket of another woman who worked in the market. The soldiers had caught her and chopped off her hands. That night I dreamt that a Buddhist monk had been shot for not wearing his hat straight.

During the month of May several public executions were carried out in the streets and in most cases the victims were usually shot. Despite these measures people continued to steal and were later taken off to jail. The soldiers would also make a man wash out his mouth if they heard him swearing. One of my girls had her mouth washed out with water and gasoline three or four times. If girls were caught smoking in public places they were made to stand in the street and smoke continuously for up to four or five hours as an example to others. If anyone deliberately sold an incorrectly weighed piece of meat in the market, they were made to eat the difference in weight, and they had to eat the meat raw.

The Saigon Radio station gave out warnings of severe punishments for theft and looting. Girls were advised not to work on the streets as prostitutes and most of the bars closed and then reopened as coffee shops. People were told not to gamble or drink on the street corners and it was announced that everyone would have to work. The crime and corruption in Saigon shocked the rather puritanical North Vietnamese. They would shun the street beggars and did not appreciate the shoe shine boys' offers to polish their shoes.

For the first few days I kept my hair covered under a scarf and then decided to dye it black when some of the soldiers told me they would like to chop off the heads of any Americans. I bought two bottles of black dye and by the time I had finished my hair was so black that it was darker than my girls' hair. At least now, when the soldiers I was nursing opened their eyes, they would not see a nurse with yellow hair. I returned to the hospital without my headscarf, confident that my disguise was a success, but the soldiers took one look at my hair and asked me why I had dyed it.

On the morning of 3 May, I went to visit the older boys in Truong Minh Ky home. One of them had reported to my girls that they had very little money left and had almost run out of rice. They were also frightened of being accused of looting and feared the penalties. I took the boys enough food for a few days and warned them not to steal and not to use drugs. I didn't know that Dick was still in Saigon and went to look for a man called 'Ong Long' to see if he could help. Before the take-over, Ong Long had worked for Father Hoang and helped administer the financial side of the Project. His office used to be in the boys' technical centre in one of the streets at the side of the airport. I cycled to the centre and found that it had been hit by a rocket and almost completely destroyed. I walked through the ruins of the building and could see the place had been looted. Chairs and tables were turned upside down, many of them broken. Papers, files and photographs littered the floor. Before I left, I took down one very old picture of a group of Dick's first boys and fastened it onto the back of the bike.

I cycled down Le Van Duyet street, one of the main streets leading into the city, and passed the cemetery where Nguyen Van Long had been buried. I decided to visit his grave and quietly entered the gates, totally unprepared for the horror inside. Outside the mortuary were the bodies of about fifty soldiers from both sides. All the bodies looked black and I could see that many had been burned to death. Some had been shot. The blood had run down the mortuary steps and had soaked into the earth. I just stood there looking in silent horror until one of the street boys led me away. I prayed at the grave of Nguyen Van Long and gave the boys what little money I had on me. I felt so sad, firstly for the boys who had to bury them and then for the soldiers who had fought for so long and had died just as the war was over.

Most of the Communist soldiers bought radios when they first came into Saigon. Many had never seen a radio before because they had spent so many years living in the jungle. Some of the soldiers we spoke to had left their homes and families in Hanoi and had spent up to seven years in the jungle, without once returning to their family. In the hospital in the evenings, the soldiers would leave their beds and gather round the bedside of a comrade who owned a radio. They would spend hours listening to it, tuning in to the different stations in turn.

Wrist watches and cameras also fascinated the soldiers and nearly every soldier bought a watch. One soldier I knew bought two watches and wore one on each wrist. The South Vietnamese sold their own watches, radios, cassettes and cameras for large sums of money. Some North Vietnamese soldiers paid ridiculously high prices for virtually worthless objects. It was almost as if the Americans had come back, with everyone engaged in buying and selling. There was a flourishing black market where people sold the goods they had looted from the abandoned American buildings and storehouses. Many of the American goods were purchased by the North Vietnamese soldiers, and I even saw some of their officials walking around in U.S. army boots. All the soldiers seemed to have plenty of money and I was soon to realise why.

Many of the soldiers had never ridden a Honda or driven a car. They stopped to ask the locals to let them have a ride. At first they didn't know how to control the vehicles and many fell off, much to the amusement of the people watching them. They would start the Honda, pull out the throttle before they got on and would have to run down the street after the machine. They were terrible drivers and I saw one soldier drive a large army truck straight into the front of a bus. No one was angry because everyone roared with laughter and the soldiers covered the cost of the damages.

When the soldiers first came into the home we offered them coffee, but they had never drunk coffee before and the girls gave them iced tea. One of the soldiers had never seen ice cubes and asked us what they were. He wondered if he would be sick if he ate one. We had to laugh. Many of the regular soldiers couldn't read or write and even some of their officials couldn't read.

It was clear that the Communists were not going to carry out any massive reprisals against the South Vietnamese. They proclaimed that it was not the South who had lost the war but the Americans. Now they wanted a reconciliation and declared that all Vietnamese would be partners in the 'Liberation' of Saigon. Every day the radio and television programmes celebrated this 'Liberation'. Broadcasts were made to the people explaining what was expected of them and urging everyone to work. The PRG went round the streets with loud speakers telling everyone to stop throwing their rubbish into the streets and organising small groups of young people to sweep the city clean. Others were given the task of directing the traffic of the main streets.

The North Vietnamese soldiers had now taken over the police station opposite us and were living there. In the evenings they used to wander down the lane and come into our homes to talk and watch television. I was lucky in that my neighbours who supported the PRG were able to explain to the soldiers my reasons for staying behind. Some of the soldiers looked at me warily at first, convinced I was an American journalist or a member of the CIA. Others, on seeing how black my hair was, thought I had a Vietnamese mother and an American father. But most of them treated me with civility. Some even came into the home and asked me to teach them English. Later I met soldiers from the North who had studied English in Hanoi and spoke it fluently.

The North Vietnamese soldiers and the Viet Cong often had friends and relatives living in the South and there was a building in a street near our home where people would gather hoping to meet their families. Many Southerners who had left their homes in the South to join the Communist troops now also returned to their own homes and villages. Every day more and more North Vietnamese moved into Saigon, including women, children and even old people. Saigon was quite a change for these people who wondered at its wide tree-lined boulevards, its air conditioned buildings, restaurants and swimming pools. A few of the soldiers even visited the bars to sleep with the girls and later I saw others drinking beer and playing cards on the street.

On Monday, 5 May, I woke up and tuned into the B.B.C. World Service to hear the sounds of Big Ben at eight o'clock, followed by Victor Sylvester. I then set off for Tu Do street, as I had been told by Dick that there was a meeting for all social workers in Saigon, but I was the only person who turned up. Opposite the National Assembly Hall the soldiers were knocking down the military statue built by the South Vietnamese army and many foreign journalists were taking photographs. They told me that all lines of communication had been cut in and out of Saigon and that no one could send out news reports.

When I arrived home the new Communist District Chief and Anh Cuong visited us. Anh Cuong told him about the home and our work in the neighbourhood. The Chief had a kind face but because of the way he was dressed, the girls and I could hardly hide our smiles—his cowboy hat and sunglasses looked strange beside his army uniform. He told the girls that they had to return to their own families and explained that everyone would be given work in return for food to eat and a place to live. He nonetheless thanked me for all the work I had done amongst the poor people and street children.

On Wednesday, 7 May, a large meeting was held in the grounds of the Presidential Palace which had been made into the new Military Headquarters. The North Vietnamese General Tran Van Tra exhorted all ex-soldiers, police and civil servants to present themselves with their identification papers between 8–31 May. He stressed that those who supported the old Government would have nothing to fear as long as they followed instructions, but that anyone who tried to run away or hide would be severely punished.

The Communists set up offices in every district in Saigon, where the old soldiers of the South Vietnamese army could go and register. Once they had registered and received their new identification papers, they were allowed to go about their normal duties. Some senior army officers were detained and sent away to special centres in the country for re-education. Many South Vietnamese soldiers had 'Sat Cong', meaning 'Kill Viet Cong', tattooed on their arms or across their chests and now lived in fear of being shot.

When the first South Vietnamese army officers left for the re-education camps, Lien and I watched them go. Their wives and children were not allowed to follow them and were not told their destination. The wives wept in the streets and many feared they would never see their husbands again. They were told that they would return in a few weeks but many of the first officers to leave had still not returned when I left Saigon eight months later. I am sure they were killed.

Later we heard stories about the re-education camps from members of the PRG. They were supposed to be somewhere in the jungle area of the Central Highlands of Vietnam. The officers were said to be stripped of their clothes on arrival and only allowed to wear one pair of shorts. They had no protection against the weather or the mosquitoes at night. Many were believed to have died from fevers and malaria. They were made to bathe in and drink water from the river and were given only two bowls of rice a day. The Communists did not kill the South Vietnamese officers outright but subjected them to conditions in which it was impossible to survive.

Our local district office was set up in one of the houses in our lane. The woman who used to live in the house had disappeared before the takeover and it was believed she had run off with a South Vietnamese officer. Immediately after the Communist victory, Anh Cuong ran the office with the help of some of the younger boys who worked for the PRG and two Communist soldiers. Their job was to watch the whole area and arrest anyone who was caught misbehaving. We did not have much freedom during those first few weeks. Lists were made of the occupants of each house and at night there were frequent house to house checks to see if anyone was missing. When some of the girls who had previously lived in the home returned to visit us I had to obtain permission for them to stay overnight. If someone did stay in the home without their name on our family paper, they were likely to be arrested. It was after the take-over that I changed my name to 'Ho Cam Tu', thus adopting the family name of 'Ho Chi Minh'. The girls and my neighbours still called me Co Nam, but for official purposes I always signed my name 'Ho Cam Tu'. Saigon was also to become 'Ho Chi Minh City'.

In the evenings we were supposed to be quiet after about nine o'clock and had to stay in our homes. We were not allowed to keep our lights on late and after about ten o'clock someone would come along and tell us to turn them off. Nor were we allowed to listen to any kind of popular music and I even had to listen to the radio very quietly. Our neighbours usually had their lights turned off by nine o'clock but my girls found it difficult to obey this rule. Lien and I were always being called into the office in the mornings because of complaints about the noise from my home at night. We were warned that if we were not quieter we could be arrested, but we still continued to make a lot of noise. We also had a small record player and used to play American records on it. If the soldiers heard us they would stand outside the home and wait until we had turned it off.

Even in our own small area a number of people were arrested for keeping firearms or for stealing. Anh Cuong knew most people in the neighbourhood and if it was a first offence he usually gave them a warning and let them go. He knew only too well the conditions they would have to suffer in jail. One night, two local boys tried to break into one of the houses by climbing over the roof. A dog barked and they were both arrested and detained in the office until the following morning. The office was kept closed and two Communist soldiers sat outside with rifles at the ready. When the boys were released they could hardly walk down the lane. Both had been beaten up and one boy's arm was broken.

The boys from Truong Minh Ky still visited us and continuously asked for help. They told us that Communist soldiers were taking care of the younger boys in Hope 5 and 6, providing them with a daily ration of rice and giving them identification papers. Some of the soldiers had moved in to the farm at Hope 6 and were living there with the boys. No one wanted to help the boys from Truong Minh Ky because of their looting raids and continued use of sleeping pills and opium. Although I had been warned not to help them I still shared out our rice. I didn't give them any money because our own funds were running low and I felt they might spend it on drugs.

Whenever I went into the city I always hoped to meet someone British who could contact my brother Dave and let him know I was safe. I heard that the British newspaper office Reuters was still open but discovered that only a few Vietnamese journalists had remained behind. They told me that the British had already left but that there was a French journalist at the Caravelle Hotel who might be able to send a message through the French Embassy. The French Embassy had remained open during the takeover and the French Ambassador Jean-Marie Merillon had stayed behind.

By the time I reached the Caravelle it was pouring with rain and I arrived soaked to the skin. Inside the hotel I met a French journalist and photographer called Jean Claude Labbé whom I had known before the take-over, as he had come to the home to take some photographs of the girls. He spoke fluent Vietnamese and had been talking to the North Vietnamese soldiers who had taken over the top floor of the hotel in order to watch the city by night. When Jean Claude saw me he came over and kissed me and started to dry me down with his towel. I felt a little embarrassed standing there in front of the soldiers but they only looked at us and laughed. Jean Claude was only about twenty-eight years old but looked a lot older. He suffered from a nervous complaint which caused his arms to twitch violently, and we often wondered how he could be such a good photographer. When he had finished drying me down he introduced me to the North Vietnamese soldiers and we all sat down and smoked cigarettes together.

To my astonishment Jean Claude told me that he was a member of the French Communist Party and had been working in Vietnam for the Revolution. He firmly believed that almost half of the population of France was sympathetic to Communism and that there would be a Communist Government in France and England in the not so distant future. Before the take-over he used to collect medicines from the Pharmacies in Saigon and steal medical supplies from the International Red Cross to smuggle out to the North Vietnamese soldiers in the jungle. When the first North Vietnamese troops came into Saigon they invited Jean Claude to go with them on the tanks to the Palace where they arrested General 'Big Minh'. After the take-over the Communists gave him an American car and a driver and eighty litres of petrol.

I asked the soldiers in the hotel if they were happy about the Revolution in South Vietnam. They said they would not rest until Communism took over the whole world and even asked Jean Claude for his address so that they could visit him in France when they finally arrived there. Jean Claude told me he was planning to visit Hanoi before returning to France and continuing to work for the Revolution in Europe. The soldiers told me that the new President of Vietnam would be a Communist leader called Nguyen Huu Tho.

On Saturday, 10 May, Saigon Radio announced that all remaining foreigners in Saigon had to register with the new authorities within fifteen days. Foreigners were forbidden to leave Saigon and could not visit the airport or any coastal ports. although most of the refugees had returned to the countryside, Saigon was still desperately overcrowded. Practically the whole of the South Vietnamese army and all former government employees were out of work. All the banks in Saigon were closed and people could not withdraw their savings. Food was more expensive as the Communists cut down the amount of produce allowed into the markets, and what was sold cost far more than most ordinary families could afford to pay. Street crime in Saigon increased as the thousands of people who had recently broken out of prison had to steal to survive. Many of Father Hoang's boys left the Project homes because they did not want to live and work for the Communist soldiers.

Schools had closed down during the take-over and were just starting to re-open. Some business premises in Saigon remained open, but employees found their salaries drastically cut and in some cases abolished. Instead, the Communists paid them a daily ration of rice. I had a friend who was married to a bank manager whose monthly salary before the take-over had been over 200,000 piasters. He now received only 14,000–15,000 piasters. Girls who worked for the Air Vietnam office used to earn 100,000 piasters per month. Now they received 8,000–10,000 piasters and their daily rations of rice.

In the home Lien and I tried to encourage as many of the girls and children as we could to return to their own families, because we feared we would not have enough money to support them. We had already started to sell off some rolls of material which had been sent over from the States to help pay our running costs. Father Chau refused to give us any of Father Hoang's money and demanded repayment of the last 100,000 piasters he had given us. I still had about twenty girls and children living in the home and by this time we were only eating rice and vegetable soup and never bought meat or fish. I had to get hold of some money somehow, and decided to sell some things on the black market. The Communists confiscated the belongings or property of anyone who had left Saigon, but I was determined to keep some of the contents of Father Hoang's house for ourselves. I felt sure he would rather we had them than the Communists or Father Chau.

I went to visit Major Trong, an ex-South Vietnamese officer who lived nearby and who had not yet registered with the new authorities. He was very brave and openly displayed his tattoo 'Sat Cong' on his chest. I asked him if he would disguise himself as a North Vietnamese soldier, tie a red Viet Cong flag on his jeep and drive us to Phulam. He could then pretend he was our new District Chief and could order Father Chau to give us the key to Father Hoang's storeroom so that we could take what belonged to the Project and use it for the benefit of the children. Major Trong agreed to the plan provided that he had a share of the profits.

The next morning Lien went to buy two big red flags, while Major Trong and I went to buy petrol. We finally bought ten litres for 10,000 piasters. The people selling the petrol were mixing it with kerosene and water and the colour of the mixture varied. We tied the red flags on to the jeep and set off for Phulam. We were lucky enough not to be stopped by the Communist soldiers, who in fact saluted to the Major as we passed, much to our amusement.

Father Chau looked really scared when he saw the jeep with

the red flags flying draw up in front of his house. The Major was a fine, well-built man and played his part superbly. Father Chau was extremely nervous and handed over the key without a murmur. For the rest of the day we made several trips to and from Phulam and took away anything we thought we could sell in the market. Some of Father Hoang's belongings were missing and Ong Nam told us later that Father Chau had been selling them himself. Father Chau had also destroyed all Father Hoang's papers, including the papers authorising me to run our two homes.

By nightfall we had collected twenty rolls of material, a cassette tape recorder, a record player, two large radios and two amplifiers. We also cleared out a lot of the clothes, soap, toothbrushes and medicines. We paid off the Major with a couple of rolls of material and some soap and kept everything else carefully hidden and locked away upstairs. So far our plan had worked well but we had to be careful not to be found out when selling the goods. We gave most of the clothes to the poor people living in the lane and whenever someone was sick they always came to the home for medicine. Ong Ngoc, who lived opposite and worked for the PRG, had seen us bring everything into the home and so we gave him a box of medicines to keep him quiet.

Two days later we were visited by an irate Ong Long. Father Chau had telephoned him, complaining that I had looted his house. Ong Long had always been quick tempered and was sometimes very mean. He had refused to give me extra funds for the various homes and had been very reluctant to supply the Truong Minh Ky home with rice. Later, I went to Dick's office and to my surprise discovered that Ong Long had left us 200,000 piasters for the running costs of our home. This money enabled us to pay our water and electricity bills which were months overdue, but because of rising prices we soon had to resort to selling the rolls of material in the market. Anh Cuong knew about this practice but agreed to turn a blind eye as long as we used the money for the girls alone. Although we warned the boys not to come anymore they continued to do so and were finally arrested.

Anh Cuong's father, now a prominent figure in our neighbourhood because of the work he had done for the take-over, pointed his gun at the boys' heads and ordered them to lift their arms while they were searched for weapons. Then Anh Cuong wrote out a paper stating why he had arrested the boys and referring their case to the main precinct office, where they would be questioned by the Communist officials. Anh Cuong felt very strongly that the boys should be working. Although there was no real employment available at this time, those who participated in working groups organized by the soldiers themselves, the PRG or volunteer groups working for them, were at least given their daily ration of rice. Boys were also encouraged to enlist in the local Communist forces. However, Father Hoang's boys had no intention of contributing in any way to the Communist cause and stubbornly refused to co-operate.

The next morning, Anh Cuong came to the home and summoned Lien and me to the precinct. He sent one of his boys to escort us but halfway down the street the boy left, saying that he could not follow Lien and me with a rifle, as if we were prisoners, after we had done so much to help the people. When we arrived at the office, the soldiers wouldn't let us in at first because we were not escorted, but once inside we were taken to see one of the officials. He spoke slowly to us in Vietnamese so that I could understand him and told us how much everyone appreciated the work we had done amongst the poor. He said that we could continue to help those who were worthy of our help, but that the boys did not deserve our support since they refused to work and abused our kindness by using the money we gave them to buy drugs. The boys had in fact been released earlier that morning and warned for the last time about coming to see us. Anh Cuong told us they might be shot if they were caught in the home again.

In the afternoon, the brother of the owner of our first home came and asked if we would give the house back to him, as he feared that the Communists would appropriate it. The owner, Mr Hieu, from whom we had rented the first home in early 1974, had been studying in the States for over a year and it seemed unlikely that he would now return to Vietnam. As Father Chau had destroyed all Father Hoang's papers, including the contracts for our two houses, we had no written, legal proof that we had either paid the rent for the first home or even purchased the second home. However, I knew that Father Hoang had paid the second year's rent of the first house in advance, and that we were therefore entitled to live there for another ten months. The second house alone was not large enough for the twenty girls and children still in my care and I refused to give back the house.

Hieu's brother angrily replied that he would refer the matter to the District Chief.

That evening we sold our gas cooker for 30,000 piasters. I split the money between the girls and we went out together to eat in the market place. We could no longer afford to buy gas cylinders and began to cook over two small charcoal fires. Our funds were running low and we could not rely on financial help from abroad any more. Although I still had some money in an account I shared with Father Hoang I was unable to withdraw it as the banks were closed. I realised that at some point the home would probably have to close, but for the moment I was determined to make the best of what little we had and continue to live happily together.

During this time house checks were a frequent occurrence. Usually one of the North Vietnamese officials from the precinct would come to the home with one of the boys working for the PRG. Sometimes they came late at night and once they came very early one morning while we were still sleeping and searched the whole house. They made a list of everything we had and even looked through the drawers where we kept our clothes. They found all the things we had taken from Father Hoang's home and asked us where they had come from. We insisted that Father Hoang had given everything to us as a gift but they still wrote everything down and forbade us to sell anything.

19 May was a public holiday to celebrate Ho Chi Minh's birthday. Every household had to fly two North Vietnamese flags and have a picture of Ho Chi Minh that stood higher on the wall than any other picture inside the house. There were many celebrations and rallies in Saigon. The children were taught to march along in straight lines with workers' groups and youth groups. People could only take part in the demonstrations if they belonged to one of these groups and had learned the Communist slogans they were required to chant. Everyone seemed happy and the children in our lane let off fire crackers all day. Anh Cuong decorated our local office and invited everyone down to sing, drink and celebrate. The next morning, I went to the Immigration Office where all foreigners were called to register with the local authorities. We had to hand over any identification papers issued by the old government and then fill out forms stating our names, addresses, reasons for staying in Vietnam, details of any property owned, etc. The Communist officials

were all very helpful and most of them spoke either English or French.

When I returned to the home just before midday, I was surprised to see Qui waiting for me. He could hardly speak because he had taken so many sleeping pills. He told us that late on Sunday evening the soldiers had visited the boys' home in Truong Minh Ky and had ordered them to leave the home that night and return to their families. The boys had refused to leave since they had nowhere else to go and the soldiers had moved in to arrest them. Two of the boys, Sinh and Qui Nor, had climbed onto the roof with a loaded rifle and had fired at the soldiers. The soldiers had immediately surrounded the home and opened fire. One boy on the roof had been hit by a bullet that just missed his heart and the other had been hit just below his right knee. Both boys had fallen off the roof and landed in the street covered in blood. The soldiers had arrested everyone else and left the two wounded boys behind, believing them to be dead. One of their neighbours had taken them to the nearest hospital.

I had to make sure that Sinh and Qui Nor were all right and so I borrowed a bicycle from one of my neighbours and went to look for them. When I arrived at the hospital I asked at the reception if the boys had been admitted. They found Qui Nor's name but there was no mention of Sinh and for a minute I thought that he had already died. One of the nurses told me where to find Qui Nor and I finally found both of them in the fourth ward. Sinh in fact recognised me and called my name. I went over to him and he just held onto me and cried. Sinh had had the bullet removed from his lung. He still had a chest tube draining a lot of bloody-looking fluid. Qui Nor's leg had been bandaged but not operated on because the bullet had gone straight through his leg. I stayed with them for two hours and bought them some iced water and a few cigarettes.

When I left the hospital, I went outside to look for my bike and couldn't find it anywhere. I could hardly believe it had been stolen because there were many soldiers around and everyone had left their bikes outside propped up against the fence. I searched everywhere but never found it and eventually returned home by bus. It was a hard blow because I had to replace the bike but felt that the little money we had left should have been kept for the girls.

The following morning Hieu's brother returned and told us

that we had to see the District Chief in the precinct. He explained to the Chief that he needed the house for his mother but that he would return the ten months' rent to us having deducted enough money for repairs. I realised full well that by the time the repairs had been paid we would have nothing left. The District Chief listened to him and after some thought decided that he could not let them reappropriate the house. I was astonished to hear this decision in our favour. The Chief told Hieu's brother that he could not evict twenty children just so that his mother could live there. He said we could continue living in the home until our second year's rent had run out. Lien and I were elated at this news but Hieu's brother and his mother left the precinct without even looking at us.

That afternoon, Lien and I bought a new bicycle for 55,000 piasters. We now had no money left. In the evening we sold some of our soap and toothbrushes to neighbours so that we could buy food the next day. We turned off the fan during the day and started to burn candles to save the electricity. The girls washed their clothes from the tap in the street to save on our own water, and we continued eating rice with just a few vegetables and perhaps a little fish if we could afford it.

On Friday, 23 May, I woke up with another fever and felt so sick and tired that I had to lie down and rest during the day. That evening I visited Sinh and Qui Nor as usual but had only been in the hospital for about half an hour when some of the boys who worked for the PRG happened to walk through the ward and recognised them. These boys had accompanied the soldiers to the Truong Minh Ky home on the night that Sinh and Qui Nor were shot. They alerted the nurses and told them to watch the cubicle and locked the doors at either end of the ward while they went off to call the soldiers. I was afraid they might be shot and sat resolutely between them. Ten minutes later, three soldiers, one official and three of the boys working for the PRG came into the cubicle. The soldiers were armed with M.16 guns and hand grenades. They questioned the boys and placed them under arrest. I was also placed under arrest because the soldiers suspected I was working for the old South Vietnamese Army. Sinh and I were taken to the local Precinct Office for questioning but Qui Nor remained behind because his leg was still too painful to move.

The soldiers were not very friendly and kept their M.16 guns pointed towards us in the jeep. I was not afraid because I knew they had no reason to shoot me but I was worried about the boys. Everyone turned to look at us as we drove through the streets with the siren sounding. It was also pouring with rain and by the time we reached the office we were cold and wet. An unsympathetic-looking official, who shouted rather than talked and never once smiled, questioned us, and I did my best to explain about the Streetboys Project and the various homes. Then Sinh was called in to see the District Chief while I waited outside. I could hear a lot of shouting inside the room and then I was called in. Luckily the Chief could speak some English and so in a mixture of English and Vietnamese I was able to tell him about my work. He asked me why the boys had tried to shoot at the soldiers and I said that since they had been taught to help each other as a family they had only been trying to protect each other. The Chief thanked me for trying to help the boys and offered me tea and cigarettes. Then he called in one of his officials and said we could go back to the hospital. The soldiers did not return with us but the boys working for the PRG stayed in the ward all night and the soldiers were just outside.

I was detained in the hospital over the week-end. On Saturday morning Lien came looking for me and returned in the afternoon with some food. Whenever I wanted to go out to buy some bread or something to drink, one of the soldiers followed me with an M.16 gun. I hadn't expected them to release me so quickly, but on the Monday morning they told me I could go home. As I left I somehow felt that I would never see Sinh and Qui Nor again. I fainted when I arrived home and my body seemed to ache so much that I couldn't even stand up. I slept for about four or five days and even eating exhausted me. Ong Ngoc, the nurse who lived opposite us, came in to give me some injections and I began to recover. I returned to the hospital the following week to see Sinh and Qui Nor, but they had already been taken away. I returned to the Precinct Office and visited eight local police stations but I never found them.

Not long after the take-over, the Communists formed their own police force in an effort to decrease the amount of crime in Saigon and to control the traffic. The police stations and all the prisons were reopened but this time conditions were even worse than before. The soldiers began to carry guns in the streets and to make known their rank. The new-found happiness of the people gradually faded and they began to fear and mistrust the soldiers. This was especially noticeable in our own neighbourhood when the soldiers gave Anh Cuong and the boys working for the PRG 200 piasters and rice each day. Anh Cuong was married with one child and his wife was expecting a second baby. Their daily ration of rice was barely enough to fill them and 200 piasters was hardly enough to buy one fish in the market. PRG supporters dropped out and spent their days getting drunk on Vietnamese whisky.

The soldiers were very strictly disciplined and expected the people to adopt their standards. Meetings were held in every neighbourhood and talks were given by Communist officials. At first attendance was not compulsory but later everyone had to go. Youth groups were organised and every morning all the young people in our neighbourhood had to sweep the lane and the street outside. They thought this was fun for a week or so but their enthusiasm soon waned. Then the soldiers started to make them go into the city and clean up various empty buildings they wanted to use. It was stressed all the time that everyone had to work hard, but when people received nothing for their efforts they soon stopped bothering.

Admittedly the soldiers themselves worked very hard and got little in return, but for them it was a way of life which they had been taught to accept. They only ate twice a day and their officials did not allow them very much food. They usually just ate rice with a little salt. Sometimes they would go to the market and buy a few vegetables and perhaps some fish, but they had to be careful not to be found out. They also started to tell the people that later they, too, would only be given rice and salt to eat.

People became edgy and quick-tempered and wondered for how long they would be able to support their families. The girls in the home became miserable and depressed and started to take sleeping pills again. They worried about their own families and about what they would do if the home had to close. Friends from Te Ban or Le Lai street started to call at the home to ask for help but we could no longer give them money as we did before. Drug addicts became desperate and some of the girls who had once lived in the home tried to steal things from us.

One morning Mai returned to visit us and stayed all day. She was still dressed in her tight fitting trousers and low necked sweater. Her nails were long and varnished, although the soldiers had told all the girls to cut their nails and remove all nail polish. Mai told us that she was still working as a prostitute but that now her customers were Communist soldiers who did not pay as much as the Americans had done. She advised us to guard our possessions since everyone was much poorer, and to make sure we didn't lose anything. That evening after supper, she suddenly left without saying goodbye to anyone. At ten o'clock I hunted for the radio to listen to the news and realised that she must have taken it with her.

A few days later, I woke up in the morning and went upstairs to get some money for Lien to go to the market. I had the shock of my life. The cassette tape recorder, the record player and amplifiers, two radios, three cameras and all our money were missing. The theft was a complete mystery. The door leading upstairs was always kept locked and I was the only one who had a key to the padlock, which was in the form of a magnet so that it could not be copied. As I kept the key pinned to my trousers I wondered if someone had taken it while I was sleeping. Lien and I slept in front of the door leading upstairs and we always heard any movement during the night, and none of our dogs had barked. However, as there was no evidence of anyone having broken in from the roof, we concluded that it must have been someone who lived in the home.

Later that morning, Yen's younger brother Hen and No's younger brother Cu Ly disappeared all day and didn't return home until evening. I then discovered that one of the children had actually seen Hen and Cu Ly carry the things out of the home early that morning and hand them over to two of Father Hoang's boys who were waiting outside. Both Hen and Cu Ly decided to leave the home and return to their own families. Later, when Yen and No went home, they found both the boys with a lot of money on them and they finally admitted they had sold everything on the black market. There was nothing I could do. If I told the soldiers the boys would have been taken to jail and I did not want that to happen. I still loved them even though we suffered as a result of the theft. Hen and Cu Ly used to visit us almost every week and always bought a chicken or duck for us to eat.

With the loss of all my money that morning, the girls and I didn't know if we would be able to eat that day. We started to sell the rest of the soap, toothpaste, toothbrushes and clothes we had and managed to get enough money to buy rice and a few other provisions at the market. In the afternoon Anh Cuong advised us to sell everything we had, divide the proceeds amongst the girls and let them return to their own families. The soldiers had started to check the contents of people's homes and were only allowing them to keep certain necessities. They even counted the cooking pots and rice bowls and permitted each household to keep the minimum for family use. They allowed each person to keep three pairs of trousers and three shirts. The soldiers took whatever they wanted when they went into a home, including cookers or refrigerators if they so wished. We therefore started to sell everything that afternoon. A cousin of Lien's bought two of our sewing machines and sold them at a profit in the market. Anh Cuong borrowed some money from his father and bought our third sewing machine for his wife and also our television set. We also sold five rolls of material. We now had 170,000 piasters.

When the soldiers entered some of the more wealthy Chinese homes they discovered that some of the Chinese owned gold bars. In one Chinese home they discovered twenty gold bars and the family handed over nineteen of them. The soldiers waited for a few days and then returned to search the house for the missing bar. When they found it, hidden in the bottom of a flower vase, they ordered the family to leave the house. All their possessions were appropriated by the soldiers. Both parents and the six children took enough poison to kill themselves.

On Thursday, 5 June, nearly all the girls and children left the home. We shared the money amongst the older girls and sent them off with enough money to start buying and selling in the market. It was heart-breaking to watch them packing their clothes before they left. I think nearly everyone cried, including some of our neighbours. Yen and No took about ten sleeping pills each because they were so sad. Lien and her two children stayed behind because they had nowhere else to go and besides, I needed someone to stay with me who could speak English. Van, an eighteen year old French-Vietnamese girl who had no family in Vietnam also remained. I also kept an eight-year-old boy called Cuong, whose father had recently died in Saigon hospital, and another little boy called Hao, who had been severely handicapped by a mine explosion.

I could not sleep that night because the house was so quiet. All I could hear was the sound of the rain as it leaked through the roof and dripped onto the floor, but I couldn't be bothered this time to get up and collect a bucket. The girls' home no longer existed, but I knew the memory of it would go on living for a long time to come. Perhaps we could never change the lives of the street children, but I hoped that at least during the time they stayed with us, we were able to bring them a little happiness. I missed them all terribly, but I knew they would always remember me. I knew they would remember how Father Hoang and I had tried to help them. I would not be sad—it had all been worthwhile.

I just felt a little empty and perhaps a little lost as I listened to the sound of the rain and not to the sound of the girls and children. I knew I would always love them, always remember them. That was why I had stayed in Vietnam—to look after the girls and children for as long as I possibly could. I had told the girls I loved them and that meant loving them for ever. That day, I felt a part of my life had ended. I felt a little older, but at the same time I knew that we had made a success of our venture. I remembered one of Dick's favourite songs, 'He ain't heavy, he's my brother.' Really that song belonged to us.

EPILOGUE

I stayed in Vietnam for a further six months. Lien and I could not help people on the same scale because we did not have the funds, but we still continued to visit patients in Saigon hospital and helped the nurses if they were short staffed. We kept in touch with the small boys living on the street and most of the girls returned to visit us.

Yen had started to go to the market every morning to buy chicken eggs which she could sell at a profit in her own neighbourhood. She lived with her boyfriend and their baby in a small house near her own parents' home. Later, the entire family moved into the countryside. The soldiers encouraged anybody living in a very poor, overcrowded part of Saigon to move out into the country and work on the land. For the first six months they were given a place to live, their daily rations of rice and salt, and enough seeds to plant to start growing crops with which to support themselves. Some of the other girls also moved out of Saigon and some already had relations in the country to whom they returned.

Only one of the girls returned to a life of street crime and was later arrested by the soldiers and sent to jail. Another girl called Hoa had a hunch back and just couldn't make any money buying and selling in the market. She came from a very poor family and her step mother took care of her baby because she never had enough money to care for the child herself. Hoa came back to visit us one day but left in the evening without saying goodbye. We discovered that she had taken four pairs of black satin pants with her—Lien and I were left with the pants we were wearing. Hoa disappeared from her home and we never saw her again.

Lien and I always looked for Mai and Jacky whenever we went into Saigon but we never saw them. Most people had moved away from Le Lai street because they were afraid the soldiers would discover their drug dealing. Tuyet and Hom also moved out to work on the land but came to see us before they left. Tuyet's boyfriend had died but although she had stopped taking opium she had become very thin and miserable looking. We still used to see Chao around. She lived with several different men who gave her sufficient money for her opium. Sometimes she was so drugged that she didn't even recognise us.

I only saw one of the boys who had been arrested from Truong Minh Ky home when Sinh and Qui Nor were shot. His name was Hung and he was released from jail just before I left Vietnam. Luckily Hung had a girlfriend who was very much in love with him and he went to live with her family. The other boys were still kept in jail and were not allowed visitors. Hung told us that they had spent their days chopping up firewood but had not been 're-educated'. No one ever saw Sinh or Qui Nor again but the rumour spread that Sinh had died in jail and that Qui Nor had lost his leg.

Shortly after we closed the home Dong Chi Tho and Anh Hai, the two Communist soldiers who looked after our area, came to visit us. Dong Chi Tho was universally liked and used to play football with the children in the lane. Whenever he came to the home he would always stay for a couple of hours and make me speak to him in Vietnamese. He had learned some English in Hanoi and tried to pronounce words with the aid of our English dictionary. He was young and very good-looking and all the boys working for the PRG. enjoyed working with him because he was so friendly. Sometimes he would bring them to the home and they would tell me how much he loved me and that he planned to take me back to Hanoi with him. Tho would just laugh and then ask me himself whether I loved him. I could only laugh with embarrassment with everyone else there—the Vietnamese often spoke openly about love and I could never tell if they were serious or not. The other soldiers who worked with Tho were just as friendly and they used to discuss amongst themselves who would be a suitable husband for me.

Anh Hai, the other soldier for our area, was a bully and nobody liked him. He even looked ugly and his fellow soldiers were just as mealy mouthed. When Anh Hai came to the home he upbraided us for having sold our sewing machines and television set without his permission. He was always threatening to send Lien and me to jail and said that he would arrest us if we sold anything else. Lien and I did not listen to him and sold our two large U.S. office desks and two swing-back chairs in order to buy food. Anh Hai was furious and made a list of the remaining items of furniture and even counted the number of books and records we had. He wanted these goods himself and declared he would return to collect them.

Anh Hai also ordered Lien and me to go to school to be 're-educated' and disciplined. We went three times a week in the evenings for two weeks and then had to go during the day. The daytime sessions were much longer and we became very bored. Sometimes Anh Hai gave the lecture and sometimes it was Dong Chi Tho. Everyone liked Dong Chi Tho's lectures because people were free to express their own opinions and ask questions, but when Anh Hai spoke no one dared say anything. It was clear that Anh Hai really hated the Americans and Thieu's government. Unlike the other soldiers, who told us that the war was over and that all Vietnamese were brothers together in the Liberation of Saigon, Anh Hai used to say that those who had shed blood owed a blood debt, and in return would have their own blood shed.

There were about fifty people in our class, most of whom we knew because they were our neighbours. One day, Anh Hai began criticising the Americans and then ordered me to stand up. He said he could not accept my presence—when I looked like an American myself—after all the destruction the Americans had brought to Vietnam. I thought for a moment and then told him how difficult it was for me to accept him as a Viet Cong after the North had fought against the South for so long. There was complete silence as Anh Hai ordered me to repeat what I had said. By the look on his face, I thought he was going to shoot me, and I am sure everyone else thought so too. To my astonishment he said I was right to have said this and gave me a cigarette.

We learned about the whole history of the Vietnamese Revolution and the meaning of Communism. Everyone had to work and in return would receive a daily ration of rice and salt and a place to live. Anyone who did not co-operate would be punished. We were encouraged to work on the land and were told that farmers were the most important people in the community. The Communists encouraged everyone to read and write and stressed the importance of sending all children to school. Schools were opened in every neighbourhood for children whose parents couldn't afford to send them to an existing school. Adults who couldn't read or write also had to attend classes with the children, and even the Chinese had to learn Vietnamese.

After some weeks of going to school during the day, the soldiers split the people into groups. All the men would attend one day, the women the next. Even the old people had to form a separate group and go to school. No one was exempt. The women were not allowed to wear their hair down at school, but had to pin it up on top of their heads. The soldiers considered that women looked untidy with their hair down. We even had to do up the top button on our shirts and no one was allowed to wear make-up or nail varnish. The soldiers would even inspect our nails and would tell us to cut them if they thought they were too long. They also gave us a specific measurement for the width of our black pants. They stated that we should wash at least three times a day and that we should wear a bra whenever we went out. This was quite ridiculous and we just used to laugh.

We were taught in an old wooden hut which became unbearably hot because there was no fan. We were usually given one five minute break during a five hour session. There were no toilet facilities and everyone would run out to relieve themselves behind the nearest tree and have a quick cigarette. In the evenings, the mosquitoes would constantly bite at our ankles. The soldiers spoke far too quickly for me to be able to understand much of what they were saying, and I found it difficult to concentrate.

Anh Cuong's father Ong Ba often came to the meetings and spoke to us about his experiences when he was working for the Revolution. On one occasion he was captured by the South Vietnamese soldiers and buried under the ground with just his head left above. He was left out in the sun for three days without food or water. Later he was imprisoned and tortured. Ong Ba used to enjoy talking to the women's groups, especially when he was a little drunk, as he often was. He even discussed personal relationships with us. He told us that one man could love one woman, but that it was quite wrong for one man to have three or four wives as was often the case in Saigon. Then one day after the meeting, Ong Ba came to the home and asked me to live with him. Although he was an old man and already married, he said that if I agreed to live with him, he would find a job for Lien and she could continue living with us. Later, whenever Ong Ba came to the home, Lien and Van would always come and sit down with me.

I used to study the Communist doctrine in my spare time. I found several books in the market, in English, about Ho Chi Minh and the history of Vietnam. One book was called *Vietcong* and it was all about the Viet Cong soldiers and General Giap, the famous Communist military leader. Later, when the soldiers came to the home, I could answer all their questions and I didn't have to go to school anymore.

The soldiers continued to come into the home and were all charming except for Anh Hai. Anh Hai summoned me to his office several times and I would have to stand in front of him and his soldiers, while he accused me of being an American journalist. My British passport made no impression on him because he couldn't read. A week later he would call for me again and accuse me of working for the CIA. He was impossible to reason with and in the end I just used to walk out.

The South Vietnamese became increasingly disillusioned with Communist propaganda and more and more distrustful of the soldiers. The Communists had promised that everyone would become equal, but they took away the people's money, their homes and their freedom. No one became equal, the rich became poor and the poor died.

At about eleven o'clock one evening, when most people were sleeping, the soldiers went round the streets with loud speakers announcing that the next day they intended to change the money notes. Everyone was to go to their local district office and get their money changed. All the local shops reopened and everyone went out to buy something to eat for the next day with the old money. Our area office was next to the cinema on Petrusky street and the soldiers called out each person's name in turn. People watched to see how much money their neighbours had. Some of my neighbours whom I had believed to be very poor went down to the office with their pockets stuffed full of money. They, too, were watching Lien and me, but to everyone's surprise we had much less than anyone else. Outside the cinema, the street was packed with queues of people. Lien and I had to wait three days and three nights before our name was called and we took it in turns to sleep on the steps of the cinema.

Much to everyone's dismay and horror, the soldiers changed the first 100,000 piasters at the rate of 500 piasters to one dong, and allowed each family a maximum of 200 dong. Lien and I only had 50,000 piasters so we only got 100 dong, but at least we didn't lose money as others had. The soldiers kept the rest of the money and it was only by special permission that a family could request more of their money to be changed. In the case of a wedding or funeral or in the event of sickness, the soldiers would allow a person to withdraw more of his savings.

The more wealthy Vietnamese had to go to one of the banks in Saigon to change their money. Lien and I went down to have a look and I could not believe that some families were so rich. They were queuing up with suitcases and whole sacks filled with money notes. What people could not change themselves or get their friends to change for them, they lost. Several suicides occurred during those few days. The people not only hated the soldiers now, but considered them thieves. Even I could not help feeling indignant as I saw families lose their entire life savings.

People started to move out of Saigon, not because they were forced to leave, but because they could no longer afford to live there. They could not sell their houses but received about 200 dong from the soldiers who appropriated the property for themselves. We felt that sooner or later everyone would have to leave Saigon and that the city would only house the soldiers and their families.

As our home consisted of two houses that were now practically empty, Anh Hai decided that Lien and I should only live in one house while he lived in the other. He decided he would prefer to live in the first house and told us to remove all our remaining furniture except for several chests of drawers which he wanted to keep for himself. No one wanted Anh Hai to live in the lane, so Lien and I told him that as we only rented the house he would have to contact the owner first. I also pointed out that we had paid our second year's rent on the house and that this rent should be returned to us if we had to move out. The soldiers could not take over a home which was still occupied but could only appropriate a house which had already been vacated, where the occupants had been turned out for a valid reason.

Lien and I told Anh Hai we didn't know the address of the owner of our house. Anh Hai then threatened to take our second house because we did not have the papers to prove it belonged to us. All our neighbours confirmed that we had bought the house, but Anh Hai said that unless we could produce the papers he would take the house from us. He gave us one week to contact the owner and get the papers. As soon as he had gone, Lien and I decided to sell all our chests of drawers because we needed the money and didn't want Anh Hai to take them.

Later that evening, Anh Cuong came to the home and we could see he had been drinking a lot. He told us he could no longer work for the Communists because they weren't giving him enough food and he could no longer afford to support his family. He asked us for a glass of water and we thought he wanted to drink it, but instead he took out a used syringe from his pocket, dropped a few crushed sleeping pills inside it and filled the syringe with water. He rolled up his sleeve and injected the pills into his arm. He was so depressed and in his semi-unconscious state cursed the revolution and told us how much he hated the soldiers. Later, Anh Cuong was no longer allowed to work for the local office and all his friends working for the PRG left at the same time. They used to spend their days getting drunk and injecting large quantities of whatever pills they could obtain into themselves—even aspirin tablets.

On several occasions in Saigon, groups of ex-South Vietnamese soldiers rose up against the Communist soldiers. Dressed in their old military uniforms, they usually waited by night for a group of passing soldiers and would then suddenly appear in the street ahead of them and open fire. Several Communists were shot and killed and the South Vietnamese soldiers either shot themselves immediately or were caught and killed by a firing squad.

Ambushes of this kind happened in the countryside for several months after the take-over, and the North Vietnamese soldiers would avoid travelling alone through isolated areas. Rumours spread through Saigon that a South Vietnamese General was still holding out in the jungle, together with several divisions of the South Vietnamese army. The people in Saigon still had great faith in their former Prime Minister Nguyen Cao Ky, and although he had left the country just before the take-over they believed that it was he who was sending in supplies and ammunition to the supposed former army. People claimed they had seen American planes fly over some jungle areas and drop supplies. It was also thought that American submarines were bringing supplies and sending them into the jungle by night.

Even in Saigon itself the soldiers avoided going into certain areas alone. They virtually cut themselves off from the people and no longer bought from the street vendors or sat round the drink stalls on the pavement. The soldiers began to realise how much everyone hated them. In the evenings they would stay in their compounds and play football or squash, rather than wander round the city as they had done first. The soldiers didn't seem to care so much about the South Vietnamese people either. If they caught someone stealing, they would still shoot after them, regardless of whether innocent bystanders were killed.

Everyone became much poorer and people could no longer afford to go to the market. Many families just lived on the rice and salt. Even our rice was rationed and we could no longer buy it in the market place, but had to obtain it from the soldiers. Every family was given a ration book and the soldiers would write down how many kilos of rice we had so that they could control the amount given to each family. They sold us a lot of the American rice that had been sent over for the refugees just before the take-over. It was very poor quality and had gone bad so that we had to spend a couple of hours picking out all the grit and the worms before we could eat it.

Lien and I used to buy a lot of Vietnamese spinach (the leaves were very small compared to English spinach) because it was very cheap and if we had any money left over we would buy a little meat or fish for the children. For two months we lived on the rice and spinach and, like everyone else, we became pretty thin. The rice blew you out but didn't fill you up, and after an hour or so we would be hungry again. I now weighed seven and a half stone and was only a little heavier than the average Vietnamese woman. I had weighed nine and a half stone on my arrival in Saigon.

Medicines became increasingly difficult to obtain because most of the medicines in Saigon had been imported from France and as stocks ran out, the pharmacies closed down. Everyone suffered from vitamin deficiencies and skin diseases. I contracted scabies and because we could not afford to buy soap for washing and didn't eat enough, I couldn't get rid of it. At night I would scratch in my sleep without knowing. My skin opened easily in the humidity and the sores began to ooze pus. Sometimes they were so itchy that I couldn't even go out. We had sores everywhere except on our faces, the palms of our hands and the soles of our feet. I still have the scars even now.

The babies became ill and stopped growing. Their mothers

couldn't produce enough of their own milk and no one could obtain a tin of condensed milk unless they went to the doctor and asked for a prescription. But who could afford to pay the doctor's fees? Even then, milk was only given to babies up to eighteen months old and after that they had to go without.

Sugar was also rationed and no one could afford to buy it in the market place. Every few weeks or so we could buy about a pound of sugar from our local office at a cheaper price. It was a real treat to be able to eat sugar with our rice instead of spinach. There were several things such as washing powder and noodles which we could buy cheaply on our ration books, and we usually sold them at a profit. Lien and I used to buy cigarettes and were able to sell them at almost twice the price we paid.

When people are hungry and have little money, they eat anything edible. We were soon to lose Lulu, one of our dogs, and we believed the soldiers had taken her and eaten her. Lien and I sold nearly everything we had and just managed to continue buying rice. We sold all our furniture, our books and records and most of our clothes. I sold my typewriter to one of my neighbours and spent a whole morning in Saigon trying to sell my camera. We sold most of our medicines on the black market. By the end of August our house was empty. We had no cooker or refrigerator, not even a chair or table. Part of our roof had fallen through and we could not afford to get it mended, so the house was flooded whenever it rained. Our fan had broken and so at night we had no protection against the mosquitoes. We had no soap, no hair shampoo and even used to clean our teeth with salt.

The soldiers in our neighbourhood would sometimes ask us to care for young children they had found wandering in the street. Then they would bring us some extra rice, but we could not live on rice alone. Later, Yen's brother Hen came to the home and suggested that we should eat Ringo, the big old dog we had bought just before the take-over. I was reluctant to eat him, but if we hadn't, someone else would have done. So that afternoon Hen killed Ringo by holding his head down under water and in the evening we ate him. I can't really say what he tasted like because we curried him, but he was a bit tough.

Anh Hai still continued to visit the home and at one stage we did move into the second house so that he could live in the first. But on the day he planned to move in our neighbours helped us to strip the house bare. We took more corrugated iron sheets off the roof so that the house would really flood when it rained, removed all the door handles and wall fittings and disconnected the electrical wires, some of which were pulled out altogether. We let all the street children play in the house and even allowed them to draw on the walls. When Anh Hai arrived that evening he was so angry that he immediately called his soldiers to arrest Lien and me. We changed our clothes ready to go to jail, but I think at that moment Anh Hai suddenly realised he would never be accepted in the lane and he changed his mind. He even started to laugh and was considerably more friendly towards us after this incident.

I tried to get a job because I thought that if I could work the soldiers would at least give us enough rice to eat. I approached several government offices in Saigon to see if I could work with the people, but there was no employment available. The Communists had their own workers—their own doctors and nurses in the hospitals and their own staff in the banks and offices. Everything was now controlled by the Communists and they didn't need further help from foreigners living in Vietnam. They still needed foreign aid in the form of farm machinery, seeds to grow crops with and medicines for the hospitals, but they wanted to develop the country in their own way. All foreigners were being encouraged to leave and I knew that I too would soon be forced to go.

I was determined to get hold of some money for Lien, Van and the children before I left. I still had the joint account with Father Hoang in one of the banks in the city, and although there was only a slim chance that we could even get hold of part of that money, I thought it was worth a try. In October Lien and I wrote letters in both English and Vietnamese to the South Vietnamese bank manager and also to the Communist officials now in charge of the bank. We rather exaggerated our situation and listed the debts we said we owed. We told them we didn't have any money to buy food for the children and said they were in desperate need of clothes, school books, etc. At first we were turned down, but every day I went to the bank to plead my case. I kept on saying that I could not leave Vietnam until I had paid all my debts.

I believe that God was on our side again because after about two weeks of pestering almost every office in every bank in Saigon, our local district office and the precinct office, I was finally allowed to withdraw money from the account. Father

Hoang and I had 750,000 piasters in the account and the Communist officials said I could withdraw the whole sum. Lien and I decided to withdraw at least half the amount there and then, just in case they changed their minds, and I put the rest of the money into a separate account for Lien. We could not believe our luck as we walked out of the bank with 375,000 piasters or 750 dong. We treated ourselves to a cyclo ride and on our way home we stopped at the market and bought two cooked ducks, French loaves and a bottle of whisky. We didn't dare tell anyone about the money, so when we invited our neighbours to share the meal we told them I had received a present from my brother in England.

The decision as to whether or not to remain in Vietnam was a hard one. I loved the people and the country; I loved Lien and the children; I loved everything about Vietnam. The soldiers told me that I could stay but that I would be permanently exiled. Some of the soldiers who were living in the lane came to the home and asked me to stay, but I explained that without work, I could not support myself. They replied that if I married one of them and returned to Hanoi, I wouldn't have to work—and some were extremely keen to marry me. Had it not been for my two brothers, Dave and Jim, I think I would have stayed in Vietnam. But we were extremely close to each other and I could not bear the thought of never seeing them again. Nor did I want to cause them the same unhappiness.

I waited several weeks before applying for an exit visa and often almost changed my mind and decided to stay. I had intended to leave at the end of October but then decided to postpone my departure until November. November came and I thought I might as well leave at the beginning of December, to be home in time to spend Christmas with Dave and Jim.

Before I left Vietnam, Lien and I made several trips to the countryside. Foreigners were not allowed to leave Saigon but I spoke to Ong Ba and he asked the soldiers to give me an official paper to carry me through the checkpoints. I asked permission to go to Vung Tau, which, being a port, was the one place where foreigners were likely to be arrested. I told the soldiers I just wanted to swim there, and they agreed to let us go. Lien and I took the children with us. Van had left the home and had gone to live with Hen and his family in the country.

I loved Vung Tau and nothing had changed. It was very

quiet and hardly anyone walked in the streets apart from the soldiers. Even they didn't seem to take much notice of me. I now dressed like a North Vietnamese woman, in a plain shirt and with my hair up, even wearing the sandals made from car tyres. We returned to Father Qui's orphanage but he had been arrested and most of the boys had left. It was sad to think I would never see him again. We walked along the beach and watched the fishing boats coming in. As I watched the people working on the boats, I understood how much I loved their simple way of life. We returned to Tay Ninh city where I had been at the height of the fighting. There were no more rockets, no more tanks and ambulances tearing along the street. It was strangely quiet, the peasants worked away in the fields and small boys tended the oxen. I loved it that way.

We also returned to the Delta and as I watched the gold and red sun setting over the green rice paddies and the people returning to their tiny thatched mud huts, I thought about London and wondered how I could ever live there again. How could I become part of Western society and do the things that everyone else did and considered normal, when I found them so irrelevant? How could I live with people with steady jobs and steady incomes, whose chief concern was the mortgage on their home or their material possessions? Did they ever stop to think about the suffering in the world or see it as I had done? Did they even know about Vietnam—or even care?

I wondered what would become of the Vietnamese people in the future; I knew we would never know. I don't think they will ever be really happy. The end of the war was only a temporary respite from misery. They will always be poor and have to work long hours for their daily ration of rice. Just before I left, the soldiers announced that no couple was allowed to have more than two children. There was no birth control available and any woman who became pregnant for the third time was forced to have her pregnancy terminated in hospital. The soldiers said the children ate too much rice.

The people had nothing they could call their own, not even the shirt on their backs. Everything belonged to the government. Although there had been no bloodbath in Saigon, many people disappeared or were killed, like the ex-South Vietnamese government officials who went away to be re-educated and never returned. Children remained in jail; some were beaten and others were strung up by their ankles. Homeless children and beggars still lived on the street. I doubt whether the Communists will show kindness to them.

I finally left Saigon in the second week of December 1975. The French Embassy cabled my brother in England to let him know I was leaving. Dave sent me enough money to cover my air fare from Saigon to Bangkok, and sent a ticket to Bangkok for the rest of the journey. I left Saigon with two empty suitcases and took nothing with me. Souvenirs were only material things and had no real meaning. The only souvenirs I had, I held in my heart. I have written everything in this book from memory. I could not forget my experiences in Vietnam and the love of the people and the children will stay with me forever. I shall always love them and I still hope that one day I will be able to return.